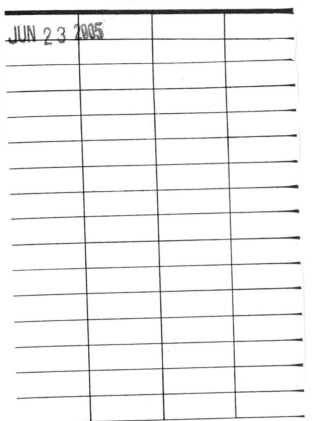

"After three decades of laboring in the governance vineyards, we at the National Association of Corporate Directors (NACD) might be forgiven if we dared complain that despite progress there is fundamentally 'nothing new under the governance sun.' After all, since our founding in 1977, we have seen cycles of scandal, reform, and rulemaking, with each new generation rediscovering the timeless truths our Association has preached all along. But *Inside the Boardroom* does indeed offer a glimpse at true change ahead, in fulfillment of its title's bold promises. Based on interviews, direct observation, and service as directors themselves, the authors describe how boards 'really' work. They see the key to excellence not in structure but in director competencies and behavior linked to corporations' strategic needs, and predict a future 'revolution' accordingly. Directors will be recruited for who they truly are, not for what predetermined slots they fill. These well chosen directors 'will demand effective continuing education and induction programs,' as well as 'proper board information and effective board mechanics and communications,' while making 'greater use of consultants, educators, and advisers.' *Inside the Boardroom* not only prophesies this change, but shows boards how to cultivate it."

~ *Alexandra Reed Lajoux, Chief Knowledge Officer, National Association of Corporate Directors, Washington, D.C.*

"*Inside the Boardroom* is based upon research involving observations of board meetings and interviews with chairmen and directors from many different types of listed companies. The analysis contained in this book provides one of the most stimulating and interesting insights into board effectiveness and dynamics in recent years. The book provides an invaluable framework for all types of boards to improve their effectiveness using board competencies and behaviours as the key to explaining why certain boards succeed whilst others fail. This is a 'must-read book' for corporate directors and corporate governance practitioners."

~ *Chris Pierce, CEO Global Governance Services Ltd., Former Professional Standards Director of the UK Institute of Directors, London*

More Praise for # INSIDE THE BOARDROOM

"*Inside the Boardroom* is an important and valuable contribution to the growing literature on corporate governance. The authors successfully bring together the growing body of research with practical and pragmatic insight. Their perspective on 'function not form' and their typology of directors is especially helpful in understanding the real issues involved in the world of boards of directors."

~ David A. Nadler, Ph.D., Chairman and CEO,
Mercer Delta Consulting, LLC

"A wonderful and pragmatic guide to building high performance boardrooms."

~ Jay A. Conger, Professor of Organizational Behaviour,
London Business School; Research Scientist,
Center for Effective Organizations, University of Southern
California; and Co-author, Corporate Boards

"Dr. Leblanc's study is one of the most important pieces of original research in governance in the last 20 years. Based on an observation of the inner workings of actual corporate boards and extensive interviews, Dr. Leblanc's conclusions take thinking about corporate governance to a new level. The implications of his work for boards, search firms, rating agencies and directors are extremely important. Dr. Leblanc turns our attention to competencies and behaviours and away from simplistic concepts of independence. The practical implications for 'building a better board'—position descriptions, competency matrices, director behaviour types, assessments, strategic alignment and recruiting—are all in this book."

~ Geoffrey Kiel, Professor of Management,
University of Queensland, Brisbane, Australia, and Co-author,
Boards that Work *and* Board, Director and CEO Evaluation

"Professors Leblanc and Gillies have pushed aside the veil that surrounds corporate boardrooms. Researchers can only examine what they can see, enabling many board realities to remain shrouded in mystery. This ground-breaking study, however, found that interactive processes, director characteristics, and structure—in that order—are important to effective governance, *ironically the reverse order of their visibility* to the outside world. From my experience, the same phenomenon holds true for nonprofit boards as well. Breaking the seal on the sanctum may hold most immediate appeal to outside observers, but the ultimate beneficiaries will be shareholders and directors themselves. In the flurry of corporate governance books now out, this one is a must-read for directors and all who observe them."

~ *John Carver, Ph.D., Author,* Boards That Make a Difference, John Carver on Board Leadership, *and Co-author of* Reinventing Your Board *and* Corporate Boards That Create Value

"I know from first-hand experience that Richard Leblanc's assessment model of boards of directors works and is leading edge. He emphasizes the right things—competency of directors and how they behave and interact as a group. If you want to build a better board, read this book."

~ *Ronald W. Tysoe, Vice Chairman,*
Federated Department Stores, Inc.

"Leblanc's remarkable incursion into the inner sanctum has produced compelling evidence of what experienced company directors know and regulators are perhaps unwilling to admit: it's not the structure of boards that drives performance; it's the people and behaviours. Is this the beginning of the end for 'trophy boards'?"

~ *Patricia Cross, Director, Qantas Airways Limited and Wesfarmers Limited; Chairman, Qantas Superannuation Limited*

"Richard Leblanc's new book offers what we've long needed in the world of corporate governance—a systematic blueprint for how boards are actually led and function, and tools for improvement."
~ *Ralph D. Ward, Publisher*, Boardroom INSIDER,
Editor, The Corporate Board

"Few individuals possess the ability to combine academic analysis, theoretical excellence and an in-depth, independent knowledge of the inner workings of boards. Professors Leblanc and Gillies achieve that and more with their ground-breaking resource. *Inside the Boardroom* is a true insight into what really drives corporate governance—competencies and behaviour."
~ *Rt. Hon. Jim Bolger ONZ, Chairman of* New Zealand Post
and former Prime Minister of New Zealand

"This is breakthrough material and the hope for meaningful research on corporate governance in the future. You have opened up a whole new world of possibilities for researchers. I remain more convinced than ever that you are pursuing a line of research that is ground-breaking in the corporate governance field, *i.e.*, the social/group dynamics of boards, and the question of leadership from the chair in making that dynamic effective."
~ *David S. R. Leighton, O.C., D.B.A., F.I.C.D., Professor Emeritus, the Richard Ivey School of Business, University of Western Ontario; and Co-author,* Making Boards Work

"Dr. Leblanc's exceptional qualitative research—including interviews with almost 200 corporate directors and dozens of board meeting observations—provides unparalleled perspective on board room dynamics that should be required reading for corporate governance practitioners. Armed with this data, Dr. Leblanc proves that the individual and collective competencies and behaviors of directors drive effective corporate governance cultures, which ultimately determine organizational success or failure."
~ *Mac Ryerse, Corporate Secretary, Potlatch Corporation*

"This book is a timely and a significant contribution to the corporate governance debate. The conclusions are both intuitively obvious to anyone with board-level experience, yet surprisingly contradictory to the normative best-practice codes and the mathematically elegant attempt to link governance with performance. In short, this book proves that in corporate governance people matter. Directors' individual character and behaviour influence board decisions. This work is also oriented towards the practitioner, rather than the academic. Intuitively it debunks much of what has passed as definitive corporate governance research to date. The verbatim quotes from directors give the work legitimacy and make it very readable. Experienced directors will readily recognize many of the points of view."

~ *Dr. R.I. (Bob) Tricker, Author of* The Essential Director: An Economist Guide

"The effectiveness of boards depends on what happens *inside* boardrooms—the capabilities, the behaviours and the way boards organise their work. It has little to do with the avalanche of governance rules now demanded by regulators and by governance vigilantes who can only focus on what is visible from the outside— which isn't much! The authors of this book have clearly been inside many boardrooms and it shows in their practical appreciation of the board task and determinants of success. Directors who want to think through the paths to improved board performance will find this a very insightful book."

~ *Colin Carter, Co-author*, Back to the Drawing Board: Designing Corporate Boards for a Complex World

"Writing in an area with few answers, Professors Leblanc & Gillies' work is nothing short of remarkable. Their insights regarding the human drivers of successful boards are simply riveting—it's difficult to believe that good people choices aren't the keys to good governance once you've finished this insightful read. A must for any professional advising in the growing field of governance."

~ *Ian A. McDougall, Director, Joint Schulich-Osgoode MBA/LL.B. Program*

"Drs. Leblanc and Gillies' book represents a high watermark in the continuing struggle to understand and improve performance in the corporate boardroom. Eschewing simple approaches, exemplified by the current crop of 'best practices' codes, they have spent countless hours delving into the innermost workings of that elite circle. In doing so, they point us to important behavioral and process dimensions, often ignored even in the best studies on officers and directors. A well balanced mixture of research informing practice, this book will serve as an enduring reference for future researchers and policymakers but more importantly a mirror for directors who are serious about their duties."

~ Phillip H. Phan, Ph.D., Warren H. Bruggeman '46 and Pauline Urban Bruggeman Distinguished Chair, The Lally School of Management and Technology, Rensselaer Polytechnic Institute, Troy, New York

"Dr. Leblanc 'gets it.' He has proposed a model of corporate governance based on competency and quality decision-making, not cronyism or the 'old boys' network.' This book is a 'must read' not only for all directors, but also for the many women with the necessary credentials who aspire to be on boards. His book should be required reading for nominating committees who want to obtain the best possible directors they can find, using the C-B-S-R model within this book. Bravo!"

~ Doreen McKenzie-Sanders, CM, Executive Director, Publisher/Editor, Women in the Lead Inc.

"In this ground breaking book, Richard Leblanc and Jim Gillies provide useful insights into the dynamics of boards, both in terms of directors themselves and of board processes. This pioneering work is essential reading for scholars of corporate governance and board directors alike."

~ Professor Chris Mallin, Editor, Corporate Governance: An International Review

"This groundbreaking text by Professors Leblanc and Gillies develops a bold new paradigm for evaluating boards of directors and assessing decision-making effectiveness. While corporate governance is not a new concept or field of inquiry, *Inside the Boardroom* is among the first books to combine successfully the best insights from theory with proven lessons from industry and practice. This indispensable reference is a welcome and timely achievement."
~ *Pamela M. Gibson, Partner, Shearman & Sterling (London) LLP*

"This book establishes through its background research the link between common sense, directors and boards. As we see when we review board performance and help identify new board members, quality people with the relevant competencies and acting together in a common purpose will produce a good 'team' in any situation. It's time to forget the emphasis on political correctness in the governance codes and move on to focus on what really will be effective: boards must review, reflect and explain, not just comply."
~ *Chris Thomas, Board Consulting Practice Group Leader,*
Egon Zehnder International, Paris

"His [Richard Leblanc's] findings give a significant boost to the thesis that board process is the most important factor, with membership (director characteristics) as next in importance, followed by board structure (a distant third). He concluded: 'Clearly, board structure is not as important a factor in determining board effectiveness as is normally believed; board membership and director competencies are quite important; and most significantly the behavioural characteristics of individual directors are crucial, if not determinant, of overall board effectiveness.' As a result of his director observations of boardroom behaviour and his interviews with directors, he developed a new categorization of director types.... [W]ith the heightened scrutiny of board actions and the threat of shareholder lawsuits and regulators' sanctions, it is doubtful that many boards will allow future researchers such as Leblanc to observe their inner workings."
~ *Lorin Letendre, in "The Dynamics of the Boardroom,"*
Academy of Management Executive

"Dr. Leblanc's eagerly awaited book establishes standards where none existed. It brings to the fore new knowledge and challenges boards to examine themselves in a stricter light. Dr. Leblanc's work is assisting us in reforming the governance of hospitals...it is a new yardstick that will lead us into a new era of governance."
~ *Virginia McLaughlin, Chair, Governance Leadership Council, Ontario Hospital Association; Chair, Sunnybrook and Women's College Health Sciences Centre; and past Chair, York Central Hospital*

"The corporate governance debate of recent years has tended to focus on readily measurable metrics of directors such as independence, age, years on the board, *etc*. Directors of specialist sub-committees such as audit committees are required to both be sufficiently skilled to add valuable insight to the board, as well as maintaining independence. Leblanc's research confirms that while director competencies and behaviours cannot be readily measured, their impact on board effectiveness is significant."
~ *Michael J. Coleman, National Managing Partner - Risk and Regulation, KPMG, Sydney, Australia*

"With the focus in recent years on boards' nomination process and the importance of quality and experienced board members, *Inside the Boardroom*'s advice on an approach to board composition that focuses on competency and behavior in relation to the corporate strategy is important reading and well worth the price of the book."
~ *Holly J. Gregory, Weil, Gotshal & Manges LLP, New York*

"A thoughtful and thought-provoking treatise on a subject of great interest to investors. It is thorough, well-researched and an interesting read."
~ *Charles M. Elson, Edgar S. Woolard, Jr., Chair in Corporate Governance, Weinberg Center for Corporate Governance, Lerner College of Business & Economics, University of Delaware*

"This book is about the chemistry of boards, the skills and abilities of directors and how they work together. The authors define their characters, styles and group roles. The research results and the process could prove useful to a number of groups who need to know how to assess the quality of boards of directors: chairmen of boards and individual directors; investors who need to assess the competence of boards; consultants and advisers, search consultants, remuneration consultants and other board advisers; investment bankers and venture capitalists and management consultants who advise on Initial Public Offerings, mergers and acquisitions and alliances; bankers and financiers; and also credit rating agencies."

~ Professor Bernard Taylor, Executive Director, Centre for Board Effectiveness, Henley Management College; and Co-author, Boards at Work

"Dr. Leblanc is in an environment where corporate governance experts around the world are attempting to explain the massive failures in governance in the United States entities that failed. He has distinguished himself by engaging in research and publishing analyses which have not been done before. By securing the trust and confidence of the boards of major public corporations, Dr. Leblanc earned the right to observe the inner workings of these boards over an extended period of time. His insight into those board dynamics which distinguish between successful and unsuccessful boards have rarely, if ever, been published. He has made a very important contribution to this science."

~ David A. Brown, Q.C., Chair, Ontario Securities Commission

"In the wake of the recent corporate governance scandals, corporate accountability has taken centre stage and it is useful to have original research as was done by Dr. Leblanc. This research can help initiate reforms and will benefit everyone who invests in capital markets."

~ Claude Lamoureux, President & Chief Executive Officer, Ontario Teachers' Pension Plan

"His [Dr. Leblanc's] seven-member examining committee, consisting of some of the top scholars in corporate governance in the world, unanimously voted to recommend that we submit his dissertation to the Graduate School for a prize. It was the first time in my long experience with Ph.D. dissertations that an examining committee has passed a candidate with distinction, requiring no revisions to be made to the manuscript that he presented for us to evaluate. ... Dr. Leblanc's work has led to a major paradigm shift in the field. I predict that hundreds of social scientists, all over the world, will radically revise their research programs to follow up on his breakthrough... His lectures are described by students as being filled with enthusiasm and energy, which, '... if they could be bottled could make us all wealthy.'"

~ *Rein Peterson, PhD, Anne & Max Tanenbaum Professor, York University*

"In my view, Dr. Leblanc is fast becoming—if he is not already—the resident expert in corporate governance. The impact of his research has reached institutional shareholders, regulators and practicing directors, as well as of course the academic community, both domestically as well as internationally. Dr. Leblanc's empirical work and the recommendations flowing therefrom are practical and make eminent sense. I have watched Richard achieve a level of recognition such that he has become the 'go to' person in corporate boardrooms for his expertise."

~ *Patrick J. Lavelle, Former Chairman, Export Development Corporation*

INSIDE THE BOARDROOM

Richard Leblanc   James Gillies

HOW BOARDS *REALLY* WORK

AND THE COMING REVOLUTION

IN CORPORATE GOVERNANCE

John Wiley & Sons Canada, Ltd.

National Library of Canada Cataloguing in Publication Data

Leblanc, Richard W., 1965-
Inside the boardroom : how boards really work and the coming revolution in corporate governance / Richard Leblanc, James Gillies.

Includes index.
ISBN-13 978-0-470-83520-6
ISBN-10 0-470-83520-6

1. Directors of corporations—Canada.   2. Corporate governance—Canada.
I. Gillies, James M., 1924-   II. Title.

HD2745.L35 2005   658.4'22'0971   C2005-900323-5

Production Credits:
Cover design: Adrian So R.G.D.
Interior text design: Mike Chan & Adrian So R.G.D.
Front cover photo: Getty Images
Printer: Friesens

John Wiley & Sons Canada, Ltd.
6045 Freemont Blvd.
Mississauga, Ontario
L5R 4J3

Printed in Canada

10 9 8 7 6 5 4 3 2 1

CONTENTS

FOREWORD

"At the regular meetings of the board, which never sat for above half an hour, two or three papers were read by Miles Grendall. Melmotte himself would speak a few slow words, intended to be cheery, and always indicative of triumph, and then everybody would agree to everything, somebody would sign something, and the 'Board' for that day would be over."

This famous quote from *The Way We Live Now*, by Anthony Trollope (1815-1882), might well have been believable by many, at least into the middle of the twentieth century. Boards of directors were little discussed by the popular press or by academia, and were not even well thought of by business people. Boards were not considered to be an important part of corporate development.

But certainly from the '60s on, with the sizable number of mergers attendant on the conglomerate movement, and carried into the '70s and '80s during the time of unfriendly tender offers, boards of directors developed a higher profile. Another factor raising that profile was the large and growing number of lawsuits aimed at corporate directors. Also in the background was the growing concentration in the corporate equity ownership of publicly owned companies by institutional investors.

By 1990, the stage had been set and an increase in the rate of change began in the structure, organization and operations of boards. Some large institutions had begun to flex their muscles in order to have a voice in the mode of board operations. CalPERS (California Public Employees' Retirement System) was in the forefront of this development in attempting to fashion "desirable" change in corporate board operations and raising the profile of board decisions. More and more controversy was publicly aired by shareholders, resulting in a response that affected the makeup and operations of boards.

All these phases in the forces of change were dramatically overshadowed by a number of corporate scandals with the opening of the twenty-first century. In very short order, Enron, WorldCom, Tyco, Global Crossing, Adelphia, etc., reported major deficits or declared bankruptcy with very large losses to shareholders and lenders. In all of these cases, and a substantial number of others of smaller magnitude, boards were accused of not operating responsibly and therefore breaching their fiduciary responsibility.

These occurrences ushered in a new era of pressure for change. The Sarbanes-Oxley legislation was passed quickly and virtually unanimously by the United States Congress. The major exchanges and the Securities and Exchange Commission (SEC) were galvanized into action, changing long-standing regulations and methods of overseeing corporate board operations and organization. The interest in board activities has grown enormously in a short period of time, from little or mild interest to top-of-mind, keen interest.

In the discussion that has ensued around the dramatic development of interest in the activities of boards of directors since the implosion of Enron, the emphasis has been on structural change. Major importance has been placed on transparency—the proportion of independent versus inside directors. The role of the audit committee in overseeing and reporting the financial condition and operating results has been greatly increased. Committee membership was mandated to be entirely of independent directors. The definition of an independent director has been much more strongly circumscribed. In the United States, institutional investors have given strong support for a separation of the CEO function from the chairmanship. The importance of the internal auditor role has increased.

These are major changes that have been centrepieces of federal legislation, new rules promulgated by the exchanges or new SEC rules. It is, therefore, very interesting to note that academic research conducted on corporate boards has been singularly unable to demonstrate a relationship between structural changes and corporate performance. This has been a difficult reality for the advocates who have championed these various changes in the structure and operations of corporate boards.

Now, along comes a new book that investigates the question of how boardroom decision-making is conducted. Richard Leblanc, as the basis of his PhD dissertation, interviewed intensively almost 200 directors and observed in real time the operation of the boards and/or committees of twenty-one enterprises. James Gillies has the personal experience of serving on the boards of thirty companies. In essence, the authors reviewed how boards actually make decisions.

The authors classify board members by behavioural characteristics and analyze the interaction of groups with differing sets of characteristics. From this analysis, they hypothesize what attitudinal and personal traits produce highly productive boards as opposed to those less so. This, of course, leads to suggestions of how to structure a board that will be conducive to a highly productive and well-functioning enterprise.

One can ask why it has taken so long for a study such as this to appear. The answer, I believe, is simply that shareholder activists could observe the action of potential and current directors through data supplied by the proxy instrument or by SEC filings. However, it has been very difficult to learn about personal attributes and how individuals respond in board discussions and, in the process of making decisions, sitting as a board of directors. Board meetings have not been open to shareholders, even large institutional investors or even regulatory bodies. Interesting data about board decision-making does occasionally become public in court records or in controversial confrontations that are fought in public view with both sides vying for shareholder support. But these forms of information cannot properly be generalized and probably cause erroneous conclusions.

This is a truly pioneering work that is not only worth study by students and academics interested in corporate governance but should also be profitably read by directors, officers, investors, regulators and professional advisers interested in the construction of well-functioning boards.

Donald P. Jacobs
Dean Emeritus
Kellogg School of Management, Northwestern University

Acknowledgements

A study such as this could never have been completed without the assistance and co-operation of a host of directors and regulators who freely gave of their time and knowledge in the course of the completion of this study. To all we are extremely grateful.

Over the years, a number of our colleagues at the Schulich School of Business have been involved in the development of this book. We are particularly indebted to Professor Gareth Morgan, without whose help on the methodological problems associated with the research we could never have completed the work, and to Professor Rein Peterson, for the incisive comments he always cheerfully provided while the book was being written. Professor Ian McDougall of Osgoode Hall Law School was a helpful constructive critic of the work.

We owe a particular debt to Professor Robert Tricker, former editor of *Corporate Governance: An International Review*, Professor Bernard Taylor of Henley College and Drs. William Dimma and Josef Fridman for reading the manuscript and providing us with useful suggestions. We are extremely grateful to Laurence D. Hebb, Q.C., a former managing partner at Osler, Hoskin & Harcourt LLP. Larry's analytical rigour and consistent support contributed immensely to this book. In addition, Professor David Leighton, one of the great scholars in the field, not only read the manuscript, for which we are grateful, but over the years has been a friend, supporter and, at times, colleague. His friendship and encouragement as one of the pioneers in the study of corporate governance in Canada cannot be sufficiently acknowledged. We are also grateful for the commentary of Peter Bartha, Carol Hansell and Paul Waitzer, who discussed various aspects of the project with one of us as it evolved over time. And we owe a very special debt of thanks to Dr. Barbara Kelley who patiently introduced us to the complexities and ambiguities associated with contemporary behavioural psychology.

We gratefully acknowledge the support of the Institute for Corporate Directors (ICD) for permitting the use of some of the data generated by an ICD-funded study on director education, conducted by Dr. Leblanc. We also thank the Australian Institute of Company Directors, the Institute of Directors (London) and the National Association for Corporate Directors (Washington) for their continuing support.

The study of corporate governance is a tricky business. The authors could never have completed this study without the great good fortune of meeting, debating, chatting and exchanging views with a great many business leaders throughout the years. Among those who were particularly helpful in formulating our views, with which many disagree and who of course have no responsibility for them, are Ronald Atkey, John Bankes, Nicholas Barnett, Matt Barrett, Isabel Bassett, David Beatty, Jalynn Bennett, Roy Bennett, Conrad Black, Bill Blundell, David Brown, Michael Brown, the late Max Clarkson, John Cleghorn, David Conklin, Purdy Crawford, Tom D'Aquino, Robert Dale, Bill Davis, Graham Day, Michael Deck, Paul Desmarais, Jr., Peter Dey, Wendy Dobson, Bill Etherington, John Evans, Ralph Evans, Don Fullerton, the late George Gardiner, the late Douglas Gibson, Peter Gleason, Bill Glikbarg, Jim Goodfellow, Fred Gorbet, Peter Gordon, Chuck Hantho, Rob Hines, Ken Hugessen, Hal Jackman, Tom Kierans, Alex Lajoux, Claude Lamoureux, Patrick Lavelle, Jack Leitch, Frank Logan, Peter Lougheed, Fiona MacDonald, Michael Mackenzie, Joe Martin, Frank McKenna, Doreen McKenzie-Sanders, Margaret McNee, John McWilliams, Michael Meagher, Gord Nixon, Mary Mogford, Brian Mulroney, David O'Brien, Patrick O'Callaghan, Tom O'Neill, Heather Osler, Sunny Pal, David Peterson, Michael

Phelps, Chris Pierce, Gary Polonsky, Alfred Powis, Rob Prichard, Bob Rae, Ced Ritchie, Mac Ryerse, Guy Saint-Pierre, Art Sawchuck, Guylaine Saucier, Francis Saville, Seymour Schulich, Maureen Stapleton, Frank and Belinda Stronach, Maurice Strong, Larry Tapp, Paul Tellier, Axel Thesberg, Chris Thomas, Richard Thomson, Beverly Topping, Denis Turcotte, John Turner, Rudy Vezer, Liz Watson, Paul Weiss, Bill Weyerhaeuser, Rick Whiler, Bernie Wilson, Red Wilson, Rob Yalden, Adam Zimmerman and John Zych.

We also wish to express our deep appreciation to Dr. Dezsö J. Horváth, the wise, experienced and energetic Dean of the Schulich School of Business, for his constant encouragement of this project and his thoughtful insights on corporate governance. Dr. Leblanc also thanks Dr. Rhonda Lenton and Professor Joanne Magee, Dean and Associate Dean of the Atkinson Faculty of Liberal and Professional Studies, and Drs. Brian Gaber and Monica Belcourt, current and former Directors of the School of Administrative Studies, York University, for their support and commitment to the study of corporate governance, law and business ethics.

We sincerely appreciate the enthusiasm and encouragement which Karen Milner, Elizabeth McCurdy, Pam Vokey, Meghan Brousseau, Erin Kelly and Michelle Bullard at John Wiley & Sons brought to this book as they managed its production from manuscript to final form in a highly efficient and effective way.

By its very nature this book is highly controversial. It also almost certainly contains mistakes, contentious conclusions and unsupportable generalizations. For these we take full responsibility, blame and, if there is any, the occasional credit.

Richard Leblanc
Atkinson Faculty of Liberal and Professional Studies

James Gillies
Schulich School of Business

York University
Toronto, Canada

INTRODUCTION

Since the early 1990s, regulators, researchers, shareholders and directors themselves have paid great attention to the governance of corporations and boards of directors. Between 1990 and 2001 alone for instance, Australia, Brazil, Canada, France, Germany, Holland, Hong Kong, India, Italy, Japan, Malaysia, Russia, Singapore, South Africa, Sweden, the United Kingdom, the United States, and possibly a few other countries that we may have missed, including some where very few corporations exist, have developed and enacted codes and guidelines for corporate governance practices.

The amazing thing about all this activity is that it has been based on very little knowledge about the relationship of corporate governance to corporate performance, and almost no knowledge about how boards actually work. Paradoxically, while regulation of, and writing about, private sector boards has increased in a dramatic fashion, actual knowledge about how boards work has increased hardly at all. The reason for this is that boards are notoriously difficult to study. Of all the major institutions in society, they are probably the most closed. Few board meetings, if any, are ever open to the public and it is seldom that outsiders are invited to attend. Hence little is really known about how and why boards make decisions. Most of the writing about boards, and it has in recent years been voluminous, has been limited to analyzing information that is publicly available through annual reports, regulatory filings and

1

corporate releases. As a result, most writing is largely about various aspects of board structure and composition; that is, whether the positions of chair and CEO should be occupied by the same person, the appropriate percentage of independent directors that should serve on a board, the size of the board, the committee structure of boards and the independence of such committees, and so on.

This book differs from other books and articles on corporate governance in that it is based on original data obtained over a period of five years, from the study of the boards of directors of twenty-nine private sector for-profit companies, four government-owned enterprises, and six not-for-profit organizations. Most significantly, the study included attendance and observation in real time of activities at board and/or committee meetings of twenty-one of these organizations, which included eleven of the private sector boards and each of the government owned and not-for-profit boards being examined. In addition, since the research upon which this book is based was completed by Dr. Leblanc, he has observed and advised corporate boards and directors in Canada, the US and other countries. His findings from this additional work tend to support the hypotheses advanced in this study.

The twenty-nine private sector companies studied operated in almost every sector of the economy and ranged in size from large, including some of the largest corporations in North America, to small and medium. The type of ownership varied from widely held to closely controlled by a dominant individual, family or a foreign parent, and the majority were publicly listed on the Toronto and/or New York stock exchanges. While being studied, the boards were dealing with issues as diverse as CEO succession, mergers, acquisitions, divestitures, unfriendly takeovers, financial distress, global expansion and new government regulations.

The data obtained from attending board and committee meetings were supplemented by interviews with 194 directors, primarily, but not exclusively, with those associated with the companies studied, and included additional interviews with directors after this study had formally concluded. Directors' backgrounds were as diverse as their companies. The group consisted of current and former regulatory officials, active and retired directors and chief executive officers, as well as other officers of boards. In addition, the group included shareholder representatives and activists, lawyers, auditors, former senior politicians and government officials, consultants, compensation experts, human resource professionals, professors, university presidents and business school deans. Many of the directors interviewed served on more than one board, including the boards of companies domiciled outside of Canada.

Since many of the observations in this book are based on the collective views of the people interviewed, a very large number of quotations from the interviews are included in the text. While many are repetitious—many directors complain of the same problems—it is essential that the many quotes be read with care. Only by savouring the comments of almost 200 directors is it possible to gain a real flavour of the state of boardroom governance at the turn of the century. It should be noted, however, that no attempt was made to draw a random sample of directors interviewed and so broad generalizations should not be drawn from their views.

Traditionally, the study of corporate governance has been limited by the perceived inability of researchers to actually attend board meetings to observe "how in fact boards make decisions." The fact that this study was completed—and the means by which it was completed—should put an end to the idea that research on boards must be limited to published data and hearsay. It is possible to study the manner in which boards function in real time. The methodology of how this can be accomplished is summarized in Appendix B in order that this type of qualitative research may be replicated and built upon in the future.

Not astonishingly, the study's data indicate that the decision-making processes of boards are greatly influenced by the behavioural characteristics of individual directors. Consequently, a classification scheme for types of directors, based on behaviour, has been developed. Not unexpectedly, directors with certain behaviour patterns are common to an ideal, "functional board," which include the Conductor–Chair, Change Agent, Consensus-Builder, Counsellor and Challenger. Similarly, certain other directors are common to a "dysfunctional board," which include the Caretaker–Chair, Controller, Conformist, Cheerleader and Critic.

Based on the study's data gained by observing boards in action and interviewing practising directors, a model of the ideal, effective board of directors is proposed. The performance of a particular board or director may be measured against this model of the effective board. It is hypothesized that if the board of directors is effective, as defined by the proposed model, other things being equal, it will make decisions that will result in the company earning superior rates of return for the shareholders.

However, because so many exogenous factors impact on the financial performance of an individual firm, *neither effective nor ineffective* governance may be a necessary nor sufficient condition to ensure positive or negative financial performance. Indeed, the majority of the studies of corporate governance have not been able to show a causal relationship between the structure and form of boards and corporate financial success. This study of board activities does not either, nor was it designed to. But common sense suggests that there is a positive relationship between the two, and this study strongly indicates that the connection may be found by studying board processes.

The basic result of this study is the development of the hypothesis that boards based on structure and form may not be optimal for providing effective governance for a corporation. Rather, if good corporate governance, when governance is defined as effective decision-making, is a prerequisite for good corporate financial performance, directors must be selected on the basis of how their competencies and behavioural characteristics complement each other and how they match the strategies that a corporation may have for achieving its goals.

This study is the first of what we hope will be many in the analysis of the relationship between board and director effectiveness and corporate financial performance. Gaining greater knowledge of how boards function—of board processes—may be the key to resolving the still unsolved major question about corporate governance—"What are the conditions of corporate governance that must be present to assure solid corporate performance?"

BOARDS OF DIRECTORS HAVE FAILED AND WE DON'T KNOW WHY

Directors are like parsley on fish—decorative but useless.
—Irving Olds, former Chair, Bethlehem Steel

The director walks a tightrope. His responsibility is to be supportive to management, but not a rubber stamp. He directs, but he does not manage. Legally he has the ultimate responsibility for both the formulation of strategy and its implementation, but as a practical matter he relies on the CEO. He and his fellow directors elected the CEO, but he may later have to remove him. He is responsible for the long-run health of the corporation but most of the information he receives on its performance relates to the short run. He has a legal responsibility to the shareholders, but he has a moral responsibility to the employees, customers, vendors and society as a whole. He is responsible for keeping the shareholders informed, but at the same time he should not disclose information that would be adverse to the company's best interests. He has personal goals, as does the CEO. However, the director must ensure that neither his goals nor those of the CEO overshadow their obligations to the corporation and its goals.
—Charles A. Anderson and Robert N. Anthony,
in *The New Corporate Director*

It was the best of times; it was the worst of times.
—Charles Dickens in *A Tale of Two Cities*

Few people buy shares in a company for the sake of buying shares. Rather they become shareholders in the expectation that the value of their shares will increase—that they will make money. When they entrust the use of their funds to the corporation, a legal entity governed by a board of directors, it is an act of trust on their part that the board will make decisions that will not only conserve their capital but also increase it. And, by taking it, a board of directors is committing itself to accepting the responsibility of using other people's money in an intelligent, prudent, honest and successful manner.

Nothing is more important to the well-being of a corporation than its board of directors. The board, by law, has the responsibility for the overall performance of the business. It has the power to appoint the management of the enterprise, to delegate to it specific responsibilities and to oversee the strategic direction and the setting of long-term goals for the company. It is a self-governing body that has the power, within very few limits, to manage its own affairs. In short, the board, by law, is the *decision-making* body of the corporation. To the extent that the directors acting collectively as a board make wise decisions, the corporation will prosper; to the extent that the board does not, the corporation will stagnate or fail. Consequently, knowing how and why boards make decisions is fundamental to an understanding of why some corporations succeed and others do not.

And yet, in spite of the importance of board decision-making in the life and death of companies, little is known about how boards work. Almost nothing is known about the decision-making characteristics of individual board members, and even less is known about the manner in which individuals act together to arrive at board decisions, either in a crisis or in the normal course of business activity. In short, almost nothing is known about arguably the most important function of boards of directors—the way in which they make decisions.

IGNORANCE ISN'T BLISS

There are many reasons why companies succeed. Sometimes it is because the board of directors has selected extraordinarily good management; sometimes it is because of a technological advantage;

sometimes it is because of extraordinary timing in the production of a particular product.

Similarly, there are many reasons why companies fail. Sometimes it is because of exogenous events that the board of directors did not foresee and over which they had no control. Occasionally it is because the board is badly advised or there is fraud that they don't know about.[1] More often it is because they do not always insist on and/or participate in the development of effective strategies and astute activities that increase shareholder value. Indeed, unfortunately, many times it is because the board does not always effectively monitor the management of the enterprise, with the result that the owners lose money. And, all too often, a board monitors the activities of a company so poorly that the shareholders lose all their investment.

Boards of directors are not made up of stupid people. To the contrary, they often have as their members some of the brightest and best members of the community—men and women who have proven their capabilities in a variety of activities. Moreover, the tasks that directors are expected to perform are not only well-known, but under normal conditions are not overly onerous. And the motivation for directors to do well is great. Certainly no one joins a board of directors to help a company fail, or indeed does when the prospects of failure are expected to be substantial. Just the opposite: people join boards to assist in guiding an enterprise to success. And yet some boards make poor decisions that lead to disaster, whereas others make good decisions that lead to success.

But why is this so? Why do some boards choose brilliant chief executive officers while others do not? Why do some pick strategies that prove effective while others never seem to get things right? Why do some seem exceptionally able to calculate the risk involved in mergers and the advantages to be found in divestitures, whereas others engage in merger activities that never turn out well? Why do some boards seem continually to make wise decisions that lead to above average returns for the shareholders, whereas others never seem to be able to make any money?

---

1. It should be noted that by law directors are not responsible for business decisions that in the fullness of time turn out to be incorrect, if, at the time they made the decision, they exercised proper business judgment.

ASKING THE RIGHT QUESTIONS

Unfortunately, no one knows the answer to the most important question about corporate governance—"How do boards of directors make decisions?" No one knows the factors that lead to good or bad decision-making. No one knows how directors work together to decide what should be done in the best interest of the corporation. No one knows the factors that lead to good decision-making by a board when good decisions are identified as improving shareholders' value and stakeholders' interests. And, most importantly, no one knows how boards should be selected to assure that their decision-making capabilities are maximized. In short, no one knows the characteristics of an effective board.

It is the thesis of this book that board decision-making is a function of the competencies and behavioural characteristics of individual directors and how they fit together. It is argued that improvement in board operations will not be achieved, as is so often contended, by the enactment of more regulations and laws governing the structure of boards; rather that it will come through the willingness of directors, managers, regulators, shareholders and corporate leaders to accept new and different, somewhat radical, criteria for the selection, appointment and evaluation of directors.

Coming out of the trials and tribulations associated with corporate governance during the first years of this century is evidence to support the proposition that there *is momentum* to adopt new approaches to the creation of boards. Whether the momentum is sufficient to bring about a true revolution in corporate governance in the twenty-first century depends, in the final analysis, on the number of "change agents" there are among directors and corporate leaders who are willing to make major changes in their own organizations–corporate boards.

THE "SUMMER OF FRAUD"

The early years of this century have not been a period of particular pleasure for North American corporations and the people responsible for their regulation and governance. To the contrary, it has been one of the most devastating periods in the modern history of corporate capitalism. Corporate malfeasance and individual scandals have rocked the capital markets and destroyed investors' confidence and faith in many of the institutions that are fundamental to making the capitalist market system work. During the two-month period from May to June of 2002, referred to as the "summer of fraud" by James B. Comey, Deputy Attorney General of the United States,[2] the headings of major stories in the leading business magazines told the story.

Table 1.1

Headlines of Major Stories in Leading Business Magazines, May–June, 2002

- "Special Report: The Crisis in Corporate Governance," *Business Week*, May 6, 2002.
- "How Corrupt Is Wall Street?" *Business Week*, May 13, 2002, 37.
- "Trouble in the Boardroom," *Fortune*, May 13, 2002, 113.
- "Enron's Demise Has Taken the Shine Off the Boardroom Table," *Financial Times*, May 30, 2002, 14.
- "Tyco Board Is Criticized for Kozlowski Dealings," *Wall Street Journal*, June 7, 2002, A5.
- "The Wickedness of Wall Street," *The Economist*, June 8, 2002, 11.
- "SEC Wants CEOs, CFOs to Vouch For Reports, Disclose More, Sooner," *Investor's Business Daily*, June 13, 2002, A1.
- "Under the Board Talk: American Companies Need Stronger Independent Directors," *The Economist*, June 15, 2002, 13–14.
- "Designed by Committee: How Can Company Boards Be Given More Spine?" Special Report on Corporate Governance, *The Economist*, June 15, 2002, 69.
- "The SEC's Accounting Reforms Won't Answer Investors' Prayers ... But Changes in the Boardroom Could Rebuild Trust," *Business Week*, June 17, 2002, 28–29.
- "When Directors Join CEOs at the Trough," *Business Week*, June 17, 2002, 57.
- "Venal Sins: Why the Bad Guys of the Boardroom Emerged en Masse," *Wall Street Journal*, June 20, 2002, A1.
- "Restoring Trust in Corporate America: Business Must Lead the Way to Real Reform," *Business Week*, June 24, 2002, 31.

Continued

2. Luncheon address: "Lessons Learned from Recent Corporate Debacles," 2004 Annual Corporate Governance Conference, National Association of Corporate Directors, Washington, DC, October 18, 2004.

- "System Failure: Corporate America, We Have a Crisis: 7 Ways to Restore Investor Confidence," *Fortune*, June 24, 2002, 62–77.
- "WorldCom's Travails Could Affect Its Directors," *Wall Street Journal*, June 28, 2002, A9.

In a chart entitled "A Question of Accountability," *The New York Times*[3] listed examples of major American companies where there were "auditing lapses," "the hiding of loans or losses," "insider trading" and "inflating revenue." It reads like a Who's Who of North American business—Arthur Andersen, Deloitte & Touche, Ernst & Young, KPMG, PricewaterhouseCoopers, Adelphia Communications, Enron, Kmart, PNC Financial Services Group, Tyco International, WorldCom, ImClone Systems, Computer Associates International, CMS Energy, Dynegy, Edison Schools, Global Crossing, Halliburton, Lucent Technologies, Network Associates, Qwest Communications International, Reliant Resources, Trump Hotels and Casino, Waste Management and Xerox. Canadian examples of corporate failures and scandals include Livent, BreX, YBM Magnex, Philips and, most recently, Hollinger.

And is there anyone who has not heard of the stock market adventures of Martha Stewart? And that some leading executives have gone to jail for fraudulent practices?

Even in the heady days of the "takeover movement" in the early 1990s, when such high-powered players as Ross Johnson and Michael Milken were in the headlines, there was never such attention paid to the corporate community and the organizations with which it is associated—investment bankers, accountants, lawyers, brokers, commercial banks and investment advisers.

By any definition, the attacks and reports have not been undeserved. The damages and losses to corporate stakeholders resulting from the above failures and abuses were widespread and incredibly damaging. Retirees, employees, shareholders, bondholders, creditors and suppliers lost upwards of tens of millions and in some cases

3. June 16, 2002, BU 12.

billions of dollars as a consequence of mismanagement, accounting fraud, false reporting and totally misleading, if not downright dishonest, investment advice. The investments and pension plans of literally thousands of individuals and families were "wiped out" or essentially rendered worthless as a result of the breakdown in the institutions of capitalism. Given these scandals, it is not astonishing that the confidence the public once had in the fairness and honesty of the economic system has been significantly eroded. Nor is it surprising in the wake of such activities that, in the early years of this century, the American public began to be less willing to invest in much lauded American companies to the extent they had in the late 1990s.

CORPORATE ACCOUNTABILITY GOES CENTRE STAGE

Naturally, as the concern for "corporate accountability" gave way to questions about "corporate responsibility" and finally "corporate corruption," there was strong political reaction. In July 2002, the President of the United States, George W. Bush, delivered a major speech—a speech billed as important as a State of the Union address—on corporate responsibility. In this address, he outlined proposals for imposing strict discipline and punishment on corporate wrongdoers, and reiterated his administration's support for corporate governance reforms. He pledged a strengthening of the Securities and Exchange Commission (SEC) and endorsed the new listing proposals being advanced by the New York Stock Exchange (NYSE). Not to be outdone, in the same month, the United States House of Representatives and the United States Senate overwhelmingly passed H.R. 3763. Widely known as the "Sarbanes-Oxley Act of 2002," this legislation called for broad new regulations, described as the most far-reaching in over seventy years, affecting issuers of publicly traded securities, corporate directors and independent advisers such as auditors and lawyers. The Act was signed by the President and enacted into law on July 30, 2002.

Unfortunately, no one knows whether the Sarbanes-Oxley legislation will do much to improve corporate governance in America, other than increase the costs of operating governments and corporations.

According to law, the major responsibility for the operations of corporations lies with the board of directors, and the plethora of new regulations are designed to impact boards' operations, even though no one knows very much about how boards of directors work.

For the first seventy-five years or so of the twentieth century, despite the fact that boards of directors had the responsibility for the actions of the corporation, the conventional wisdom was that boards of directors actually did not have much impact on corporate operations. In fact, as long ago as 1932, Adolph Berle and Gardiner Means claimed in their book *The Modern Corporation and Private Property*[4] that the amount and spread of share ownership of the American corporation had become so great that owners no longer controlled the organizations that they owned.

It was not news that, as a result of the rise of American capitalism and the spread of share ownership, the vast majority of the owners of the modern corporation had little to do with the actual management of the companies that they owned. But what was new and absolutely startling in Berle and Means' book was the assertion that boards of directors no longer represented the interests of the owners, if they ever did, but rather they had become nothing more than the handmaidens of the managers of enterprises, *i.e.*, that there was a real separation between control and ownership. This was truly revolutionary thinking because, by law, directors were elected by the shareholders and paid to represent their interests. They were responsible for overseeing the well-being of the enterprise, including the appointment and firing of senior management, selecting strategies and protecting the investments of the owners. To the extent that they failed to fulfill these duties in a proper fashion, the shareholders could sue them, and occasionally they did.

LEGALLY POWERFUL, BUT NOT REALISTICALLY POWERFUL

As usual, the conventional wisdom was correct. While by law the directors had all the power, directors exerted practically none. Their

4. Adolph Berle and Gardiner Means, *The Modern Corporation and Private Property* (Buffalo, New York: Macmillan and Company, 1933).

nomination and election was dictated by management, with the result that boards were controlled by management instead of the other way around. And since management controlled the directors, management was able to run the organization in its own interest, rather than the shareholders'.

Consequently, Olds' characterization of directors being "like parsley on fish—decorative but useless," while somewhat exaggerated was basically true. The men (and sometimes women) directors showed up three or four times a year at the headquarters of the corporation an hour or so before lunch to sign the financial statements, exchange friendly banter and smoke cigars, and then headed out for a good golf game. Even though they were legally responsible for monitoring the enterprise, they really had nothing to do with the operations of the company.

BOARDS HISTORICALLY WERE PAID LITTLE ATTENTION

Given this reality, it is not astonishing that for at least half a century—from the end of World War II until the mid-1980s—little attention was paid to the role of the board in the governing of the corporation, or indeed to any aspect of corporate governance. General business histories of the period seldom mentioned boards. For example, Michael Bliss' *Northern Enterprise: Five Centuries of Canadian Business*,[5] considered by some to be the most exhaustive history of Canadian business ever written, does not even list boards of directors in the index.

Perhaps even more striking is that, for nearly half a century, management scholars paid almost no attention to boards and directors. In fact the term "corporate governance" was not even used until well into the 1980s.[6] Management texts and courses devoted almost no time to the study of boards. Koontz and O'Donnell's *Management* (1980)[7] one of, if not the best-selling of the texts in

---

5. Michael Bliss, *Northern Enterprise: Five Centuries of Canadian Business* (Toronto: McClelland and Stewart, 1987).
6. Robert Tricker, *The Pocket Director* (London: The Economist and Profile Books, 1993). The first book with the title *Corporate Governance* was published in 1984 and the academic journal, *Corporate Governance: An International Review*, began publishing in 1993.
7. Harold Koontz, Cyril O'Donnell, and Heinz Weihrich, *Management*, 7th ed. (New York: McGraw-Hill, 1980).

general management in the post—World War II period, had only a few pages on the role of the board. And it is not astonishing that perhaps the most important scholar in strategy and management writing during the period, Alfred Chandler, in his great classics *Strategy and Structure: Chapters in the History of the Industrial Enterprise*[8] and *The Visible Hand: The Managerial Revolution in American Business*,[9] focuses on the role of management and gives little importance to the role of boards, providing further confirmation that boards were essentially unimportant factors in the governing of most corporations.

Boards, of course, were not totally dismissed. In 1971, Miles Mace of the Harvard Business School published *Directors: Myth and Reality*,[10] in which he generally agreed that boards did not do much and there were occasional articles about the role of boards, but by and large they were more or less ignored through the first three-quarters of the twentieth century by scholars, chief executive officers and everyone else interested in business. They were basically treated as something that the law required incorporated organizations to have—something not of any real consequence and about which very little was known. In the first three-quarters of the twentieth century, boards of directors played a very limited role in monitoring and assisting the management of the corporation, despite the law.

Given that so much of today's regulations and codes are directed at improving governance through "improving the board of directors," the significant questions with respect to corporate governance now have to be: "Has the role of the board of directors changed dramatically in the past quarter of a century?"; "Do directors have any, let alone a major, impact on the way in which corporations are governed?"; and "Do directors exercise the power they legally have?" If the answer to these questions is "yes," then concentrating on regulating and reforming boards makes considerable

---

8. Alfred Chandler, *Strategy and Structure: Chapters in the History of the Industrial Enterprise* (Cambridge, Mass.: MIT Press, 1962).

9. Alfred Chandler, *The Visible Hand: The Managerial Revolution in American Business* (Cambridge, Mass.: Kelknap Press, 1988).

10. Miles Mace, *Directors: Myth and Reality* (Boston, Mass: Division of Research, Harvard Business School, 1971).

sense. But if the answer is no, then it is not likely that governance will improve markedly.

INTEREST INCREASES IN BOARD ACTIVITIES

Before the very serious problems in governance developed in the early years of this century, the conventional view was that, for a number of reasons, the not-terribly-important role of the board in the governance of enterprises was at least increasing, and that, by-and-large, directors were beginning to exercise considerably more influence on the governance of the corporations of which they were directors.

MERGERS AND ACQUISITIONS

One of the most important phenomena leading to the increasing role of boards in corporations' activities (and giving boards a good deal of publicity) was the beginning in the mid-1980s of the unfriendly takeovers movement. Traditionally, mergers and acquisitions among companies were usually, at least on the surface, relatively friendly, but by the mid-1980s, with the development of junk bond financing and other financial schemes, there were few major publicly-held companies that did not have a controlling shareholder that were safe from, or uninvolved in, a takeover bid. In order to protect what many managers felt was "their company" from an unfriendly takeover bid, many managements recommended to their boards that they put in place "a poison pill," otherwise known as a shareholder rights plan, or some other restriction designed to make it more difficult for takeover offers to be made, let alone succeed.

Historically, when change of control of companies took place, it was usually done, at least publicly, in a friendly manner. The chief executive officers would get together and work out the terms of the deal, then present them to their boards, which usually automatically endorsed the arrangement and recommended to the shareholders that they approve the transaction. It was all very straightforward, with a few major law firms and investment houses providing the professional services necessary to get the deals completed. Indeed, from the 1930s until the 1980s, no prestigious corporation would get involved in an unfriendly takeover and, if

Continued

some extraordinarily ambitious chief executive officer tried to mount an attack on a rival corporation, it is doubtful that any of the outstanding law or investment firms would support him. It was all very polite.

In the 1980s, this rather cozy situation changed as unfriendly takeovers became very common. Some of the largest companies in the United States and Canada either became the object of an unfriendly takeover, or conversely tried, and often succeeded, in taking over an enterprise that simply did not want to merge with them. Seagram's, Dupont, Mobile Oil, United States Steel, Hiram Walker and Occidental Petroleum, to mention only a few, were all involved in transactions where control was gained or lost. The battles were often quite fierce and the rewards and losses extremely high.

If corporate boards did decide to grant approval for so-called poison pills, as many boards did, in order to deter or prevent takeovers, boards had to be careful that they did not do anything that might make it more difficult for shareholders to maximize the value of their shares in the future. To the extent that they did, they were not fulfilling their fiduciary responsibilities to the shareholders to maximize shareholder value over time. In the case of a takeover threat, boards normally hire their own professional advisers, lawyers and investment bankers—and, if there is more than one bidder, try to arrange an auction so that the highest possible price is obtained for the shareholders. The board does all these things independent of the management, because these matters are the board's responsibilities, not management's.

When a company is faced with an unwanted takeover bid, shareholders look (and still do) to the board to determine whether the company should be sold and whether the price offered is appropriate. If the directors decide that the company should not be sold to the "raider," they may put in place various defensive efforts that can involve selling off particular assets or finding alternative, more suitable, buyers for the company. Then and now, the board must decide what to recommend to the shareholders—to accept the bid or to fight it—because, by law, only the shareholders can sell the company. Giving a recommendation is not easy, since management often was, and usually still is, opposed to a change in control, if for no other reason than they want to protect their jobs.

Institutional Investors

Another significant reason for the increased interest in boards of directors was the increasing importance of institutional investors, primarily mutual and pension funds, in the marketplace. Historically, the funds paid little attention to the governance of corporations. However, as they became larger and began holding an ever increasing percentage of shares in various companies, it became more difficult for them to divest of shares if they were unhappy with a company's current or expected future performance, without causing a serious deterioration in share prices. For a variety of "conflict of interest" problems, they are not able to have direct representation on boards, but, because of their large shareholdings, they are able to bring pressure on corporations with respect to various governance matters. It has become the practice of organizations such as the California Public Employees' Retirement System (CalPERS) to take positions with respect to who should be on boards, by withholding their vote for directors recommended by management when they believe that such directors are not properly fulfilling their duties. The message they sent and are sending is clear: directors have to be real directors or their election will not be supported.

And the threat has not been an idle one. General Motors, Xerox, Kodak, Westinghouse, Disney and many other major American corporations have been influenced in director selection and other matters of governance by the position taken by large institutional investors. Needless to say, nominating committees are much more careful in selecting candidates for a board position, and current directors are much more conscious of their performance when they know they are being assessed by very powerful shareholders.

Directors' Legal Liability

Moreover, the possibility of a lawsuit because of failure to fulfill one's duty of care and loyalty to the corporation has increased immensely during the past two decades. In their own interest, directors have had to take a more active role in the affairs of the corporation. While directors are protected by the business judgment rule and cannot be successfully sued for making a business mistake, if they use the rule as a defence they must, ever since the famous *Van Gorkom* case in the United States, demonstrate that they did in fact use their informed business judgment when they made the decision that is being questioned.[11] In addition, in recent years there has been a great increase in the statutory obligations of directors. Directors must be concerned about their personal financial obligations for possible unpaid wages if a corporation becomes bankrupt; about certain environmental damages that may result from actions of the company; about unpaid taxes; and about unpaid contributions to pension, unemployment and social security funds. The risks of not being a vigilant and responsible director are very much higher now than they were in the 1970s.

PRESSURE FOR EFFICIENT, EFFECTIVE OPERATIONS

Finally, there have also been enormous positive reasons to expect major enterprises to be governed more effectively. During the past quarter of a century, because of the progress in the transmission of information, the increase in the speed of transportation and the elimination of many tariffs, the market for almost every good and service has become worldwide. For most companies this has meant a substantial increase in competition. No longer can firms be content to be the low-cost producers in their local market. They have to be the low-cost producers in the world. If they are not, someone will come and take their domestic market share away from them. Modern firms need modern strategies or they will not survive.

The clever chief executive officer and wise board of directors know this. As a result, they are constantly looking for directors who can help them evolve the optimum competitive policies for their firm. They do not want, and cannot survive, with a board composed of members who have no interest in the company and bring nothing to the table to make it operate better in the interests of all its stakeholders. Competition is a driving force in increasing the importance of boards and the quality of directors in modern corporations.

As a result, at the beginning of the twenty-first century it was broadly believed that corporate governance in general was better

11. *Smith v. Van Gorkom*, 488 A. (2d) 858 (Del. 1985).

understood and much improved, and that regulations governing various aspects of corporate activity were becoming more effective—that, in general, all was relatively well in the corporate world as directors went about their task of maximizing values for shareholders, and the economy and stock market both set new records in levels of activity.

THE "CORPORATE GOVERNANCE BUBBLE" BURSTS

Unlike in the period from 1930 to 1980, when boards, directors and the concept of corporate governance were generally ignored, one of the consequences of the takeovers movement, the growth of institutional investors, *etc.,* has been that the study, analysis and popularization of the corporation has increased tremendously. Biographies and autobiographies of top corporate executives such as Jack Welch of General Electric[12] and Thomas Watson[13] of IBM headed the bestseller lists. Participants in takeover battles became famous. *Barbarians at the Gate,*[14] by Bryan Burrough and John Helyar, chronicling the battle for control of RJR Nabisco, was on the *New York Times'* bestseller list for months and eventually was made into a movie for television. Connie Bruck's *The Predators' Ball*[15] provides a highly entertaining account of several takeovers, with great emphasis given to the part played by Michael Milken. Newly minted investment firms like Drexel Burnham Lambert and law firms such as Skadden Arps became noted for advising on takeovers.

Not astonishingly, at the same time, a number of academic studies and articles on corporate governance began to appear. Gillies,[16] Leighton and Thain[17] and Dimma[18] used a wealth of personal experience as the basis of their writing, while Lorsch, author of probably the most popular of all the texts on the subject, *Pawns or Potentates,*[19]

12. Jack Welch and John A. Byrne, *Jack: Straight From the Gut* (New York: Warner Business Books, 2001).

13. Thomas Watson, *Father, Son and Company* (New York: Bantam Books, 1990).

14. Bryan Burroughs and John Helyar, *Barbarians at the Gate: The Fall of RJR Nabisco* (New York: Harper and Row: 1990).

15. Connie Bruck, *The Predator's Ball* (New York: The American Lawyer/Simon and Schuster, 1988).

16. James Gillies, *Boardroom Renaissance: Power, Morality and Performance in the Modern Corporation* (Toronto: McGraw-Hill Ryerson Ltd., 1992).

17. D. S. R. Leighton and D. H. Thain, *Making Boards Work: What Directors Must Do to Make Canadian Boards Effective* (Toronto: McGraw-Hill Ryerson, 1997).

18. W. A. Dimma, *Excellence in the Boardroom: Best Practices in Corporate Directorship* (Toronto: Wiley, 2002).

19. J. W. Lorsch and E. MacIvar, *Pawns or Potentates: The Reality of America's Corporate Boards* (Boston: Harvard Business School Press, 1989).

based his work on interviews with nearly one hundred directors. Literally hundreds of articles on corporate governance appeared in the business journals and popular press. All had the underlying theme that governance was improving and boards were getting better—that directors were more conscious of their responsibilities to their stakeholders, and particularly to shareholders, the owners of the enterprises. And the slogan "maximizing shareholder value" became the theme of everyone associated with corporate governance.

And yet, despite all the work and analysis, and all the reports and commissions, little was learned during the period about how boards actually work. Numerous kinds of assumptions were made about corporate governance, and on the basis of these unproven assumptions, regulations and laws were passed that impacted directly on the structure and activities of boards of directors.

In short, during the last decade of the twentieth century, just as there was a "stock market bubble" and a "new technology bubble," there was a bubble in "corporate governance analysis." This bubble, based on few facts, suggested that, in spite of problems here and there, corporate governance in general had improved, new and significant regulations had been put in place that ensured that it would improve even more, and all was well for stakeholders in major widely-held public corporations. It, like the first two bubbles, also burst.

CRISIS MANAGEMENT LEADS TO NEW REGULATIONS

There were two major results of the extensive attention paid to corporate governance in the 1990s. First, it was increasingly believed, at least by academics, that the role of the board of directors, if any, implicitly if not explicitly, was really important only when a company was in crisis.[20] It was assumed that, as long as things were going reasonably well, there really was no significant function for the board to play. As a result, the focus on corporate governance from the point of view of the internal management of the firm was more on crisis

---

20. Savan Chatterjee and Jeffrey S. Harrison, "Corporate Governance" in Michael A. Hitt, R. Edward Freeman and Jeffrey S. Harrison, eds., *The Blackwell Handbook of Strategic Management* (Oxford: Blackwell Publishers, 2001), Chapter 19.

management than on the positive, traditional tasks associated with the board working with and monitoring management to increase the value of the enterprise on behalf of the shareholders. Second, it was generally accepted that in a capitalist system with free markets, the failure of major firms was still quite understandable and acceptable, as long as the failures were the result of market forces, but quite unacceptable if they resulted from 1) inadequacies in the institutional and legal framework within which corporations operated or 2) fraudulent behaviour on the part of the enterprises' management.

As a result of the emphasis on crisis management, which largely centred on how boards should act in the face of takeovers, a series of laws and regulations were developed that outlined acceptable procedures for dealing with such situations. Eventually it became accepted that a takeover crisis was best managed through the appointment of a special committee of the board, with the power to retain its own advisers, who, if it were decided to sell the company, would arrange to do so to the highest bidder through an auction process. While there was a modest amount of legislation associated with the crisis aspects of corporate governance, the evolution of the handling of crises was basically driven more by corporate law than by the tenets of corporate governance.[21]

Such was not the case with respect to dealing with corporate failures and perceived corporate abuses. These were dealt with through public policy and, in country after country, codes of conduct for boards were written and either enacted into law or made a condition for a company to be registered on a major exchange. In Great Britain, a committee chaired by Sir Adrian Cadbury prepared a report on appropriate corporate governance.[22] It was followed by similar committees chaired by James Treadway[23] in the U.S. and by Peter Dey[24] in Canada.

---

21. See various securities acts with reference to takeover bids and issuer bids, *e.g.*, Part XX of the *Ontario Securities Act*.

22. A. Cadbury, "Highlights of the Proposals of the Committee on Financial Aspects of Corporate Governance" in D. D. Prentice and P. R. J. Holland, eds., *Contemporary Issues in Corporate Governance* (Oxford: Clarendon Press, 1993).

23. The Committee of Sponsoring Organizations (COSO), "The Report of the National Commission on Fraudulent Financial Reporting," otherwise known as the "Treadway Report," after the Chairman of the Commission, former SEC Commissioner, James C. Treadway, October 1987.

24. The Toronto Stock Exchange Committee on Corporate Governance in Canada, "Report: 'Where Were the Directors?' Guidelines for Improved Corporate Governance in Canada," otherwise known as "The Dey Report" (Toronto: Toronto Stock Exchange, December, 1994).

All the reports, not unexpectedly and correctly, focused on the board of directors, for after all it is the board that makes the decisions that determine how the corporation functions. The underlying assumption of all codes, regulations and reports was that, if a company fails, it was basically because of poor decision-making by the board. Consequently, it was argued quite correctly that it follows that, if board decision-making were improved, corporate performance would improve. The question was, therefore, how to improve board decision-making. All the major reports emphasized that regulating the structure of the board could best do it. By this they meant, to one degree or another, that

- it was essential that directors be independent from management and that the majority come from outside the firm;
- the position of the chair of the board and the chief executive officer of the company be held by different people;
- the board be organized into committees to fulfill certain functions such as nominating new directors;
- where it was not already required by law, an audit committee composed of a majority of independent directors be formed.

Basically, the recommended changes in the form and structure of boards were made on the assumption that such changes would lead to better corporate governance through better decision-making by the board in performing its responsibilities in monitoring the activities of the corporation. They were not in any way developed to ensure that the corporation would be better able, through a different board structure, to earn a higher rate of return for the shareholders. It was clearly assumed, if it were thought of at all, that improved internal monitoring of the activities of the corporation should improve the performance of the firm, on the simple assumption that if activities are not monitored effectively, the firm may well fail.

So, the important questions about corporate governance, arising from the rash of regulations and law impinging on the structure of the board are:

1. Have all the new regulations providing for more effective monitoring of corporations by the board of directors resulted in fewer board failures?

2. Have the new regulations had any impact on the performance of corporations?

The answer to the first question is, nobody knows.

It is impossible to prove the negative. Without the increased regulations designed primarily to prevent conflicts of interest and to maintain a balance of real power between the board and management, there may well have been much more malfeasance in the operation of companies. Given the rash of failures and problems of major corporations such as Enron, Nortel, WorldCom, Adelphia, ImClone, Global Crossings, *et al.*, many of which carefully followed the rules of good governance as recommended by regulators, it is difficult, however, to believe that the regulations made much difference.

On the other hand, there is little doubt that the regulations have had an impact on the structure of boards. The number of outside directors on boards has increased markedly; there has been a rash of separations of the office of chair and chief executive officer; and much more attention is being paid to issues of corporate governance by many more companies. Whether or not the changes in the structure of boards have had any major impact on the decision-making capacities of boards of directors is another question. At any rate, however, the evidence does not support the view that the results of the regulations and rules have had any positive relationship to corporate performance.

BOARDS OF DIRECTORS AND CORPORATE PERFORMANCE: IF THERE IS A CONNECTION, THEN WHY CAN'T WE EXPLAIN IT?

There are several reasons why studies to date have not been able to demonstrate a relationship between various recommendations about board structure and corporate performance. First, the cynics may be correct—none may exist. Second, there may be so many internal and external contingencies and intervening and moderating factors causing a corporate failure or success, such as a natural disaster or war, that to demonstrate a causal link between board performance and corporate financial performance may simply be impossible. Complex regression analysis equations may be incapable of resolving this issue because they are not capable of handling so many variables. Third, many of the factors involved in board performance may not be able to be expressed in measurable forms. Fourth, there may be time lags between when boards act and when company performance responds that may make any relationship difficult to find.

Another reason for the lack of studies demonstrating a relationship between corporate governance and corporate financial performance may be a political one. Professor Westphal suggests that leaders of the corporate governance reform movement, including "corporate leaders, public policy makers, institutional investors and other corporate stakeholders," have ignored the findings of academic research (see Chapter 5) and "have already chosen board independence as a rallying cry or unifying theme of the governance reform movement, and to change the message now would diminish the focus, unity and credibility of the movement."[25] Dr. Westphal goes on to state that "[a] focus on independence may also attract more attention to the movement, as it taps into popular suspicions about corporate leaders and concerns about the apparently "excessive" CEO pay and perquisites. A focus on director capabilities may be less effective as a lightning rod to mobilize the governance reform movement." In addition, Westphal remarks that "[r]egulators seem more concerned about the impressions that their policies will create than about formulating policies grounded in rational principles and empirical evidence.[26] Professor Donald Thain in Canada was equally critical of the empirical foundation of the Toronto Stock Exchange corporate governance guidelines when they were initially enacted in 1994, when he wrote, "The result is recommendations that have no systematic base in fact and stated logic."[27]

---

25. J. D. Westphal, "Second Thoughts On Board Independence: Why Do So Many Demand Board Independence When It Does So Little Good?" *The Corporate Board* 23:136 (September/October 2002): 10.
26. *Ibid.*
27. D. H. Thain, "The TSE Corporate Governance Report: Disappointing" *Business Quarterly* 59:1 (1994): 80.

LACK OF KNOWLEDGE OF BOARD PERFORMANCE

Some (most) of the above explanations may not be particularly compelling, and perhaps a few are overstated. A much more likely reason for the lack of knowledge is that in all the research that has been done, there is almost no analysis of how boards perform as boards. Surely "the human dynamics of boards as social systems where leadership character, individual values, decision-making processes, conflict management, and strategic thinking"[28] at play are as important, if not more so, as the structural composition of the board in determining the nature of the governance of the entity. And yet, in all of the research and analysis of the performance of boards that has been done, an explanation of how boards make decisions is missing although this may well be the *most important factor in determining the effectiveness of the governance of an enterprise.*

The major reason this gaping hole in knowledge about boards exists is that there is almost no public knowledge about the manner in which boards operate. No semi-public (in the sense that they have hundreds of shareholders) institutions are more removed from public inspection than are corporate boards. Meetings of every level of government—municipal, state or provincial, federal and international—are open to the public and often televised, and yet meetings of the boards of companies in which people have invested their money are shrouded in secrecy. The few times when shareholders observe the board members of the companies they own are at carefully planned and conducted annual meetings. The only people who actually know how boards operate are directors themselves, and they, of course, can only reflect on the quality of the decision-making process for the boards of which they are members.[29]

Consequently, boards are extremely difficult to study. As a class they tend to be closed groups, bound by confidentiality, privilege and customs, and are very difficult to access. Few people other than directors have ever attended a board meeting. Corporate directors tend to be fairly homogeneous in terms of gender, race, socio-economic

---

28. J. Sonnenfeld, "Good Governance and the Misleading Myths of Bad Metrics" *Academy of Management Executive* 18:1 (2004): 112.

29. Various tables in Chapter 3 cite directors' views on the effectiveness of the boards on which they serve and that of individual directors.

level, *etc.* A board is a relatively small, concentrated and interrelated group of individuals who have a common interest in maintaining their privacy, with linkages and associations not commonly apparent to most laypeople or academics. As a result, gaining access to board meetings to study directors' behaviour is very difficult, and almost all the empirical work on boards of directors has been based on material that can be obtained from outside the boardroom—annual reports, proxy circulars, press releases and court hearings. The "human factors" in governance have been left out.

Table 1.2

Some Directors' Observations on Corporate Governance: the Good, the Cautious and the Disillusioned

"The real issue in corporate governance . . . is that 10 percent of the corporate governance is outstanding whereas 90 percent of it is not." (director)

"Good governance leads to good performance." (chair and CEO of a financial institution)

"Good governance contributes to superior corporate performance—there's no doubt in my mind." (director)

"Boards matter all the time. There's no question that better companies have the best boards. In times of crisis, the intensity of activity heightens. Strong companies were built by having strong boards and good management and good strategy." (director)

"Stakeholders are popular normatively but shareholders are the reality." (director)

"Boards consider stakeholders only if it's in their interest to do so." (director)

"Nothing is more important than good corporate governance. It's shareholder value. . . . Stakeholder value is also important. The corporation has a big responsibility to stakeholder value. It's not shareholder value by itself, but includes stakeholder value such as society, communities, etc., who produce dividends for shareholders. You have to weigh these things for good corporate governance. It's also timeframe, short term versus long term. There's a tendency to focus on the short term, but we're here for the long term." (director)

"[T]here are no hard and fast rules on corporate governance. . . . It is not an exact science. It's an ability to analyze and decide whether it's the right thing for the people affected. It's not short term, but a weighing. The legal, moral and ethical are there to balance when you're a board member, and ultimately voting. You're always weighing. It's the same in Cabinet, from a governance standpoint. You're weighing. What's the net-net benefit to the country over the longer term? I practised corporate governance all the time . . . every minute of every hour of every day. . . . Very seldom is it win-win. There are tradeoffs and it's a question of degree of win and loss. So corporate governance is judgment and net-net over the longer term." (director)

"It's foolish to think that good governance keeps you out of trouble. You will lessen the likelihood of trouble and maximize performance but with good governance you can still have judgmental errors by the board and errors of management, which tend to be errors of timing rather than errors of product or service. Good governance alone does not protect institutions from making mistakes and legitimate mistakes. It's one of the tools." (director)

"The measurability of governance? It's not measurable. This is an art form. Even some of the very best boards go through bad luck, extraordinarily adverse conditions, which contaminate the data, and you don't know if there was a deeper downside." (director)

"In the correlation between corporate governance and financial performance, what's the causal event? In many cases it's not doing something. For example, the board says 'no.' How do you measure this? What's the negative correlation to a non-event?" (director)

"[C]orporate governance is the most difficult part of business to quantify. Although it has a great effect on the success of the venture, it does not have a measurement like EPS or cash flow. There is nothing in business that is so related to basic human nature as an independent outside board of directors." (CEO)

Continued

"[The] quantitative rigour ignores 80 percent of what matters." (director)

"The smartest boards can be caught off base to a certain degree, so good governance is not enough." (director)

"Good governance does not get you there and good governance does not grow a company." (director)

"Institutional shareholders don't give a _____ [30] about the stakeholders, yet if I'm CEO of [Company ABC], I have to worry about consumers, creditors, communities, governments. . . . I'm very careful. Institutional shareholders don't give a _____ . They're in it for the short-term hype. Six months and they're out. . . . Let's start to focus on institutions. Where's your corporate governance, you holier than thou _____ ?" (director)

"It's a country club—you bring your friends in, not who is most effective. This exists because the board does not truly acknowledge what its role is and the needs and demands of shareholders are not highest. . . . Rare is the case when people are brought on to the board based on what they can contribute. It's payback for a favour, throwing a bone, a good name, not competence or value." (director)

"The result is recommendations [by the "Dey Committee"] that have no systematic base in fact and stated logic." (D. H. Thain, "The TSE Corporate Governance Report: Disappointing" *Business Quarterly* 59:1 (1994): 80.

"This governance stuff has been all blown out of whack." (controlling shareholder)

"If I hear one more thing about corporate governance, I think I'm going to puke." (chair)

And yet, gaining an understanding of the internal workings of boards, which Leighton and Thain refer to as "the black box of corporate governance,"[31] through observing boards at work in real

---

30. Profanity and expletives exist within some of the quotations. Although only a small minority of respondents used foul language, by excising the existence of swear words, the integrity and meaning of some of the commentary and trustworthiness of the data might be affected. The decision was made, therefore, not to tamper with the quotations, other than by succinct editing.

31. Leighton and Thain, *Making Boards Work: What Directors Must Do to Make Canadian Boards Effective*: xviii.

time is probably the only way of obtaining a truly comprehensive understanding of the role the board plays in determining the corporation's performance. Almost nothing is known about how directors relate to one another as a group, how the board interacts with management or how decisions actually get made, both inside and outside of the boardroom. And yet it is the work of the board and the way that it is done that is the most important factor in determining the relationship between corporate governance and corporate performance. The current reality of corporate governance knowledge is that the "what" and "how" of a board of directors—its work and its processes—are still unknown.

It is interesting that the inability to find a positive relationship between most of the recommendations for changes in the structure of boards and better corporate performance has not in any way lessened the general view of directors, chief executive officers, politicians and regulators that one exists. In fact, only one respondent, of the almost 200 interviewed for this book, was of the view that better boards *do not* make for better companies. This prominent director remarked that "boards negatively impact financial performance, as currently constituted" and were "grotesque orgies of self-protection." Overwhelmingly, however, directors persist in believing that there is a persuasive relationship between corporate governance and corporate performance, and yet no one knows what it is.

And their intuition and experiences are probably quite correct. It may well turn out that the much sought after "missing link" between corporate governance and corporate performance will be found in "board process." It may well be that when more is learned about board process—the appropriate interaction of boards for successful decision-making—that directors, nomination committee chairs, institutional and private investors, regulators and lawmakers will be able to make the decisions and regulations that will lead to more effective corporate governance performance, which, in turn, will lead to better corporate performance.

THE MANY FORMS OF THE MODERN CORPORATION

A corporation "is a collection of individuals united in one collective body under a special name and possessing certain ... capacities in its collective character which do not belong to the natural persons composing it. Among other things it possesses the capacity of perpetual succession and of acting by the collective vote or will of its members. . . . In short it is an artificial being existing in contemplation of the law and endowed with certain powers . . . as distinctly as if it were a real personage."
—Chief Justice Marshall, *The Dartmouth College Case, 1819*

The modern corporation, as we know it today, is a creature of the law. It cannot exist outside of organized government and it cannot operate where the rule of law does not exist. In all countries with, and even some without, modern economies where there are organized governments and the rule of law, legislation has been enacted under which corporations can be created. In most countries these acts are relatively permissive in the sense that they make it very easy for a corporation to be chartered.[1] Usually, all that is required of

---

1. The analysis in this book is limited to corporations incorporated under English common law. For a number of years following World War II, with the globalization of business, there was a general feeling that "corporate law" and "corporate practices" would converge among the leading trading nations of the world. Since the major difference in corporate governance between Europe (with the exception of the United Kingdom) and the countries where English common law prevailed is the existence of the two-tiered board (administrative and management) there was some thought that with the development of the European Common Market there might be a general movement to a one-tiered type of governance. In fact, such a change has not happened.

31

people seeking to form a company is that they be of legal age, not bankrupt and of sound mind. In short, individuals are given the right to create an organization that to all intents and purposes is a form of private government—a legal entity, separate from its members, with a permanent existence.

A modern corporation has the following characteristics:

- the right to acquire other corporations and engage in activities of its own choice;
- a separation of ownership and management and division of authority between management and a board of directors, governors or overseers;
- limited liability for those who invest in it.

Through the years, literally tens of thousands of laws and regulations have been enacted that impact upon the corporation, but the fundamental concept of the institution over the centuries has not changed.[2]

A VAST ARRAY OF SIMILARITIES AND DIFFERENCES

Because economies have become so complex and the law is so permissive with respect to the organization of corporations, it is not astonishing that almost every type of corporation that can be imagined has, at some time or in some place, been created. They can range in size from one-person companies selling one product or providing one service in a small town, to gigantic organizations with sales larger than the gross national product of some countries, selling a multitude of different products throughout the world, *e.g.*, General Motors and Walmart, and there is every type in between. But regardless of their shape or form, all corporations have two things in common: they have a shareholder or shareholders whose liability is limited to the investment they make in the enterprise, and they have a board of directors.

2. The Code of Hammurabi in 2083 B.C. is the first known set of laws governing the organization of entities for the carrying on of commercial transactions.

Although the basic concept of the corporation, *i.e.*, that the corporation is owned by shareholders who elect a board of directors to oversee the operations of the enterprise in their interests, continues to be the basis from which the myriad of laws governing the corporation flow, it is an empirical reality that the concept is far from a true reflection of the way in which many (most) modern corporations operate. The vast majority of people who buy shares in corporations do not perceive themselves as owners, but rather as investors.[3] If they are dissatisfied with the manner in which the corporation is managed, they do not act as owners and change the management, because in reality they have no feasible way of doing so; rather, they act as investors and sell their shares. Similarly, the board of directors, certainly for most of the twentieth century and the early years of the twenty-first, have generally been believed to be the *handmaidens* of the executives of the firm rather than the effective *representatives* of the shareholders.[4] Even the large institutional investors—it is interesting that they are seldom referred to as institutional owners—that are the largest single shareholders in a company often do not have representation on the boards of corporations in which they have an important interest.[5]

This difference between concept and reality is one of the reasons why analyzing and regulating corporations has, through the years, proven to be very difficult. Since it is quite clear that the situation is not going to change—the laws and regulations governing the corporation continue to be based on the ancient concept of shareholders with limited liability depending on boards of directors that they elect to protect their interest—it is important to know precisely what the law and the continuing court interpretations define as the basic legal duties of directors and a board of directors.

THE LEGAL DUTIES OF DIRECTORS AND BOARDS
While the amount of work required of directors varies enormously among companies of different sizes and in different industries, the

---

3. Michael Lewis, "The Immorality of Investors," *The New York Times Magazine* (June 8, 2004): 68 *et seq.*

4. See Berle and Means, *The Modern Corporation and Private Property*, and Chapter 1.

5. In many jurisdictions, there are various legal requirements that prevent certain types of institutional investors from sitting on boards of directors. Institutional investors have, of course, attempted to influence the election of directors on some boards, but their impact on corporate governance, relative to their size, has been modest.

fundamental legal duties of directors are relatively few, vary very little from company to company and have not changed much over time. It is, however, important to note that while through the years the definition of the legal duties of directors has changed relatively little, its application has grown immensely. Obviously, anyone contemplating serving as a director should be knowledgeable of the major laws governing the activities of directors and boards in the jurisdictions within which the company of which he or she is a director operates.

The board of directors of a corporation is responsible for the overall well-being of the company. The board has the legal authority to manage, or supervise the management of, the business and affairs of the corporation. In doing so, each director and officer is required by law 1) to act honestly and in good faith with a view to the best interests of the company (otherwise known as the director's fiduciary duty) and 2) to exercise the care, diligence and skill that a reasonably prudent person would exercise in comparable circumstances (the director's duty of care).

The responsibility for management of a company is legally entrusted to the board of directors and the board and the directors are legally required to act always with a view to the best interests of the company and not in their own interests. For example, directors are prohibited from using insider information—information that is not available to the public—when buying or selling securities of the corporation, or from participating in the awarding of contracts when they have a personal interest in the contract that conflicts with the interests of the company, or in any way benefiting in a personal matter from information they learn as a director of the company. Their first duty is to the company of which they are a director. If a conflict, or even the appearance of a conflict, arises, the conflict must be managed. In some instances the conflict may be so great that the director must resign; in others it may only require that the director refrain from voting on the issue creating the conflict, and in still others it may require the forming of a special committee to resolve the issue.

Directors also have a duty of care to the company. This means that they must perform all the functions essential for the effective operation of the corporation. Normally it requires, among other things: that directors attend and prepare for all board meetings and meetings of committees of which they are a member; that they are, or become, fully informed about the business and activities of the company; that they participate actively in the discussion of issues before the board, and in the formulation of policy and strategy for the company; and ensure that the minutes of previous meetings accurately represent the discussions that took place and the resolutions that were passed.

Through the years the laws governing the operations of corporations have grown to such an extent that it is often suggested that "legal decisions rather than business decisions" are the driving force behind business activity. While this is not the case, it is a fact that directors must be conscious in all their actions of the growing amount of litigation that is surrounding corporate operations and have a strong appreciation that many of their decisions may have significant legal implications. Consequently, they must be well aware that there are certain "statutory laws" that must be met—dealing with the environment, making certain that all taxes are paid, assuring that wages are paid as insolvency approaches, *etc.* Moreover, they must be certain that in the performance of their other functions—monitoring the activities of the enterprise, setting its strategies, and assuring that all governance requirements are properly met—all laws and regulations relating to these activities are followed. Litigation has become part of the landscape of corporate governance and all directors should assure themselves that they are properly informed of and protected by director and officer liability insurance, and perhaps even more importantly, that they are well advised, when making complicated decisions, by competent legal counsel and other outside advisers.

DIFFERENT FORMS OF CORPORATIONS

While the nature of the ownership of corporations can be classified in an infinite number of ways, the four forms of corporate structure that are perhaps most common are:

1. family or individually owned and controlled corporations;

2. family or individually controlled corporations with public share-holders;

3. publicly owned corporations with a controlling parent shareholder;

4. publicly owned corporations with widely spread share ownership.

The responsibilities of the directors are the same, regardless of the structure of the ownership, but the manner in which they are able to carry them out differs to a great degree depending upon the nature of the ownership.

FAMILY OR INDIVIDUALLY OWNED ENTERPRISES
Decision-making is about power. In a company dominated by a family or individual owner, the final decision on any and every issue can be made by the controlling shareholder(s). Whether or not the final decision is taken by the controlling shareholder does not, in any way, change the fundamental power relationship between the board of directors and the owner. In the final analysis, the owner can literally fire the board if the board persists in promoting a decision that the owner does not want.

In such situations, the board of directors functions as an advisory group to the owner, who may or may not take the board's advice. The directors have influence and can attempt to exercise it in various ways, but it is the controlling owner(s) who decides. Board members of family firms usually are representatives of various branches of the family, family lawyers, one or two business friends of the founder, and the professional managers of the company, if there are any. Not unexpectedly, a major problem for outside directors on such boards is that they may easily be drawn into serious company problems that develop because of family difficulties. The two seldom can be separated.

The most difficult problems are usually associated with succession, for it is not unusual, when a company is being built, for shares to be distributed (and promises made) in various ways among family members. As time goes by, absolute control may still exist with one person but it may well be that family developments—marriages, births, divorces, special contracts—result in the creation of a variety of shareholder agreements, which by limiting the use of control to certain purposes provide protections for minority interests.

The holders of these minority blocks of shares may have considerably different opinions about significant business decisions. At some point, it is inevitable that new management for a privately owned family enterprise is needed. Unfortunately, it is often not easy 1) to persuade the existing controlling shareholder to bring in new management and/or retire; 2) to gain agreement on an appropriate successor; and 3) after new management has been brought in, to convince the existing controlling shareholder to stop managing the enterprise. In many instances it is not qualifications for filling the job but the position in the family that determines the outcome of the debate. And it is not unusual for outside directors to be drawn into the succession discussion.

Moreover, it is also not unusual for the succession problem to be linked to the sale or retention of the company. Through time, certain family members may no longer wish to have their assets invested in what may be highly illiquid shares of a family business, so they favour some type of divestment that often can occur only if the entire business is sold. Obtaining agreement around such an emotional issue as the sale of a family firm is not easy. Indeed, settling such issues often takes the Wisdom of Solomon and the skills of a psychiatrist. In short, the role of the director in a family-owned firm can encompass a world of decisions that are far removed from the normal range of responsibilities of a corporate director. People considering joining the board of a family company should be well-aware of the not-exactly-business problems that they may be getting into. Some of the major legal battles in the field of corporate governance have been associated with great family battles for control of a family-founded and -built firm. The evidence is clear—money is much thicker than blood.

FAMILY OR INDIVIDUALLY CONTROLLED ENTERPRISES WITH PUBLIC SHAREHOLDERS

For many reasons, not the least of which is the desire on the part of the original owners of a family-built business to take some equity out of the firm, it is not unusual for there to be family or individually controlled firms with public shareholders. Once the company is public, *i.e.*, has shares trading on exchanges, it must disseminate considerable information about its affairs to its shareholders and it must make annual public reports on its operations.

> The preponderance of this type of ownership varies substantially country by country. Usually, the reasons for the variations are found in the historical development of the nation. In Canada, for example, it is estimated that anywhere from 70 to 80 percent of the corporations on the Toronto Stock Exchange have a controlling shareholder; the equivalent number in the United States is 10 to 20 percent. The high level of controlling ownership in Canada is a result of the high level of foreign control in many industries in the country, and the ability of owners to issues two classes of stock—multiple and single voting—on the Toronto Stock Exchange. Many of the major Canadian-controlled firms fall in this category.

The directors' fiduciary duties of care and loyalty in a totally privately held firm, and those where there are also public shareholders, are the same as in any company. In reality, however, the situation is somewhat different from the situation in which all the shareholders are known or related to one another. Directors have responsibilities to shareholders who are not members of the family and who have interests in the company that have nothing to do with family matters. Not surprisingly, though, given the fact that the majority shareholder controls the outcome of the election, a characteristic feature of the board of many family-controlled public enterprises is that the directors are close to the owner. Indeed, reciprocal arrangements among friendly controlling owners—X agrees to serve on Y's board if Y agrees to serve on X's—are not unknown.[6]

Because of the concentration of control, directors elected in "owner-controlled" public enterprises are not particularly inclined to act as a check on management. This is especially true if the controlling owner also holds a management position as president or chair. And yet, for the directors to have any real impact on strategy and

---

6. A widely told story has it that two very well-known chairs of boards that they controlled had a wager as to who could hold the shortest Annual Meeting. Apparently, the all-time winner was an annual meeting that lasted less than four minutes.

decision-making, the controlling shareholder must truly believe in good governance not only in form but in fact. Even in situations where controlling shareholders are convinced they are devotees and exponents of good governance, when push comes to shove, power may overweigh principle. For example, in a well-known company, the chair, who was the controlling shareholder, appointed with the consent of the board a committee to prepare detailed terms of reference for directors and a succession plan for filling director positions as the retirement date of various directors inevitably approached. A senior experienced director chaired the committee and a complete plan of action was prepared and presented to the board. At about the same time, the controlling shareholder closed another company. When the report was presented, he informed the committee (and the board) that he had simply asked all the directors from the closed company to join the board, and so the director succession plan was no longer needed. Not astonishingly, the senior director who had worked diligently on the plan argued long but ineffectively against the controlling shareholder's decision, stating that it violated every principle of good corporate governance, which it did.

Often the board in family or individually controlled companies with public shareholders is created simply because the law requires that there be one, and it exists only to sign the statements and fulfill other legal obligations. There is a tendency on such boards for directors, knowing that they have no real power and no membership in or relationship to the family, to treat their responsibilities lightly. Interest in the affairs of the company is something that may be less than total, attendance at board meetings may be spotty, deference to management's plans may be great, and debate on issues may be much more restrained than in a totally public company. A common approach taken by directors (and, given their power position, is quite understandable) with respect to most issues is "I wouldn't do it, but if you think it is the right thing to do, go ahead."

Serving on such a board can create very difficult problems for a director. The controlling owner usually has control because there are two classes of shares—one with multiple votes and one carrying only a single vote. Consequently, the controlling shareholder usually has control of the company with less than half of the equity, and many times very much less than half. And yet the directors have a fiduciary duty to all the shareholders with "preference toward none." If the controlling shareholder decides on a course of action that a director believes is contrary to the interests of the minority shareholders, what can he or she do?

The answer is to try to persuade the controlling shareholder to follow a different course of action. If the major shareholder persists, then directors, presuming the difference in opinion is sufficiently great, have to decide whether to resign. If they do resign, who then is left to protect the interests of the minority shareholders? Moreover, the very fact of their resignation may well send a signal to the marketplace that all is not well within the company and cause a decline in the value of the shares—something that no director wishes to precipitate. And directors may find that resignation is particularly difficult if the controlling shareholder is a close personal friend.

> The selling of shares by insiders must be reported at a specific time. A director who knows that there are serious problems within an owner-controlled public company that he or she cannot do anything about and that the shares are inevitably going to decline, and indeed be worth nothing, faces a serious moral question. If the shares are sold, a signal is sent to the marketplace that there is a serious problem with the company—a problem that might not be solved. If the shares are not sold, the director may, and probably will, suffer a serious monetary loss.

One of the major problems that can overtake management of any enterprise is hubris[7]—a condition that seemed to be overwhelmingly present in the technology boom of the late 1990s and early years of the twenty-first century. While it is a characteristic of many chief executive officers in companies without a controlling shareholder, it seems almost endemic among companies with a family or individual controlling shareholder. It often leads to plans and dreams for growth or expansion that have no basis in reality, but are followed anyway.

7. See Peter Munk, "The Barrick Story: Corporate Entrepreneurship on a Global Level" in James Gillies, ed., *Success: Canadian Leaders Prepare for the Next Century* (Toronto: Key Porter Books, 2000), Chapter 6.

Unfortunately, in such situations the tendency is often for directors to do nothing. They do not wish to end their friendship with the owner-controller and their fellow directors, and because there has been no culture of debate and discussion about issues in the boardroom and because they know that in the final analysis they have no power to change things, they often take the position that they cannot do anything anyway. The results can be disastrous.

A passive position on the part of directors is understandable but hardly acceptable. Directors, regardless of the control situation, do have a continuous fiduciary duty to the minority shareholders. While they may not be able to change the situation, if directors are convinced that a strategy or some other action being proposed is clearly incorrect, they should certainly try. If someone is not prepared for the problems that are implicit in serving on such a board, they should decline to do so in the first place, regardless of their relationship with the controlling owner.

COMPANY–CONTROLLED PUBLIC SUBSIDIARIES

The role of a director in decision-making in a company-controlled subsidiary varies from that in a family or individually controlled public enterprise by a matter of degree. In both, the individual director does not have power, only influence. If the owner of the subsidiary wishes to make major strategic changes and chooses to close or expand the subsidiary, he can and will do so; there is nothing that a director can do, other than provide advice on how to proceed. On the other hand, when the controlling shareholder in a family or individually controlled enterprise takes action, a director can sometimes have some influence on the decision through strong personal relationships with the owner. Board members of a controlled subsidiary usually do not have such a close relationship with the management and owners of the parent company.

The parent company exercises control of the subsidiary by appointing, sometimes even without consultation with the board, the chief executive officer; by establishing the capital expenditure program; and by having representation on the board. If the subsidiary's directors disagree with the direction that the subsidiary is taking, they find it much easier to resign than if they were resigning from a family-owned company where they have close personal relationships with the management and owners.

On the other hand, the responsibilities to the minority shareholders always exist, and when the company is a subsidiary of a foreign corporation, it is not unusual for shareholders to look to the national directors to protect their interests. This is particularly true in cases when the owner decides to take the subsidiary private through buying in and cancelling all the shares of a publicly held subsidiary. In many jurisdictions, minority shareholders are given some protection through "oppression remedy laws," but even with this protection, it is not unusual for shareholders of a subsidiary to look to the directors for assurances that they be properly compensated for their shares.

In Canada, "minority investors" are legally protected by the ability to apply, through the oppression remedy laws, for relief from perceived mistreatment. One of the places where "oppression" is often claimed is when a majority owner decides to buy all the minority shares, usually when it decides to delist the stock from a local exchange. The question then becomes, "What are the minority shares worth?" It is not unusual for the national directors to become involved in what may become a very bitter debate on this matter, because the minority shareholders have always perceived such directors as having a particular duty to look after their interests. It is assumed that the majority shareholders can look after themselves.

Directors of subsidiary companies are seldom expected to make a major contribution to the oversight or the management of the company, or to the strategic direction that it will take. They are, however, expected to enhance value by serving as advisers on the social, cultural and political trends in the country, and providing contacts for the management of the subsidiary (and often the owner) with various influential people and organizations in the country. It is for this reason that former politicians are often asked to serve on such boards.

Table 2.1

Some Directors' and Controlling Shareholders' Views on Controlled Boards

"It's [the controlling shareholder's way] or the highway." (director)

"If I own [Company ABC] do I want constraints? No _____ way! Never in a million years will I own a company and someone will limit my ability to run my company. What I want is a group of advisers who tell me their thinking—people I respect, who add value, who have industry knowledge and who challenge my authority and direction. But, at the end of the day, if I don't like their advice, I'll do what the _____ I want." (controlling shareholder)

"Having a public company with a large shareholder is the biggest single difficulty in Canadian corporate governance." (director)

"With the few major shareholder companies I've been involved with, the decision-making process could be improved. First, the majority shareholder should not make decisions before the board meeting. And second, the independent directors should speak up. This is a tough problem—independent directors and majority shareholders—because 75 percent of Canadian companies have a majority shareholder." (director)

"My board meets once a year for a few days. We have made a planning book of issues to discipline and clarify our thinking. I get the odd insight from the better directors but I can easily live without them. And there hasn't been a difference over the years." (controlling shareholder)

"If investors want to, they can buy apples." (controlling shareholder)

"[…] has asked me to … advise you that he thinks the subject of corporate governance is overworked. There are criminal and securities statutes in place and beyond that its [sic] his opinion that its [sic] the company's performance that is chiefly important." (eerily foretelling remarks from a controlling shareholder declining to participate in Dr. Leblanc's study)

"For U.S. parents, they call the shots. You go through the motions. It becomes a legal maneuver. . . . The better-run companies are widely held. There are exceptions. Again there's a huge gap [between those companies that have effective corporate governance and those that don't]." (director)

Continued

"The ... independent directors defer to the wishes of the majority share-holder. I'm happy to defer the big decisions to [the U.S. parent], particularly when the shareholder is in the identical business. We set the agenda independent of the majority shareholder for certain topics. If there is anything contentious, then it's discussed in advance so there is less dialogue at the meeting itself." (chair and CEO of Canadian subsidiary)

"'Who calls the shots, you ask? The [X] percent majority shareholder, in terms of the agenda, the board meeting, composition, compensation and major initiatives such as acquisitions or divestitures. . . . Only routine items appear on the agenda. If they are non-routine items, the significant shareholder must approve them, for example, a share buy-back. [The controlling shareholder] talks to [the chairman and CEO] and [he] talks to me. In the end it's approved. . . . If it's on the agenda, buy-in by the significant shareholder has been created and most times it's approved." (management)

"I was the only outspoken person who didn't agree that we should sell off the ... assets. . . . I spoke out against it. . . . Every single member of the board disagreed so I let it go. In court we were all sued. . . . Never again will I go on a control board. You're not an independent director." (director)

"We know that we have a good parent. We wanted to protect Canadian policy holders. . . . We had some impact on global strategy. . . . With dominant shareholders you want to protect minority shareholders. Widely held companies have the most responsible corporate governance." (director)

"The constant acid test is ... 'can I influence the process?' Yes, yes, yes. You may not do it to the full degree you want, but do you influence the process? If the [controlling shareholder] was on his own many things would have happened. If you're a total thorn in [the controlling shareholder's] side you don't get re-elected. The [controlling shareholder] is good at having reasonable outside directors on the board. The bottom line is that in the end [the controlling shareholder] does the right thing largely because of the board. But he is the controlling shareholder. . . . It's a delicate balance." (director)

"I only go on the boards of broadly held companies." (director)

"It's bull _____ . They're not real boards." (director)

THE PUBLICLY OWNED, WIDELY HELD CORPORATION

Not surprisingly, it is in the publicly owned, widely held corporation that all the duties and responsibilities of directors come together. When there is no controlling shareholder, the boards of directors are required by law to take the place of the owner. They have the legal responsibility to choose the management and the chief officers of the corporation, oversee what they do and generally act prudently, as any owner would, to increase the value of the shares. And so the board of directors in a widely held public corporation, unlike the directors of firms where there are controlling shareholders, are not simply advisers devoid of real power. By law, they are the decision-makers who, through their actions, usually determine the success or failure of the enterprise. The legal power to manage the enterprise lies with the board and nowhere else. The fact that boards may not, in many (most) cases, exercise that power does not in any way detract from the fact that they have it. The board of directors is expected to fulfill all the duties listed above, and indeed, very effective boards in well-run companies succeed in doing so.

Through the years, as corporations have grown in size and complexity, the relationship between shareholders and directors has evolved. Many of the changes have been driven by public policy, perhaps even more by court decisions. As a result, a vast amount of case-law governing the actions of directors has developed—indeed so much so that the claim is sometimes made that corporate governance has been "hijacked by the law"—and directors in public corporations, for their own protection, often feel they must pay more attention to their legal responsibilities than they do to guiding and monitoring the manner in which the corporation is performing. Although this is not true, certainly, the increase in litigation against directors, and the concomitant increase in interest in, and importance of, liability insurance and other forms of financial protection for directors, lends some credence to the proposition.

And as the relationship between shareholders and directors has changed dramatically through the years, the relationship between the board of directors and the managers of the corporation has also changed. Indeed, it is argued that, with the widespread separation of ownership and control, a principal characteristic of the modern corporation is that the power of the executives is to all intents and purposes as great as any controlling owner. It has long been the conviction—one based on a great deal of evidence—that while the directors by law have all the power, in reality it is held by the management. In the final analysis, it is claimed, it is the management that controls the board, and not the other way around.

Consequently, it can be argued that the difference between the role of the board in a widely held corporation and in one where there is a controlling shareholder is only a matter of degree. In one case, the power is held by the executives; in the other, by the controlling owner. Such, however, is not the fact. When the shares are widely held, the role of a board of directors is much different, because in the final analysis the power does lie with the board. And although the power relationship in the boardroom that is contemplated in the law has been, and in many cases still is, different from the reality, this does not mean that the situation is acceptable or that it cannot change. The principles of governance, as expressed through the law and regulations, are based on, seek to assure, and expect that the boards of directors exercise their power to fulfill their responsibilities.

Responsible persons joining boards of public companies should understand their fiduciary duties of care and loyalty and should have very little difficulty in living up to them. Obviously directors know that shareholders buy shares of the enterprise with the expectation that they will, as the company prospers, grow in value. They should easily understand that, as directors, they have a responsibility to act in a prudent fashion, always within the law and respecting the economic and social responsibilities of the corporation to its various stakeholder groups, including employees, customers, suppliers and local communities, in order that shareholder value be maximized.

The role of individual directors does, however, become more difficult when the directors must fill their collective responsibilities as members of the board. Most, if not all, of the significant activities that a board member is involved in—the serious issues, such as selecting or firing the chief executive officer, determining the appropriate levels of compensation for senior management, ensuring the credibility of the financial statements, by their very nature entail collective decision-making by the entire board or a board committee. And although the degree to which individual board members should be involved in the development of strategy is a matter of debate, there is no debate that the board as an entity is responsible for the approval of the strategy followed by the company, and in the final analysis must take responsibility for its implementation.

According to the law, unless it is specifically indicated in writing in the minutes that they voted against a motion, individual directors are assumed to agree with any and all actions taken by the board as an entity. Even if a director is absent from a meeting, unless he or she has submitted in writing an objection, the director is assumed to be in agreement with the collective action of the board. In short, boards act as entities. If a company falls into difficult times, regardless of the nature of the issue, it is all the members of the board who are sued, not a selected few.

THE MISSING LINK IN BOARD ANALYSIS

Clearly, how boards make decisions and the role of individual directors in the decision-making processes are critical factors in determining how successful an enterprise will be. If a corporation does well, as primarily measured by its financial performance, it is only logical to conclude that the decision-making process works well. On the other hand, many corporations do not do well—they fail or underperform. When they underperform, it is reasonable to assume that except in cases of "acts of God" and other extenuating circumstances, it is so because the directors do not fulfill their responsibilities and make the proper decisions.

Unfortunately, we do not know if this broad generalization is true, because we do not know much about how boards function in large, widely held corporations. The fact that little is known about board processes—about how boards work—means that regulators, board chairs and chairs of nominating committees are making decisions about the factors affecting board performance in somewhat of a vacuum.

In short, what should be the heart and soul of any discussion about how to improve corporate governance in the interests of shareholders and the public is impossible because so little is known about board processes—about how boards of directors actually work.

Yet despite the fact that the performance of many boards of companies has, in many respects, been disappointing, there are many reasons to believe that a major change in the role of boards of directors in the operations of public companies will occur in the early twenty-first century. The reasons to be optimistic about change are:

1. much more is beginning to be known about how boards make decisions and what types of boards are most likely to make good decisions;

2. the recommendations about boards that are coming from new knowledge do not challenge the traditional assumptions of corporate governance—that corporations are owned by shareholders with limited liability who elect a board of directors that oversees the operations of enterprise in their interest;

3. the changes are not dependent upon more regulations, nor outside pressure from shareholders. Rather the changes are coming from boards themselves. It is an increase in knowledge about how to build better boards and an internal desire on the part of boards to perform better that is driving change.

Because of the enormous importance of the widely held public companies in the economy—their activities affect almost every citizen—this book focuses on the role of the board of directors in widely held public enterprises.

CONTEMPORARY DIRECTORS: WHO ARE THEY, WHAT DO THEY DO AND HOW WELL DO THEY DO IT?

In many instances the chief executive officer, instead of seeing the board as a great asset, capable of providing solid and valuable service as to how to solve many of the problems facing the company, perceives the board as an impediment—a group of individuals that must be tolerated and that add little of value. Many are particularly dismissive of the input from the outside directors simply because they do not believe that they have sufficient experience or knowledge to add much valuable input to the decision-making process.

—Director

How do you behave as a director? Find out how the board works, how the dynamic works. The worse thing you can have is inside and outside or tier-one and tier-two directors.

—Director

Every citizen, either directly or indirectly, is affected by the activities of corporations, yet relatively little is known about the most important part of their management team—the board of directors. Other than members of management who are invited, as appropriate, almost no one who is not a member of a board has ever attended a board meeting or has any real idea of what boards of directors actually do. Indeed, the degree of anonymity that directors enjoy, given their enormous power in the economy, is amazing. The media rarely refers to individual directors by name, but rather under the security of "the board."[1]

The shareholders give the board virtually unlimited power to look after their money and yet only the smallest percentage of shareholders, in terms of number, have any idea who actually *are* the directors of the companies that they own. And in many respects they do not seem to care. On the one occasion—the annual meeting of the company—when shareholders have the opportunity to question directors, the attendance is usually sparse. Even when special attempts are made to get shareholders to come to a meeting to question management about such things as bonuses, stock options, executive pay, *etc.*, the turnout is often low.[2]

WHY BOARDS ARE PAID LITTLE ATTENTION
There are many reasons for this indifference. Partly it arises from the fact that for many years, the capacity of directors to use their power has been limited; partly because many people who own shares think of themselves as investors rather than owners who, because of the liquidity of the stock market, can quickly dispose of their shares if they are concerned about the management of a company; and, finally, because the thousands of owners with only a few shares believe, correctly, that if the board does something that they don't like, there is nothing they can do about it other than sell their shares, and so they don't care who the directors happen to be.

While all of the above reasons may explain "shareholder lack of interest in boards," the fact remains that who the directors are can make a great deal of difference to the fate of an individual company and to the economy as a whole. When boards make good decisions, companies prosper, and when companies prosper, the nation prospers. Who the directors are, what boards of directors do

---

1. It is fascinating that in many reports of corporate wrongdoing or problems, the newspaper reports seldom mention the directors by name—probably because the reporters have no idea who they are. For example, in a column on page 2 in the Report on Business section of *The Globe and Mail*, May 29, 2004, it is stated "this is about Nortel's board— possibly the worst in Canadian history"; no directors are mentioned by name. The five Nortel directors who later resigned, however, were identified by name. See *e.g.*, *The Wall Street Journal*, January 12, 2005 on page A8.

2. Some shareholder meetings where there are very significant issues being decided can be very large and lively. At the 2004 Annual Meeting of the Walt Disney Corporation, for example, there was a concerted effort to reduce the power of the chair, who also served as CEO. On the other hand, as was the case at a meeting of Magna Corporation, where after criticism of his large salary, chair Frank Stronach publicly invited his critics to attend, the turnout was very small.

and how well they do it *are* important issues, not only for all share-holders, but for everyone dependent upon a vigorous economy for their well-being, which is to say, everyone.

WHO ARE DIRECTORS?

Although very little is known about the way in which boards actually operate from information filed with various regulatory agencies, the annual reports and proxy circulars of publicly traded companies and various books on corporate governance, a great deal is known, in a general sense, about what boards are legally supposed to do (see Chapter 2), their structure and their members. The vast majority of directors are men who have experience as senior officers in business. While the precise proportions vary slightly over the years and from country to country, chief executive officers, representatives of major shareholders (who are usually businessmen) and retired business executives hold more than 80 percent of all directorships. In much smaller numbers, lawyers, former politicians and educators follow them. The proportion of directors who are women is increasing but the percentage is still very low.[3]

Directors, by law, are elected by the shareholders at the annual meeting of the company, usually, but not always, for a one-year term. Some corporations stagger the membership on the board by having a certain proportion elected each year for a two- or three-year term. In fact, it really does not make much difference if election is for one or two years because management controls the nomination and election process and solicits proxies from the shareholders in support of the candidates whom they nominate,[4] and historically the chief executive officer of the enterprise has had almost complete control over the selection of nominees. In recent years, however, it has become usual for boards to establish a nominating committee to search out and recommend candidates for election to the board. While nominating committees have led to a more structured

---

3. There is a large body of literature on this topic. See, for example, D. S. R. Leighton and Donald Thain, "The Role of the Corporate Director," *Business Quarterly* (Autumn 1990); James Gillies, *Boardroom Renaissance: Power Morality and Performance in the Modern Corporation*, 46–55; J. W. Lorsch with E. MacIver, *Pawns or Potentates: The Realities of America's Corporate Boards* and R. J. Burke & M. C. Mattis (eds.), *Women on Corporate Boards of Directors: International Challenges and Opportunities* (Dordrecht: Kluwer, 2000).
4. For a discussion of this phenomenon, see Chapter 1.

approach to board selection, the result, in terms of the background of directors, has not changed much from what it was when the CEOs alone chose board members. The fact is that people choose people they know for colleagues, and since the vast majority of board members are businessmen, now at least, they choose businessmen to become fellow directors.

The fact that the management and the existing board of a company usually controls the election of directors means that elected directors who do not seriously challenge management or their fellow directors have a relatively secure position until they reach the mandatory retirement age, if any, specified in the corporation's bylaws. The reality is that it is very difficult, if not impossible, for shareholders to remove non-performing individual directors, and management seldom requests that directors stand down. While this is a rather pleasant situation for a director, it does mean that, unless a company actually fails, it is very difficult to hold directors accountable for their actions, *i.e.*, fire them if they do not do their job.

One of the startling observations from interviews with almost 200 directors is the large number of directors who believe that some of their fellow directors are very incompetent. The overwhelming view is that it is far easier to allow a non-performing director to stay until retirement age than to go to all the trouble involved in removing him or her from the board. Individual directors are basically only accountable to themselves.

Because there are no regulatory requirements when a director does leave a board that the reasons for his or her resignation must be reported in the information circular sent to all shareholders, there is very little public information about voluntary resignations of directors. That some do resign, on principle, is certainly true. People closely associated with the corporate community all know of situations where individual board members have resigned over principle, *e.g.*, when a corporation broke a stand-still agreement that was negotiated by a lawyer who was on the board; when board members were offended that executives charged expenses to the company that were clearly not associated with the company's operations; or when company resources were not used for company purposes.

There is, however, little evidence to indicate that many directors feel they should resign when they fail to perform their functions, as indicated by the performance of the enterprise. If board members consistently appoint incompetent CEOs, if as members of the audit committee they continually approve incorrect statements of the corporation, or if they approve strategies that do not work, they should resign—and they should not wait until the corporation is in a desperate situation to do so.[5] Nor should they wait until they reach some specified retirement age. With power goes responsibility and the responsibility of every director is to assess continually if his or her contribution through the board is adding value to the enterprise. Resignation over principle may well be the practice among some directors; resignation on the basis of incompetence does not seem to be, as yet, a widely accepted practice.

At the same time, if a company has fallen into such a sorry state that shareholders may be taking legal action against the directors, resignation is not easy. Directors cannot escape problems by resigning, and if they do resign because they believe that they are not doing an adequate job as directors, they clearly place themselves in great personal jeopardy. If at a trial the first question is "Why did you resign?" and the director answers "Because I felt that I was not doing an effective job," the trial may soon be over. Moreover, when directors resign, they must be very careful that it does not impact their Directors and Officers Insurance or any indemnity agreements that they may have with the company.

WHAT DO DIRECTORS ACTUALLY DO?

While the responsibilities of a board are clearly specified by law and regulation, what, in fact, do directors actually do? Again, the mechanics of being a director are relatively well-known. Because the number and complexity of corporations is so vast, it is difficult to generalize. However, in most companies of moderate size that are managed well, directors attend seven to nine meetings or so a year.

---

5. Interestingly, there was not a cascade of resignations of directors from the myriad of companies that were forced to restate their earnings after the rash of problems in the early 2000s. What level of difficulties must be reached before directors recognize that they may not have the capabilities to fulfill their duties?

They receive an agenda and the relevant information about the items to be discussed at the meeting well in advance and they are expected to have read all the material and to contribute to the discussion associated with making decisions.

Under normal circumstances, agendas are remarkably similar. They consist of:

- a review of the minutes of the previous meeting;
- a discussion of issues arising from the minutes that are not contained on the agenda;
- a report from the chief executive officer;
- a review of the financial statements;
- reports from various committees, *e.g.*, audit, compensation, nominating/governance, executive, finance and environment;
- any new business.

The extent of time and effort that must be devoted by board members to company business does, of course, vary enormously depending upon the size and complexity of the operations of the company and the particular issues it may be facing. The board meetings of well-managed, relatively small companies might well last no more than two or three hours, and can become relatively routine. On the other hand, a director of a large transnational organization with operations in many countries through many subsidiaries and with many products may well find that being an active director or chair of an important committee is very time consuming, even when the company has sound management and is operating without any special problems. Committee and board meetings may extend over a two-day period. The consensus view of respondents interviewed for this study was that the average time commitment, exclusive of travel and special situations, for a director on the board of a major company, was upwards of twenty to twenty-five working days a year.

While, on the surface, the standard agenda appears relatively bland, it is developed to permit the directors to fulfill their major responsibility of advising and exercising oversight and control over management—to make certain that the management is operating the company in the interests of all the stakeholders rather than their own, and to ensure that it is pursuing the most effective strategies and administrative practices to support the growth and development of the company.

Most boards operate through a number of committees. Indeed, in most jurisdictions, all public companies are required by law to have an audit committee with the members being independent directors and, while law does not require it, most companies also have a compensation committee to determine the pay of their senior executives. Many have, depending on the nature, scope and scale of their activities, executive, nomination, risk management, environment, health and safety, finance and donations committees, among others. Obviously, a good deal of the detailed examination of issues is done by board members at the committee level.

FOCUS ON FINANCES

Inasmuch as the directors are particularly concerned about the financial well-being of the enterprise—after all, financial performance is one of the important measures of the success and progress of the company—a considerable amount of time at most board meetings is devoted to a discussion of the financial statements. Has the company met its financial plan for the quarter? If not, why not? Is it in line to meet its financial goals for the year? Which divisions are doing well? Which are lagging behind? Why? What are the plans to correct shortfalls in earnings in particular divisions?

The board of directors depends on the financial statements prepared by the management as a basis for its analysis of the company's activities. Needless to say, the requirement that such statements be accurate is absolutely critical and cannot be overemphasized.[6] They are the basis upon which an understanding of the operations of the organization is made and the foundation upon which almost every decision that the board makes rests. Responsibility for reviewing, assessing and reporting on the veracity of the statements is delegated by the board to

---

6. Whether or not audit committees can do all the things that they are asked to is a matter of some debate. For a full discussion of the problems associated with audit committees, see Paul Wayne, *The History and Evolution of Audit Committees* (Toronto: Schulich School of Business, York University, 2004).

an audit committee that in turn is usually advised by professional auditors. Once the committee has satisfied itself that the statements truly reflect the financial situation of the company, it recommends them to the board for approval and public distribution to the shareholders.

The problems, scandals and failures of many enterprises in the early 2000s were, in many (most) cases, related to incorrect, dishonest and inappropriate financial statements and accounting practices. It is an extreme understatement to state that many audit committees, as they then operated, were not doing their job properly. One of the consequences of the failure of appropriate monitoring activities by boards and dubious activities by some accounting firms was that a major accounting firm in the United States, Arthur Andersen, was forced out of business.

As a result, regulators and directors are giving a great deal more attention to the activities of the audit committees. It is now the practice of most corporations to publish in the information circular containing the agenda for the Annual Meeting, the charter of their audit committee, the names of the members of the committee, the number of times the committee met in the previous year and a report on its most significant activities. It is also normal practice for corporations to pay the chair of the audit committee an additional stipend for serving as chair of the committee, in recognition of the amount of work that it is expected the committee will do. And, finally, legislation in many jurisdictions, such as the *Sarbanes-Oxley Act* passed in 2002 in the United States, established by law several new relationships between auditors and the corporations which they audit, between the audit committee and the board of directors, and far greater formal responsibility on the part of executives for the reliability of the statements.

Despite these changes, many directors are not certain that they and their fellow directors have the ability to assure that the financial statements truly reflect the financial condition of the corporation. As one chair interviewed for this study stated, "The universe of financial manipulation has become extraordinarily complex and Machiavellian and is changing at a much greater rate than in the past." Consequently, even the most qualified and conscientious director may well have serious trouble dealing with the issues brought before the audit committee. Under such circumstances, it is no surprise that most of the scandals associated with corporate governance in the early part of the twenty-first century were associated with audit committee failures.

At the same time, it is important to note that many of the major and most well-known corporate collapses occurred where the board not only contained some very sophisticated financial people, but had access to the best possible financial advice. In such cases, it would not appear to be lack of financial sophistication that caused the companies to fail. Indeed, no amount of financial literacy or regulation can ever prevent against outright fraud or executive corruption, nor should it be expected to.

Table 3.1

Some Directors' Views on the Financial Literacy of Colleagues and the Functions of Audit Committees

"Do people understand enough to be able to question? No. I chair the investment committee but I don't understand why [the CEO] buys what he buys. He generally makes money. I make sure we adhere to policies but I have no _____ clue what to invest in." (director of a financial services firm)

"The problem is that we trust management and we don't have the financial literacy on the audit committee." (chair of a financial services firm)

"I guess you can tell that not many of us are experienced board members." (chair of an audit committee)

"We need a better numbers guy. None of us know the numbers. I'm a strategy guy." (chair of two audit committees and former chair of a financial services firm)

"There's a great need for financially literate businesspeople on boards. It's ego. Many are successful businesspeople in their own right and they don't want to be seen as not knowing, not critical. . . . We need some real depth to understand the subtleties and the accounting issues." (director)

Continued

"Today, most sophisticated financial practitioners privately admit that they have to re-read the forms before client meetings because of the complications underlying them. . . . It's crypto-babble. . . . I have a [business degree] and I'm a [professional] and I find it difficult to read. If I acknowledge that I'm not up to speed, my credibility is put at risk. They create ambiguities to create schemes and create more schemes to create more ambiguities. There has to be a test of commonly accepted accounting practices and the ability of the industry to explain itself. The board of directors can't and won't follow [under present conditions]." (chair and CEO)

"If you don't have financial literacy, you shouldn't be on the board." (director)

"The typical business executive is highly unlikely to have much more than a clue, although he won't admit it. You ask educated people to provide judgment, oversight on overly complex, unclear, maybe fraudulent or criminal transactions—it's very troubling. . . . We need to get rid of the veil of comfort, ego and embarrassment. It's very difficult to say, 'I don't know what you're talking about and don't understand what I've just read!'" (chair and CEO)

"So few people really understand . . . the rewards of doing business . . . penalties are zero . . . the motivational system . . . pressure of loosening controls. . . . Very few people have the discipline or knowledge at the board level to cause reporting to deal with this issue. Why the most brilliant minds in the financial world—the Swiss, Germans, Japanese—every smart financial person in the world got caught up moving down within authorized parameters. . . . But I have to certify . . . The real issue is the committee is either in place and doing its job or the full board, and no one says the full board, because that would be intolerable, so it boils down to the committee. . . . You've got to access all the knowledge you have, management and the board level, and have ready access to people who have seen operations. . . . " (director)

"It's not my responsibility to train directors of audit committees." (chair of the board)

"A continual challenge is digesting complex information." (director)

The quotes in this and succeeding chapters are from interviews with practising directors. For a summary of the methodology, please see

Appendix B. It is important to remember that this is a study based on a "qualitative methodology." No attempt was made to draw a representative sample from a general population. Consequently, it is impossible to generalize from the responses of the interviewees to the population as a whole. Given the fact that approximately two hundred directors were asked on average ten to fifteen questions, it is not astonishing that there is such a wide range of opinions. After all the number of permutations that are possible is large.

OTHER COMMITTEE WORK

The same concerns are developing with respect to the work of the compensation committee. Given the tremendously complicated and varied forms of executive compensation that developed at the end of the twentieth and the beginning of the twenty-first century, and the great debate that has ranged over the appropriateness of high levels of management compensation, it is not astonishing that compensation committees have come under serious scrutiny. Many companies now provide in their information circulars detailed descriptions of how the senior officers' compensation is determined, with a variety of charts relating compensation to performance, rates of compensation in similar-sized companies in the same industry, extenuating circumstances and so on.[7] However, according to one expert, "You will not understand the mechanics of executive compensation unless you give up your day job."

More and more, recommendations of regulators and trading exchanges are calling for the majority of the members of the compensation and audit committees to be independent directors, so a serious dilemma is developing. Outside and independent directors are being required to undertake tasks that they feel, and usually are, ill-equipped to do. As one CEO exclaimed, "How far do you push the depth and commitment versus the breadth and detachment,

7. For example, the Management Resources and Compensation committee report in the Notice of 2004 Annual and Special Shareholder Meeting and Management Proxy Circular of Bell Canada Enterprises covers fifteen of forty-five pages, or almost one-third of the entire information circular. The Information Circular explaining how compensation figures were determined at Burlington Resources covers nine out of nineteen pages, and for Brascan eight out of twenty-eight pages. It is also interesting to note that almost every major corporation in its Annual Report reviews how it is dealing with various corporate governance issues.

given the time and knowledge, *etc.*, of the non-executive directors? Can we make non-executive directors into something they're not designed to be?" To the extent that several of the new regulations require audit and compensation committees to assume responsibilities that many directors feel they, as members of such committees, cannot fulfill, they are contributing to the growing problem of many capable people being less and less willing to accept invitations to join a board of directors.[8]

Table 3.2

Some Directors' Views on Executive Compensation

"I've been chair of two compensation committees. . . . The technical competence of directors is lacking." (director)

"Directors need a more sophisticated knowledge of compensation, a technical sophistication." (director)

"Directors' understanding of compensation is poor. It's a responsibility because people don't know . . . indexed options for example. Ninety-nine percent don't understand. . . . They don't know that the business system model doesn't work on a standard basis and it's mathematically frail. No one's telling them. You listen to these fools come in. I know the proxy circular says, 'The purpose of the committee is to ensure we attract and retain. . . . ' It's meaningless if you're destroying value for shareholders for fifteen years. . . . We're 1,000 miles away. Compensation consultants provide the data, but they don't do the separation, nor do they put emphasis on the HR committee to set things. . . . It's all bull____. I've been on [over two dozen] boards since [the late 1980s]. The board ratifies the objectives without understanding the endogenous or exogenous variable and the bonuses flow with the exogenous to a greater or lesser extent. As a percentage of salary for the CEO, it's usually between 1 and 3X, but it should be 0X to 3X. So that way, they don't get anything. It's very hard to measure." (director)

---

8. See, for example, Patrick O'Callaghan *et al.*, "Special Report: Is There a Shortage of Qualified Canadian Directors?" *Corporate Governance and Director Compensation in Canada* (Vancouver: P. O'Callaghan & Associates and Korn/Ferry International, 2003), 12: "61% of directors believe Canadian Boards face a shortage of qualified directors."

"Prostitution would be a step up for them [compensation consultants]."
(director)

"Compensation is also a time bomb. We're out of reason. There are
incredible disparities. Look at the exorbitant pay some people are getting." (director)

"Good management doesn't come cheap." (highly paid controlling shareholder)

"What's important is how to work with the CEO and corporate management to agree on setting objectives for the year coming, two to three
years out maybe; how to measure success and how to tie variable compensation to the attainment of objectives you're prepared to discuss
publicly. In measuring and monitoring performance, normally the board
has three or four high-priority items, and another five or six that are important, but lower in priority. You need places where well-thought-out
objectives are debated by the board, accepted by the board and accepted by the CEO and the management team. When the compensation
team sits down at the end of February for variable compensation, at 0 to
2X target, what was the explicit, open process achieved with the objectives a year ago? Well over half the boards don't do this or don't do it
well." (director)

"It's____ that nothing counts other than the results. The entire system
had . . . no discipline in it whatsoever. Everyone is uncomfortable. . . . 'If
we don't go along, we'll lose good people.' At least 50 percent of the
problems . . . is because we have no discipline in our compensation
schemes. . . . To adopt the correct policy, you have to accept the risk that
certain people may well leave and those people [harm] the organization
and [increase] their own interests, their own pocketbook, and therefore
get rid of them." (director)

"Directors need to understand executive compensation. To drive the right
performance, you need an appropriate peer group. It can't be a get-rich-
quick scheme." (CEO)

"We are not addressing the risks of the future . . . the greed, the competitive pressure, the desire for power, the supreme CEO. The opportunities
for rewards are beyond anyone's imagination. The payoff is so big, all of

Continued

> these controls and circumstances . . . are overwhelmed by that 'great big sucker.' Otherwise we'll see bigger, more complex schemes to satisfy power and greed." (director)
>
> "I would rather make my living in a whorehouse than make that argument [that stock options should not be expensed]. And I'm not kidding. It's not a joke." (director)
>
> "There are [issues] we don't understand and we're on the . . . committee." (director)

In recent years, two additional committees (and they may be combined) have taken on added significance—the nomination and the governance committees. It is the responsibility of the nominating committee to recommend to the shareholders candidates for election to the board. A well-functioning nominating committee reviews the board's needs and tries to find people who meet them—not always an easy task. It is, however, one of the most important committees of the board, for without the proper mix of directors, it is highly unlikely that the corporation will fill its potential. Sometimes the work of the nominating committee is combined with that of a governance committee, which primarily assesses the extent to which the board is fulfilling its "governance duties" and its responsibilities to all its stakeholders.

DIRECTORS AND STRATEGY DEVELOPMENT

Whereas most boards of directors are probably over-occupied with trying to fulfill their monitoring responsibility, they are probably underutilized in the development and review of the corporate strategy of their company.[9]

With the growing complexity of business, one would expect that directors would be drawn more and more into strategic planning. In some of the more effective boards, they are, but from the

9. See Sayan Chatterjee and Jeffrey S. Harrison, "Corporate Governance" in Michael Hitt, R. Edward Freeman and Jeffrey S. Harrison (eds.), *The Blackwell Handbook of Strategic Management* (Oxford: Blackwell, 2001). The popularity of "agency theory" in the field of corporate governance in the 1990s, at the time of the unfriendly takeovers movement, did much to move the "monitoring aspect" of corporate governance to prime importance in the field at the expense of attention being paid to the value-adding role of boards.

interviews with many directors and the examination of various boards in action, it appears that in many firms, directors play a very small role in the formulation and implementation of basic strategy. Directors spoke of their desire to move beyond their "compliance" (monitoring) role to a more "value-added" (strategic) role. In many of the companies observed for this study, management developed the strategy and brought it to the board for approval and in most cases such approval appeared to be more perfunctory than critical.

In the entire strategic formulation process, boards appear to have limited input, often only at a one- or two-day general retreat where the future of the company is discussed. Not astonishingly, board members who have not been involved in the thinking behind strategic developments are not capable of making anything more than modest suggestions for change.

> A board of directors is responsible for overseeing the strategic issues and long-term goals of a company. While the nature and extent of a board's involvement in strategy will depend on the particular size and circumstances of a company and the industry in which it is operating, there should be a cooperative, interactive strategic planning process with management, including the identification and setting of goals and expectations. This process includes the constructive engagement of a board to ensure the appropriate development, modification, approval, execution and reporting of a company's strategy. Working with management, a board provides input on and establishes policy and strategic direction, debates and approves the strategies presented by the CEO and ensures that management carries out these strategies effectively. The strategic tasks of a board also include the critical consideration of the principal areas of risk to which the company is exposed, together with oversight of a risk management system and ethics program to identify and mitigate such risks.

In many instances, the board is cut out of what can be argued should be one of its most, if not the most, important function— assuring that the company follows a strategy designed to conserve and increase assets for the shareholders, the owners of the company, while at the same time providing superior products or services for its customers, continuing employment for its employees and behaving as a responsible citizen within its community.

This is not astonishing, because through the years in almost every possible way, the role of the board in the strategic processes of the firm has been downplayed. There are several reasons for this. For years, many CEOs held the strong view that the board should have no role in developing the strategy of the firm.[10] Moreover, in their emphasis on structure, regulators have paid almost no attention to the strategic role of the board. Indeed, it may be argued that some of the regulations, particularly those associated with the independence of board members, have unwittingly worked against appointing directors who would bring strengths in developing strategies to the board. The most common complaint by CEOs interviewed for this study is that "directors don't understand the business." This opinion was often supported by observations of directors in action in real time during board meetings. In some sort of perhaps perverse sense, the fixation by regulators on the need for more "independent" directors, because of the assumption that they can fulfill the monitoring role, has not been without a cost when it comes to the fulfillment of the board's strategic function.[11] And, of course, there are directors who do not wish to be involved in the making of strategic decisions.

Table 3.3

Questions to Assess Whether Your Board Is Effective at Strategy Development[12]

1. Are the company's philosophy, mission, strategic plan and operating plan thoroughly understood and discussed by the board?

2. Does the board appropriately engage in reviewing and approving the company's strategic plan? Is an appropriate percentage of time being

---

10. The insignificance of the board of directors in the eyes of strong CEOs is never better demonstrated than in their autobiographies—boards of directors are seldom mentioned. See, for example, Thomas Watson, *Father, Son and Company* (New York: Bantam Books, 1990). In Watson, Geneen and other biographies, boards are not even mentioned.
11. See also, for example, Westphal, "Second Thoughts."
12. The items in this list are based on observing the boards in action as part of this study—including strategic success and failure—together with interviews of individual directors.

devoted during board meetings to in-depth strategic business presentations and discussions? Are critical issues and current and prospective problems regularly addressed?

3. Has management responded properly to directors' comments, questions, criticisms and suggestions regarding the strategic plan and the actions to carry them out?

4. Are there performance benchmarks and metrics that are based on the strategic plan? Is executive compensation, in turn, based on achievement of these benchmarks?

5. Does the board adequately monitor financial indicators to ensure that the company performs as projected? For example, does the board devote adequate time to reviewing annual budgets, capital spending and the financial integrity of the company? Is the performance of the company against the operating and capital budgets regularly monitored?

6. Does the board regularly review the operating performance of major segments of the company against targets and inquire into the factors contributing to major performance variations? Is the board effective in reviewing annual operating plans?

7. Does the board ensure that, through management succession planning, the management team has the bench strength necessary to execute the company's strategic plan?

8. Is a strategic update given by the CEO to the board on a regular basis? Do appropriate operating managers report on subjects of interest to the board? Is the CEO candid with the board in discussing the company's strategy? In other words, is the strategic "posture" such that the CEO desires and values a strategic input by the board?

9. Is there a shared understanding between the board and the CEO as to what, when and how strategic recommendations by the CEO and management team come to the board? In other words, are key strategic issues, to the extent possible, presented to the board with adequate time for reflective thought, off-line communication among directors and effective questioning of management during board meetings?

Continued

10. As part of major strategic initiatives, does the board receive a summary or report of what options were considered by management, on what basis, and why they were rejected? Are "exit" strategies part of management's strategic recommendations to the board?

11. Do directors uphold their duty of confidentiality regarding strategic issues? Have strategic "leaks" occurred by directors, which have the effect of "chilling" management in being strategically candid?

12. Does the board have an excellent knowledge of the fundamental key drivers of the business? Does the board stay abreast of trends and issues affecting the company's strategic performance and properly focus on competitive, financial and other challenges that the company faces?

13. Does the board have an annual directors' governance and strategy retreat, in which the draft strategic plan is presented by management, discussed, reviewed, amended and ultimately approved by the board, including any final instructions and directions from the board?

14. Do board members have adequate opportunities to visit company facilities?; and

15. While it is very difficult for the company and the board to anticipate specific situations, is the board organized and prepared to handle a crisis situation? Has the board formally approved a crisis response procedure put forward by management?

OTHER RESPONSIBILITIES

Most directors will one day be faced with the necessity of dealing with a crisis of some sort. When it occurs, regardless of its nature, the responsibilities and the amount of time that must be devoted to company issues increases dramatically. How does one handle an unsolicited takeover bid? How does one react when a chief executive officer is suddenly incapable of continuing? What does one do when fraud is suspected? How does one deal with rumours of an internal scandal? How does one respond to a major lawsuit? And how does one initiate the removal and hiring of a new chief executive officer? All these and similar crises test the mettle of directors and change the job of being a director from one of relative routine to one of intense pressure, both in terms of the time that is spent on the company's problems and the stress involved.[13] Indeed, as the board wrestles with a decision relating to such questions, the discussion can become far ranging and often cantankerous.

Meetings, of course, are only one part of the director's chores. Wise management constantly calls upon good directors for advice and help. Because of their many contacts, directors arrange for meetings between executives of the company and public officials; obtain speaking engagements for company representatives; appear at a wide variety of company functions; represent the company at various meetings; occasionally meet with shareholders; and occasionally may be asked to present the company's position before a regulating body on a topic in which they have special knowledge. And in many corporations, the board meets from time to time at different divisions or spends a day visiting various operations.

HOW COMPETENT ARE DIRECTORS?

The most astonishing, and quite alarming, information derived from the approximately two hundred interviews with directors was that a large number were deeply disturbed about how the boards of which they were or had been members were functioning. While it is impossible to generalize from the results of the interviews, it is interesting to note that 1) several directors assess many of their colleagues, the outside directors, in particular, as not sufficiently knowledgeable about business to make major contributions to board decision-making, and that 2) several felt that the boards on which they themselves were serving were quite dysfunctional.

All types of problems were commented upon—lack of trust between management and board members, lack of commitment and work on the part of many directors, strong personality conflicts between and among directors, and complaints about the manner in which boards were managed. Among many other things, directors complained of obtaining too little information to permit them to be

13. For a discussion of the problems for directors when boards move into a crisis, see Carol Hansell and James Gillies, "Nearing the Brink: Financial Crisis and Issues for the Unrelated Director," *Corporate Structure, Finance and Operations: Essays on the Law and Business Practice*, vol. 9 (1996).

able to make significant contributions to board decisions and of the lack of specific terms of reference for their positions.

There appears to be misunderstanding between some CEOs and their boards about the precise duties of boards. Some of the former believe that boards should be major contributors in the development of the overall strategies of the corporation; others believe that strategy is no business of the board at all. And many CEOs feel that boards have a tendency to become ossified and out-of-date rather rapidly because many members, even with rich business experience behind them, are not currently involved in business activities.

Table 3.4

Some Directors' Views on Ineffective Boards

"There's a lack of trust and good working relationships among all directors. Because of this, certain discussions are not happening. And we, as a board, must have these discussions given the state that the company and the . . . industry is in." (chair)

"The board is drifting. . . . The board meets primarily by phone. The committees are not working . . . and don't meet regularly. There are no formal reporting requirements." (director)

"Does the board add value? Not always. They are outsiders in understanding our business. . . . They have common sense. They love strategy. In the [strategy], the board provided good common sense. But it's not their business." (chair and CEO)

"They're generally busy people and don't take their role seriously. There is rarely a stated mandate for the board, a structure or policy for tenure on the board, for nomination to the board, or clarifying how bringing this particular individual responds to that mandate." (CEO)

"Some of the directors won't even speak to one another." (director)

"The board ceased adding value about twelve months ago." (director)

"Information is leaking and certain directors are undermining the board." (director)

"The board does not add value directly." (director)

"The board lacks talent." (director)

"We need new blood, skill sets, ideas. We're getting conscript responses." (director)

"Management looks at directors and says, 'What do they do?'" (CEO)

"Outside directors aren't very effective. They only know five to twenty-five percent of what they need to know. Power is in information and knowledge. Either they're in the kitchen or they're not. . . . " (CEO and controlling shareholder)

"There's a decreasing understanding of the strategic environment. The board's responses are predictable. [Director X] is a cheerleader. [Director Y] sings the same governance song–'do it faster, cheaper and smarter. ' And [Director Z] tells us we're focussing on too many things. There's not a lot of value added." (CEO)

"The outside directors don't add much value from a strategic point of view. Number one, they don't know the industry well enough and number two, they don't know who the players and the personalities are." (chair and CEO)

"Directors don't know what the____is going on." (chair)

"The outside directors are not adding value. . . . There's a lack of understanding of the commercial process, the development of technology to product. . . . We've outgrown the board." (CFO)

"Very few chairs and boards of directors I know have a job description. And the ones that do [find the descriptions] are pretty pathetic." (director)

"Bank mergers are an economic issue." (director)

"The role of the boards in financial mergers? Politics. Not the politics of New York, Chicago or London. It's an antagonistic political environment, a politically misunderstood environment by the board. Boards have a positive responsibility to be aware and bring perspective into the boardroom. Some boards thought Paul Martin was the most powerful Minister

Continued

of Finance since Bud Abbott [the Honourable Douglas Charles Abbott, Dec. 10, 1946 to June 30, 1954], and you don't stick your fingers up his nostrils. I know they said they tried to get hold of him. Slowing down, assessing the environment and politics is the role of the board. These are the dynamics of Canada." (former regulator)

It is not surprising to obtain, from many lengthy interviews with directors about their experiences on dozens of boards of different sizes in dozens of industries, a range of views that is as disparate as one can imagine. Indeed, it would be astonishing if it were not so. Every board is different and every board member and chief executive officer perceives in his or her own individual way the manner in which a board operates. So it is perfectly normal that some board members find that their board is badly run, while others think that their board is perfect; that some believe outside directors add value, whereas others do not; that some believe boards add value, while others disagree.

However, a common theme that runs through many interviews is that many directors believe the boards on which they sit are dysfunctional—that they do not operate as effective decision-making bodies in the best interests of the company and the shareholders. Several factors were cited as contributing to this perception.

First, in many cases there is very little preparation required for joining a board, and companies have not been deeply involved in providing remedial education for new and continuing directors. Consequently, many aspects of being a director are simply unknown to some new directors. Apparently, some directors attending their first board meeting are totally unfamiliar with the most fundamental aspects of corporate law. Few fully realize their relationship to the management of the organization and that they can replace the chief executive officer, the person who probably invited them on the board in the first place. Many do not know that by law they are entitled to receive an answer to any question that they may ask and to obtain any information about the organization that they wish. And, on rare occasions, someone may be appointed to a board who is incapable of understanding elementary financial statements.

Second, many new directors often know very little about the companies to which they are elected as a director and relatively few companies have comprehensive, formal and effective director orientation programs. It is assumed that a new board member will simply learn all that he or she needs to know about the organization through the discussion around the board table—an assumption that the interviews with existing directors suggested is possibly true in the long run—but learning everything on the job is a very inefficient method for introducing new directors to their responsibilities.

Table 3.5

Some Directors' Views on the Competency of Their Peers

"Boards don't know enough about the business. They need access to independent advisers, based on their instincts regarding the major issues. . . . It's all about information. You're so subservient to what management gives you [that] you're responsive. Directors need to know more about the business and the sector." (director)

"Directors need to thoroughly understand the nature of the business and businesses. Each new director should have a substantive written briefing on the business, its nature, and over the first year it's best to schedule half a day at each of the major manufacturing sites to get up to speed. You need to develop an understanding [rather] than through osmosis and put significant time into it. Get external information as well, from third parties and analysts. Management has a strategic plan, but it helps to have third-party assessments." (director)

"I couldn't understand Enron without help." (director)

"It takes a lot of effort to really understand the business, and a lot of attention." (director)

"The nature of the specific business and keeping current [and] informed . . . People don't know much of what they've read, although they're loath to admit it if they're experienced. It's okay no matter who you are. A refresher is knowledge-building." (director)

Continued

"Too many directors go on boards because simply they know someone not because they understand their role and responsibilities and it's too late when it's in a court case. . . . " (chair)

"The CFO can pull the wool over the eyes of the CEO and the CEO can pull the wool over the eyes of the board. You can't prevent it. You need validity of the numbers . . . the right questions and the right process. The failure of the auditors is a big issue—'Enronitis.' I meet one-on-one once a quarter, not once a year any more. The auditors should be the cops." (CEO)

"So like geniuses in a room, they sit there like Moses, nodding their heads—and I can describe a couple of them—when they don't know what they're looking at, especially lately. It's not likely to be intuitive. It's like the CEO asking the CFO—you feel uneasy. What if it's legal, rational but just bad judgment? It's allowed because there's an orderly way to unwind it." (chair and CEO)

"The board should ensure that management stays within control limits, whatever they might be, which the board put in place. 'Are you within the control limits approved by the board?' It might be embarrassing but it will not jeopardize the corporation." (director)

"There needs to be a course in acquisitions, valuing them and under-standing why so many of them go wrong, from a governance point of view." (director)

"With the takeover of [Company ABC], the board would have sold it too cheaply. The board was split. The offer was increased because of a director. If that director had not have been on the board, we would have lost millions." (director)

"Corporations are getting bigger than they ever were and the stakes are increasing. Outside directors understanding of the complexity of the organization has changed. . . . The requirements of outside directors to see the flags is partly a matter of experience and partly a matter of asking the right questions. It simply heightens the process the guy goes through when he joins the board and increases his understanding and behav-iours, especially in the early years. It takes a few years to understand where the washrooms are—the business and the plays. It takes time. Shortening this would help the process." (director)

> "Shareholder democracy is a farce, still. Proxies are ineffective. Annual general meetings are a sound and light show and the slate of directors is re-elected." (director)
>
> "I don't know____about the Internet." (director of a technology-based company)
>
> "It is not clear how to make directors accountable for lack of adequate preparation." (director)

Moreover, even the more experienced directors often know little about specific situations they may have to deal with. Until they are personally involved, few directors know much about unfriendly takeovers, acquisitions, bankruptcies, failures, lawsuits or the dismissal or hiring of a chief executive officer. As a result of this situation, a large number of the directors interviewed are in favour of more training of directors; a few even go so far as to suggest that educational programs leading to the certification of directors would be a welcome development.[14]

Table 3.6

> Some Directors' Views on Education and Training
>
> "Training? We have no training!" (director)
>
> "My orientation was one hour before the board meeting." (director)
>
> "Board training and education is non-existent. I'm shocked. . . . There's basically no training or education. I am very disappointed." (director)
>
> "We give them their binders and that's it." (corporate secretary)
>
> "Directors learn after they get the job, unfortunately." (director)

Continued

14. The Institute of Directors in the United Kingdom has for many years run a major educational program for directors and many of its affiliated or autonomous branches are also doing so in Japan, Australia and other countries. In Canada, at the completion of a prescribed set of courses and a peer review, participants are given a certificate and designation they can use from the Institute of Corporate Directors.

"It's double the time and zero orientation." (director)

"Training of directors is very limited. . . . Boards I've been on often have no orientation, plant visits, industry training, *etc.* Ongoing education for directors is terrible as well. Take derivatives. Frankly I still have no understanding of what I am looking at. Information systems? None of us could even operate PowerPoint. The continuing upgrading of knowledge is done very poorly by boards. The whole pension area is another example." (director)

"We should admit that the training is inadequate. We don't know what we don't know." (director)

"Too often committee rotation is seen as an education opportunity when you think they're adding value but they're really learning on the job. Good boards educate their members. You need at least half an hour per board meeting on education. Being average is not good enough. You need to be competent and excel in the audit function and the HR and comp committees. It's specialization—there are specialized committee competencies here." (professional adviser)

"This [financial institution] doesn't have an orientation for new directors that is sufficient. It needs to be industry specific and culturally specific. It's a big hole in training directors." (director)

"After twenty years, I still have questions. To whom should I talk?" (director)

"We need to customize the orientation to the businessperson or the past CEO, understanding the individual's strengths and weakness, for example, financial literacy. We should tailor-make it to the individual." (chair)

"The learning curve on this committee is steeper than any other board committee on all of the other boards I am and have been on." (director)

"We should devote more time to being educated as we approach a decision, in reviewing and understanding a subject. The roadblock is time. It's a Catch-22, as we have only busy activist people on the board and they have the least amount of time." (director)

"Sometimes you're embarrassed to ask." (director)

"As you try to train directors . . . it's highly unlikely to be sufficient knowledge about the inner workings. . . . Even if you do, you are 'unsure' versus the experts and uncomfortable in challenging. You go away, and don't come back until one month, two or three, and their retention level decreases and the product changes. Boards don't really deal with this." (director)

"[I don't have] time to go to 'school.'" (director)

"For education of directors, the problem is not the theory but the application. Setting aside one day is hard. . . . One of the issues is the time to gain the skills." (business school dean and director)

"You want the people who have no time to get accredited." (director)

"Directors love strategy sessions and strategy retreats because that is where they learn." (CEO)

INCREASING DIRECTORS' EFFECTIVENESS

Most people when they are invited to join a board are neither unemployed nor totally uninformed about business activities. Most have some basic ideas about their responsibilities, and most are aware from reading about lawsuits against directors of some of the difficulties that are associated with being a director. But as pointed out above, directors express strong concerns over their level of knowledge. As a result, many far-sighted boards are not only developing relatively precise job descriptions for directors and other positions associated with governance of the corporation, (see Chapter 4) but are providing effective orientation and education programs for new directors.

Successful director orientation and education programs must be tailored to the individual director's or directors' needs and collectively to the board's needs: they must be aligned with the specific needs of that director(s) on that board, in that business, and in that industry. The program should contain information about 1) the corporate governance practices of the company—its position on disclosure, expectations from directors, policy on communications with stakeholders, plans for succession of management, *etc.*; 2) the industry in which the business operates and the competitive position of the company within the industry; 3) the major features of the company—its past and present financial performance, current strategy and operational strengths and weaknesses; and 4) the ethical and cultural environment within which the board operates. Depending on the size and nature of the company, an orientation program may also contain visits to some of the major operations of the company— for example, mines, factory sites or retail stores—and meetings with members of management and external advisers. Finally, while all new board members will have met current members of the board during the selection process, it is valuable to have one-on-one meetings with two or three current directors to discuss some of the "soft sides" of the operations—details about how various directors contribute to the board, the process by which decisions are reached, the qualms and quirks of the chair, and other such matters.

It is also important that continuing education should be available to directors on an ongoing basis. Properly oriented and educated directors make for better directors; better directors make for better boards; and engaged boards provide strategic value to the corporation. Moreover, as well as being a source of assistance and support for management, knowledgeable directors, through informative questioning and challenging, may well prevent the chief executive officer from making that one big mistake that could easily fatally damage the company. Forward-thinking managers welcome this sort of input. Designing and implementing effective orientation programs and encouraging and financing continuing education is a wise use of shareholders' money.

However, the scarcest resource that many directors have is time and few appeared to be prepared to spend a substantial amount of time away from their enterprises to take educational programs. In addition, many of the most ardent supporters of greater formal education for directors were quick to realize that getting prospective, let alone incumbent, board members to take more training could be difficult, given the general feeling among many directors and potential directors that they know all they need to know from their business experience to fulfill their responsibilities effectively.

Table 3.7

Some Directors' Observations on the Problems of Being a Director

"The most precious commodity a director has is time." (director)

"One of the mistakes I made was not absorbing the detail of a given study. I started too late—again, 'time' as I said. I have the mental acumen and resolved to do it. The learning curve was steep—where to look for what. . . . Time is your most valuable asset as a director. You cannot misuse your time. I did change—I prepare very carefully and raise questions by phone before I come." (director)

"The amount of reading is night and day compared to five years ago. Now, it's six inches per meeting. Ten hours a day, yes, two days a month, two hours this morning, half an hour here with you now. It's the same at [Company ABC] and [Company DEF]. In many sectors the industry and competition is moving so quickly. There's the information from the analysts. . . . Next year we will start our meetings at 8:00 a.m., versus 9:30 or 10:00 a.m." (director)

"Time is a problem. Being a director demands so much time of a person, especially when you move to smaller boards of fifteen or sixteen people and have to staff committees." (director)

"The business . . . is so complex. We look for people who have the time, such as a former CEO—someone who is independent and objective. Time is the constraint but it's taking unreasonably more time [to serve on the board]. It's between two and three days a month. Next week is Sunday through Tuesday and the annual general meeting. The annual two-day strategy session. Committee meetings. It's one-twelfth of my time." (lead director)

"I have to spend too much time here. My directors don't want me on any other board. How can a CEO running a significant corporation sit on four or five boards?" (CEO)

"[A] CEO should sit on no more than two boards. I'm now on twelve boards. I was on sixteen boards. It comes down to scheduling. I have no problem keeping up with sixteen boards." (a busy director)

Continued

"Directors are overcompensated for what they do and undercompensated for what they should be doing." (director)

"Boards are paid appallingly low. It's futile." (chair and CEO)

"We are paid so well that we pay attention and it gets to the top of our schedule." (director)

"It's a job for people who are semi-retired. People want an improvement in the remuneration, but you don't want people doing it for the money. Let's say four or five boards, max, at good compensation, say, $150,000 each. So $150,000 times five is $750,000, right? So let's say $500,000 to $600,000, which is enough retirement income because you're not active. No one wants to be a director while they're working, if they can." (retired CEO and director)

"There is a price for good governance . . . We've increased in size from a $1 billion to a $2 billion a year company and gone from 5,000 to 8,000 employees. With the travel, intense preparation, we need to attract the best and the brightest directors." (chair)

"The fees have to increase. The insurance has to improve. The liability has to get better. All to make things more attractive for serving on a board. Directors need to be paid more." (director)

"Personal liability of directors is the number one impediment to good corporate governance in Canada." (director)

"I have more work to do to feel more competent." (director)

"I'm very cynical about being an independent trustee these days; there's no relationship between the risks and the rewards." (director)

As a result of the increased expectations on the part of shareholders, managers and regulators, many individual directors are being forced to reassess their activities as directors. Generally speaking, boards are getting somewhat smaller and directors have an increasing number of committee assignments, which, in turn, requires more preparation for meetings and a better understanding of various problems that the company may be facing. As well, on better boards, they are increasingly expected to make a substantial input into the process of making decisions about the future of the company, which also means more preparation time. And so, astute and conscientious directors are finding that being a director, particularly if they are serving on several boards, is rapidly becoming close to a full-time job. To the extent that these trends continue, the difficulty of finding competent, part-time directors increases dramatically, and there will be many more "career directors."

THE CHANGING CHALLENGES
IN BEING A DIRECTOR

Directors' fees are becoming higher, the tasks and the time required to accomplish them are becoming greater, and the regulations governing directors and their actions are becoming more extensive. All these changes have important implications for directors.

First, with the payment of higher fees, there is an expectation of better performance. It is one thing for a board to tolerate an incompetent member when meeting fees are a few hundred dollars and the retainer is in the low thousands. It is quite another when meeting fees, retainers and other perquisites, including stock options, are in the tens and in some cases hundreds of thousands.

Second, when directors are expected to analyze complex problems, they may need staff assistance to do so. This raises complex questions with respect to the relationship between management and the board—questions that in many instances are not easy to resolve. While the age of the "imperial chief executive officer" appears to be coming to a close, and the old battle about directors encroaching on the role of the CEO is more of an issue for textbooks and classrooms than modern boardrooms, it is easy to imagine the problems that can arise for a chief executive officer if one or two members of the board are previous CEOs, albeit from different companies, with staff support to analyze (and second-guess) every decision that he or she recommends.

Third, a much less obvious, but more distressing trend, at least for thoughtful directors, is the view among regulators and other analysts that, given the increasing size and complexity of many corporations, boards, as they have traditionally functioned, may not be able to fulfill their legal "duty of care" to monitor adequately the activities of the management of the enterprise.[15] In order to resolve this apparent difficulty, new regulations and laws have been enacted that specify various relationships among directors, auditors and chief executive officers. Many of the changes relate to questions of independence and conflicts of interest, which have inevitably resulted in more "outside directors" being appointed to boards. This is very troublesome for some directors; indeed a common assertion running through numerous interviews with active chief executive officers and directors was that outside directors—appointees from outside the industry, particularly from outside of business—simply do not know enough about the specific business or business in general to make a major contribution to board deliberations.

Perhaps of equal concern is that the emphasis placed on the "monitoring" portion of corporate governance has led inadvertently to a decline in emphasis on the other central task of governance—the creation of shareholder wealth. Consequently, there is yet another paradox in corporate governance: in an effort to improve the monitoring responsibility of the board through regulating its structure, the capacity of the board to fulfill all its tasks—particularly the major fiduciary task of maintaining and increasing the wealth of the shareholders—may be restricted.

Being a member of a board of directors is not nearly as pleasant and fulfilling as it used to be. Not only are directors spending more time at their job, but the amount of compensation they receive, while higher, has not increased nearly as rapidly as their responsibilities and potential liabilities. As well, instead of it being automatically assumed that an appointment to a board is a sufficient indication of ability to fulfill the job of a director in a competent fashion, more and more directors, particularly, but by no means exclusively, those from outside the business sectors, are being formally evaluated and found wanting. Moreover, the scandals that have been endemic to boardrooms over the past twenty years have taken some of the

15. See Paul Wayne, *The History and Evolution of Audit Committees.*

lustre off the position, and the ever-increasing number of shareholder lawsuits against directors are, even when one holds a substantial amount of directors' and officers' liability insurance, sufficient to make one pause before agreeing to join a board.

In short, while it is impossible to draw generalizations from the extensive interviews for this study, the majority of those interviewed expressed serious concern about the quality of the governance provided by many boards and strong skepticism about the capacity of regulations and rules to have a substantial impact on improving corporate performance. Among the current directors, chief executive officers and students of corporate boards, the implicit support for a totally new approach to the formation and operation of boards of directors was palpable.

BEST BOARD PRACTICES
AND ASSESSMENTS:
NECESSARY BUT NOT ENOUGH

What gets measured gets managed.
—Shareholder

We need to set out 1) the director performance criteria, 2) a way to measure them and 3) have action based on their measurement.
—Director

Installing and measuring best practices of boards is neither the stuff of corporate war-stories nor the work that attracts stellar people to boards. At the same time it is not astonishing, given the general dissatisfaction of many board members with the manner in which their boards operate, and indeed with the activities of their fellow directors, that in recent years a growing amount of attention is being paid by far-sighted board members, regulators, consultants and students of corporate governance to what may well be defined as "best board practices." While getting all the "practices" of board operations correct may not lead to an effective board, certainly it is an essential, if not a sufficient condition, for effective board operations.

Although the words "best practices" are certainly overused, in the context of this study, "best practices" reflect empirically grounded best-in-class practices. *Best practices* may be defined here as the result of observing some of the "best" and "less-than-effective" boards and individual directors in action, over an extended period of time, supported by extensive interviews and review. Several boards and directors examined for this study received independent peer recognition for their effectiveness. Conversely, others were characterized by directors themselves and through observation as being minimally effective, and in some instances, not at all.

WHAT THE BEST DIRECTORS HAVE IN COMMON

The specification and assessment of the duties and responsibilities— of an effective chair of a board, chair of a committee, individual director and CEO—must be undertaken to ensure efficient board operations. These duties and responsibilities involve such routine activities as attendance at board and committee meetings by directors, consultation between the chair and the chief executive officer when the two positions are filled by different people, the actions that committees should take, and so forth. Elementary as they may sound, experience indicates that unless such duties are specified, and measured, there is a very good chance that they will not be properly accomplished. Rather than leaving the fulfillment of responsibilities to chance, many boards are adopting and many regulatory bodies are requiring, or at least recommending, that boards prepare official job descriptions that precisely outline for directors, for the board and its committees, and for the chair, what they are expected to do.

Putting such documents together is not an easy task. Truly effective "best practices" descriptions are dynamic, evolve over time and are definitely not something that can be "dashed off" at an afternoon's special meeting of the board.

There are many important reasons why the preparation and adoption of job descriptions is essential for any board that aspires to operate efficiently and to provide good corporate governance, but two are overwhelming—first, it is the only way to ensure that all the elements essential for the proper operation of a board of directors are being dealt with; and, second, without specific performance requirements, it is impossible to make sound judgments about the effectiveness of various people involved in, and activities associated with, the board's functions. Rumours and reflections can be replaced by facts only when assessments of performance are made against specified standards.

A major distinction is made in this book between "structural boards" and "functional boards."[1] While there is a great difference between the two, all the discussion of the relative merits of each is based on the assumption that good "board practices " are followed equally well in both. This assumption does not mean that all, or indeed most, boards and directors operate according to all the best practices required for sound board operations. To the contrary, the evidence suggests that they do not.[2] But it does mean that 1) "best practices" are a necessary, although not sufficient, condition for effective governance, and 2) putting them in place underscores the fact that basic reform in corporate governance is not to be found only in better practices, important as they may be as a foundation for good governance, but in a totally different and somewhat radical method of selecting directors and patterns of board operations.

The job descriptions outlined in this book have been developed over time from a variety of sources: observations of boards in action; interviews with directors and corporate executives; several special studies of individual boards and the writings of many scholars of board practices. They provide a useful template for ensuring the major functions of directors, boards and their committees and other officers are being performed at an optimum level. Adopting, and insisting upon, best practices of governance is an important way that a company can ensure that the fiduciary duty and duty of loyalty and care discussed in Chapter 2 will be fulfilled.

JOB DESCRIPTIONS FOR KEY POSITIONS

A MODEL JOB DESCRIPTION FOR DIRECTORS

In the final analysis, the responsibility for the success or failure of a company rests primarily with the board of directors and how it fulfills its duties. Boards are basically small decision-making bodies

---

1. See Chapters 5 and 6.
2. See Chapter 3.

whose effectiveness depends not only on the competencies and behavioural characteristics of their members, but on the manner in which directors complete all their tasks. The evidence suggests that on many (most) boards there are directors who for a great many reasons do not do so, and one may be because they are not fully informed as to what they are expected to do. It is relatively easy to understand the concept of the duties of care and loyalty to the corporation that every director must meet. It is another thing to comprehend and to complete the work that is involved in translating an understanding of these responsibilities into action. Given the reality that many boards do not have clear position description for directors, it is not astonishing that many directors, by even the loosest standards of measurement, are viewed by some of their contemporaries as being less than competent.

Basically, directors, in the process of fulfilling all their responsibilities to the many different stakeholders associated with a modern corporation, must:

- Contribute to fulfilling the fiduciary, oversight, strategic and governance tasks of the board, as outlined in the company's corporate governance guidelines
- Attend all board of directors and committee meetings of which he or she is a member
- Attend the annual general meeting and the directors' annual governance and strategy retreat
- Prepare fully for the meetings of the board of directors and committees of the board of which they are a member
- Participate knowledgeably and meaningfully at board and committee deliberations inside and outside of meetings
- Ask appropriate questions of management
- Insist on receiving satisfactory answers to all pertinent questions
- Listen carefully and bring personal skills, experience and knowledge to discussions regarding the strategic issues facing the company
- Work constructively with board colleagues
- Encourage discussion of key issues

- Introduce items for discussion that that are not on the agenda
- Initiate meetings with fellow directors to discuss critical issues
- Exercise mature business judgment, not emotion, in discussion of issues
- Refrain from interfering in the day-to-day responsibilities of management
- Be available when needed for consultation and advice
- Not panic over a crisis
- Comply with the company's Code of Business Conduct
- Act with integrity and high ethical standards.

On the basis of interviews with directors and observation of boards in action, it appears that one of the major functions of directors that is often neglected is that of asking pertinent questions. There are many reasons for this. A director may feel unsure whether the question is sufficiently important to take the time of the board and may not wish to risk the possibility of being embarrassed before fellow-directors. The reality is, however, that almost invariably if something is concerning one director it is concerning several and is something that needs to be addressed.

A famous example of the importance of questioning is provided by the experience of the outside directors on a wholly owned subsidiary of a major company. The CEO of the subsidiary always arranged for one board meeting a year to be held at the head office in New York. On one occasion, all the outside directors, who arrived in New York the evening before the meeting, met for dinner. While chatting, one mentioned in a very circumspect manner that he was less than satisfied with the performance of the CEO, who also chaired the board of the subsidiary, but had not wanted to raise too many questions about his activities. Much to his astonishment, the other two outside directors immediately stated that they had the same concerns about the same activities. The next day the three met with the chair of the parent company, outlined their problems with the management of the subsidiary and within days a new CEO was appointed for the subsidiary.

A MODEL JOB DESCRIPTION FOR THE LEADER OF THE BOARD—THE CHAIR

While one of the most strongly debated issues in corporate governance is whether the positions of chair and chief executive officer of a company should be held by one or two people, there is no debate, indeed there is strong agreement, that the most important requirement for the effective operation of a board of directors is a highly competent chair.

The following terms of reference, or position description, are for a non-executive chair, that is a chair who is separate from the chief executive officer. The chair should:

- Ensure that the board of directors discharges its principal areas of responsibilities as articulated in the corporate governance guidelines
- Adopt procedures and ensure that resources are available to the board of directors in order that it can conduct its work effectively and efficiently, including deciding committee structure and composition, agenda-setting, scheduling and the management and operations of meetings
- Chair all meetings of the board of directors, executive sessions of non-management directors, annual general meetings and any other special meetings
- Ensure that the responsibilities of the board of directors as outlined in corporate governance guidelines, committee charters and position descriptions are well understood by both the board and management and are executed effectively
- Serve as the "hub" of all board of directors activity and provide effective leadership, overseeing all aspects of the board's direction and administration and ensuring that the board of directors works as a cohesive team and builds a healthy corporate governance culture
- Provide the source of independence for outside directors, ensuring that the board is sufficiently independent from management, and oversee the standards and processes to promote such independence
- Arrange for the executive sessions of the board of directors of the company to occur on a regular basis

- Allot sufficient time during board meetings for serious discussion of agenda items and relevant issues of importance to directors
- Encourage outside directors to ask questions and express viewpoints during board meetings
- Deal effectively with dissent and work constructively towards achieving consensus and arriving at decisions
- Facilitate effective communication between directors and management, both inside and outside of board meetings
- Ensure, in cooperation with the corporate secretary/chief governance officer, that directors are receiving information from management that is high in quality, in the appropriate quantity, in a timely fashion, in a convenient format and from suitable sources
- Ensure that the boundaries between board and management responsibilities are clearly understood and respected and that relationships between the board and management are conducted in a professional and constructive manner
- Schedule, in consultation with committee chairs, the chief executive officer and the corporate secretary/chief governance officer, meetings of the board of directors and committees
- Set, in consultation with the chief executive officer, other committee chairs, the corporate secretary/chief governance officer, other directors and members of management as appropriate, the agenda for the meetings of the board of directors
- Ensure that where functions are delegated to appropriate committees of the board, the functions are carried out and results are reported to the board of directors
- Oversee the corporate governance guidelines, committee charters and the structure, composition, membership and activities of the board of directors and its committees, including the work delegated to such committees
- Evaluate, along with members of the human resources and compensation committee, the chief executive officer's performance and meet with the chief executive officer, in conjunction with the chair of the human resources and compensation committee, to discuss this evaluation

- Set, together with members of the human resources and compensation committee, and in consultation, if necessary, with independent advisers, the compensation of the chief executive officer
- Plan for, together with the chief executive officer and the board (or a specific committee), the succession of the incumbent chief executive officer
- Recruit, in conjunction with the nominating and corporate governance committee members, prospective directors, and recommend such candidates for membership to the full board of directors
- Have an effective working relationship with the chief executive officer of the company
- Set the agenda for and chair the directors' annual governance and strategy retreat
- Ensure that one's industry and committee knowledge remains current
- Work with and assist the chief executive officer, as appropriate, in representing the company to its shareholders and other stakeholders, such as customers, creditors, suppliers, the media, governments and the public
- Oversee the preparation and distribution of communication materials to outside stakeholders when required
- Monitor and periodically suggest amendments to the position descriptions for the chair of the board of directors, the chief executive officer, committee chairs, individual directors and the corporate secretary/corporate governance officer
- Regularly lead revisions to the corporate governance guidelines and the committee charters, in consultation with committee chairs and the chief executive officer
- Decide, in consultation with other directors, issues of director remuneration, other than that of the chair of the board
- Oversee the administration of the annual board, committee and director effectiveness assessments, other than that of the chair of the board
- Ensure that an assessment is conducted on the effectiveness of the chair of the board of directors with input from all directors and plan for the succession of the incumbent chair
- Participate in the orientation and mentoring of new and continuing education of current directors

- Retain independent advisers on behalf of the board of directors when needed
- Respond to potential conflict-of-interest situations, including ensuring that a system exists for the detection, disclosure and management of conflicts of interest by directors, management and other employees and that any waivers by such individuals of the Code of Business Conduct are disclosed and approved by the board of directors of the company.

Properly executing all the duties of the chair of the board has become so time-consuming and critical to the effective management of the board of directors that non-executive chairs, especially for larger companies, have an office in the company headquarters and are well-compensated for their work.

GETTING THE GOVERNANCE WORK DONE— A JOB DESCRIPTION FOR COMMITTEE CHAIRS

An ever increasing amount of the important work of the board of directors is done by committees of the board. Indeed, being chair of the audit, compensation and the nomination committee involves the acceptance of great responsibilities and with the increasing regulation of companies an enormous amount of time (see Chapter 3).

The board is greatly dependent on the work of the audit committee for assurance that their "monitoring duties" are properly fulfilled and on the nomination committee for finding and recommending directors for appointment who add value to the board. In the past decade, with the escalation of executive salaries and the introduction of a great number of changes in the manner in which executives and board members are paid, the work of the compensation committee has not only increased tremendously, but also in many cases, members have become the subject of public attack.[3]

Chairing these and other committees, therefore, must be done well. The responsibilities of committee chairs are basically to:

- Provide effective committee leadership, overseeing all aspects of the committee's direction and administration in fulfilling its charter

---

3. See Chapter 3.

- Oversee the structure, composition, membership and activities delegated to the committee
- Ensure that the committee membership meets all legal requirements
- Report the results of each committee meeting to the next board of directors meeting
- Ensure that committee minutes are available to each director
- Schedule committee meetings, in consultation with the chair of the board of directors, other committee members, the chief executive officer, the corporate secretary/chief governance officer and independent advisers and members of management, as appropriate
- Set the agenda for committee meetings, in consultation with the chair of the board of directors, other committee members, the chief executive officer, the corporate secretary/chief governance officer and independent advisers and members of management, as appropriate
- Ensure that one's industry and committee knowledge remains current
- Retain, oversee and terminate, in conjunction with the committee and in consultation with the chair of board of directors, as appropriate, independent advisers to assist the committee in its activities or assist an individual member of the committee if and when necessary
- Ensure that the committee meets in non-management executive sessions, as necessary and appropriate
- Chair all meetings and executive sessions of the committee
- Communicate with appropriate members of management in fulfilling the charter of the committee
- Ensure that committee members are receiving written information and are exposed to presentations from management consistent with fulfilling the charter of the committee
- Allot sufficient time during committee meetings to discuss fully the agenda items of relevance and importance to directors
- Oversee the assessment of the performance of the committee annually, including that of the incumbent chair.

THE MOST DIFFICULT ROLE ON A BOARD— A JOB DESCRIPTION FOR A CHIEF EXECUTIVE OFFICER WHO IS NOT CHAIR OF THE BOARD

It is almost unheard of for the chief executive officer of the corporation not to be a member of the board of directors. Indeed, in many companies, particularly in the United States, it is not unusual for the role of chairman of the board and CEO to be combined. In such situations, it is not astonishing that persons holding the combined position have long been recognized as extremely powerful players within their companies, and, indeed, in the economy. Their exploits are often chronicled in autobiographies, biographies and business histories; they are called on to serve in and advise governments; they lead charitable foundations and involve themselves in all types of public service; they become media stars. And occasionally folk heroes. But, regardless of their fame and notoriety, the fundamental and number one task of all chief executive officers is to lead the enterprise that employs them.

In spite of the apparent differences among CEOs, all basically have similar responsibilities. While obviously there are differences in emphasis among different companies and among industries and the way in which different individuals fulfill them, by and large, the duties of the chief executive officer, as they relate to the board of directors, are to:

- Provide leadership in setting, in conjunction with the board of directors, the mission and values of the company
- Manage the business and affairs of the company within the guidelines established by the board of directors
- Develop and recommend to the board of directors strategies that are intended to result in the maximization of shareholder value
- Develop and recommend to the board of directors the business plans, operational requirements, organizational structure, staffing and budgets that support such strategies
- Implement the strategies approved by the board of directors and report to the board in a timely manner on deviations of such strategies from the parameters established by the board
- Direct and monitor the activities and resources of the company consistent with the strategic direction, financial limits and operating objectives adopted by the board of directors
- Provide to the board of directors assurance that the proper systems and actions are in place to identify and manage business risks

and that such risks are within the guidelines established by the board of directors

- Participate, in conjunction with the board of directors, in the development of a position description and objectives for the chief executive officer, as well as indicators to measure the chief executive officer's performance
- Ensure, in cooperation with the board of directors, that the company has an effective senior management team, that the board has regular contact with such persons, and that there exists an effective plan of succession and development for the chief executive officer and senior management
- Ensure the accuracy, completeness and integrity of the company's financial information, reporting and disclosure requirements, and internal control and management information systems through appropriate policies and procedures, and that the legal requirements in respect of the above have been complied with
- Provide to the board of directors a communications policy for board approval
- Meet regularly with the chair of the board and other directors to ensure that these responsibilities are being fully complied with and that directors are being provided with information necessary so as to fulfill their responsibilities and statutory obligations
- Work with the chair of the board of directors in the development of the company's corporate governance guidelines and its committee charters
- Work with the chair of the board of directors in the development of an orientation program for new directors and a continuing education program for current directors
- Serve as the external spokesperson for the company, including aligning interests and managing relations effectively with the company's shareholders and other stakeholders, such as customers, creditors, suppliers, the media, governments and the public
- Set the ethical tone of the company, including directly overseeing the administration and implementation of, and the compliance with, the company's code of business conduct.

ADMINISTRATION OF THE BOARD'S ACTIVITIES— A JOB DESCRIPTION FOR THE CORPORATE SECRETARY/CHIEF GOVERNANCE OFFICER OF THE BOARD

The board of directors has often been defined as the collective brains of the company.[4] All the crucial decisions regarding the company are made by the board and it is the board that has the final responsibility for the actions of the company. There is a great deal of administrative work associated with the activities of the board and, needless to say, it is imperative that complete and correct records of the decisions and deliberations[5] of the board be maintained. Making certain that the board functions well in an administrative sense and that records are flawless is the responsibility of the corporate secretary, who in more and more companies is also designated, formally or informally, as the chief governance officer of the corporation.

More specifically, it is the job of the corporate secretary to:

- Provide resources, information and communication links between the board and management, with particular emphasis on facilitating the flow of required information, reporting and disclosure requirements
- Report to, and have an effective working relationship with, the chair of the board
- Participate, in conjunction with the chair of the board and chief executive officer, in the development of a position description and objectives for the corporate secretary/chief governance officer
- Serve as the chief governance officer of the company, including:
  - assisting the board of directors and its committees as a source of expertise and advice on new developments in corporate governance and compliance that are being employed in other corporations
  - serving as the company's principal governance liaison for stock exchanges, regulatory bodies, corporate governance rating agencies and independent advisers to the company

4. Lord Denning, quoted in J. Gillies, *Boardroom Renaissance*: 32.
5. There is considerable debate among corporate lawyers about how extensive the minutes of the meeting should be. Some prefer the simple recording of decisions, while others believe there should be a record of all discussion. In case of a lawsuit all relevant documents must be produced.

- developing professional relationships with governance associations
- coordinating and developing, under the oversight of the board, orientation and continuing education programs and sessions for incoming directors and current directors
- assisting in other governance program development, as appropriate, under the oversight of the chair of the board, chief executive officer and the board of directors

- Attend all board of directors meetings, committee meetings where possible, annual general meetings and special meetings, if and where appropriate, and act as corporate secretary at such meetings or appoint a delegate to do so when this is not possible
- Report to the chair of the board of and service all board of directors meetings, committee meetings, annual general meetings and special meetings in accordance with procedures agreed upon by the board, including the following:
  - preparation and distribution of notices of meetings, agendas of meetings, minutes of meetings, certification of resolutions and details of decisions made, information circulars, proxy material, and share issuances and transfers
  - maintenance of shareholder records and lists
  - any supporting documentation as instructed by directors or required by law
- Ensure proper and timely documentary filings and fulfillment of disclosure requirements to statutory authorities under applicable legislation, including working with the company's external counsel and other independent advisers when necessary
- Maintain the company's books and records, ensure the security and regulate the application of the corporate seal and sign documents on behalf of the company as authorized by the board of directors or by-laws.

MEASURING BEST PRACTICES: HOW CAN IT BE DONE?

The adoption of job descriptions and other best practices should lead to better performance on the part of directors and of boards. Clear-cut descriptions spell out what is expected from directors and, most importantly, they provide very clear guidelines against which a director's and board's performance may be measured. In the final analysis, it may be argued, and often is, that the only measure of a company's performance that really matters are its earnings. Annual profits or losses, however, are rather blunt instruments against which to measure whether or not an individual director is adding value to the board.

Competent chairs and board members intuitively know if a director is fulfilling his or her responsibilities. But only if there are well-understood and accepted standards in place against which performance may be measured is it possible to confirm intuition with fact. When there are formalized governance procedures, meaningful assessments—assessments that even the most skeptical director must accept as creditable—of the performance of boards and directors can be conducted.

While there is much opposition, as Table 4.1 indicates, on the part of some director's to individual and collective performance assessments, given the far-ranging attacks[6] that have been levelled against boards of directors, it is not surprising that a great deal of attention is being given to the need for formal board and director evaluations. Indeed, a key part of various reports by commissions and regulators, who have been somewhat reluctant to move to more outright regulation of various board activities, has been the recommendation that boards should undertake formal evaluations of their effectiveness and that of their members. And yet, although since 1994 and 2002, the inaugural Toronto and New York Stock Exchange guidelines, respectively, have requested boards and key committees to assess their effectiveness on an annual basis, the most formal recent regulatory survey of Canadian corporate governance practices,[7] completed in 1999, indicated that only 18 percent of the boards reporting had a process for assessing board effectiveness and only 24 percent had any process for evaluating director effectiveness, other than through *ad hoc* discussions with the chair.

---

6. See Chapter 1.
7. See The Toronto Stock Exchange and Institute of Corporate Directors, *Report on Corporate Governance, 1999: Five Years to the Dey* (Toronto: Toronto Stock Exchange, 1999), 3.

Table 4.1

Some Directors' Views of the Challenges Posed by Board and Director Assessments

On Board Assessments:

"We're evaluating our board and committees and we started in the last few years. I don't believe in individual evaluations because of disharmony. How can you perform when someone holds an axe to your neck?" (director)

"[Company ABC] does have a board performance assessment process. . . . It's a questionnaire, but it's not composite and there's no feedback. You submit it every year. Committees are evaluated as well." (director)

"For the board evaluating itself, there's a conflict if the chair is also the CEO, and so you need a lead director. . . . It's easier to evaluate the board than for individual directors." (director)

On the Reluctance for Director Assessments:

"Evaluation of the board? What about litigation? You want me to serve a personal evaluation? You're nuts!" (director)

"There is so much pride and ego with high-rollers that it is worse than death to be embarrassed or lose face in front of their peers. So you must manage the process of board and peer assessments so there is no war path or sabotage." (professional adviser)

"Never have I been subject to an evaluation as a director. A Code of Conduct was recently mailed to me that I was required to sign outlining my responsibilities as a director. It was the first time in thirty-five years." (director)

"For director evaluations, the two questions are 'on what basis?' and 'by whom?'" (director)

"The peer appraisal is a smoking gun on both sides." (director)

"Directors are reluctant to pass judgment on their peers." (regulator)

"I have never seen a really effective board evaluation that works. They have floundered on peculiar aspects that boards have with individual directors whose relative importance is outside of that board. The chairman needs to say . . . 'Look [Director Y] you're not pulling your weight.' It's tough with golf and their wives being friends." (director)

"For instance, some directors perform in committee. Some directors perform more one on one. Some directors use their outside expertise. Some directors are active in the community. So effectiveness measurements should measure the different ways the directors contribute." (director)

"So the issues are [threefold:] One, what do you assess against? Two, how do you assess, given the backgrounds, thoughts and biases? And three, then what do you do? With management, it's two years or you're gone." (director)

A recent survey indicates that the number of boards conducting assessments is increasing. However, since companies tend not to share the details of how these evaluations are conducted, no one knows how reliable they may be—they could consist of nothing more than a simple self-evaluation check list.[8] *The Financial Times* (of London) reported that "So far, reporting on board evaluation in the annual report tends to be bland, with little information on responses to findings."[9] Professor Jeffrey Sonnenfeld at Yale University has remarked, "I can't think of a single work group whose performance is assessed less rigorously than corporate boards."[10] Some respondents interviewed for this study, based on their experience, estimate the figure for assessing the effectiveness of individual directors in a rigorous manner to be quite low—5 percent.

Why boards do not assess their own, committee and director performance in an "effective" fashion and implement the recommendations, when 1) presumably they are in the assessment business—one of their duties is constantly to assess management, 2) those that do make regular assessments find them very valuable, and 3) they are requested to do so by the Exchanges, is an interesting question.

8. See, for example, Spencer Stuart and the Rotman School of Management, *Canadian Board Trends and Practices at Leading Canadian Companies* (Toronto, 2003), 7: "The current nature of evaluations raises some important issues. Performance evaluations are useful only if they are conducted objectively and provide constructive feedback to directors . . . this raises questions as to how effective they are."

9. *The Financial Times*, January 20, 2005, London Edition, business life section, page 12.

10. J. Sonnenfeld, "What Makes Great Boards Great" *Harvard Business Review* 80:9 (September 2002), 113.

The answers offered by most directors for not undertaking self-assessments of the quality of the board's performance and their own individual contributions include:

1. Concern that there is a general lack of criteria for conducting proper assessments

2. Uneasiness about the manner in which the information collected may be interpreted and administered

3. Fear of the potential damage that assessment may have on the chemistry of the board

4. Concern about the confidentiality of results, and

5. Worry that results might be subsequently "discoverable" by the lawyers of plaintiffs in litigation against company directors.[11]

Underlying all these objections, however, are the realities that assessments make directors uncomfortable, that directors do not think they need them, and possibly that directors have a concern for what they might disclose about themselves. Many experienced directors, particularly those from smaller companies, believe that *ad hoc* discussions between a non-executive chair or lead director and other directors is all that is needed to ensure that the board and individual directors are performing well. A formal process of review, they believe, is simply not necessary and would accomplish little.

---

11. The raw data—be they from board or director assessments—should be kept confidential. However, legal consensus, given there is a lack of jurisprudence in this area at present, appears to be that board and director evaluation documentation are not privileged and may therefore be subsequently discoverable in the event of litigation, assuming relevance can be established. Practices emerging in this area are that the data from board evaluations are best disclosed to, and discussed by, the entire board in aggregate form. For director "self"-assessments, the non-executive chair or lead director may see the data under appropriate circumstances, *i.e.*, with consent of the director, as may a trusted corporate secretary for data compilation or filing purposes. However, for "peer" assessments (directors assessing one another), the full results are not normally shared with other directors, although, of course, directors see their own individual results. Dr. Leblanc predicts—based on boards with which he works—that as assessments of individual directors become more commonplace and boards become more comfortable assessing individual members and their respective contributions, results from individual director assessments, *e.g.*, chair, committee chairs, individual directors, *etc.*, will be shared more broadly with other directors on the board or committee, as appropriate, and in a highly constructive manner with which directors are psychologically as well as intellectually comfortable.

Boards that conduct rigorous formal reviews of board and director performance, however, find the process valuable. First, it compels the chair or lead director and directors to look inward to assess what factors are relevant for superior board performance and how they should be measured, *e.g.*, the adequacy of the information that board members receive before and at meetings, the appropriateness of the agendas, the effectiveness of committee operations, *etc.*

Second, conducting assessments also compels board members to consider how well the board is dealing with its strategic tasks, how well it is making decisions, the state of the company's relationship with its stakeholders, *etc.* Assessments are not simply meaningless acts with no operational substance. They bring about tangible enhancements of overall board operations, which, of course, is what they are designed to do.

Third, the boards that engage in assessment find that it increases the level of discussion about governance, encourages opinions to be shared by all directors—both orally and in writing, and enables attention to be paid to specific governance issues that might otherwise have been neglected.

Fourth, they find that, when the board makes its expectations explicit in the form of position descriptions and subjects itself to internal review, it signals to shareholders, management and other corporate stakeholders that the board is an active and engaged one, and that it has set explicit internal goals and priorities for which it is responsible.

There is a strong view among these boards that a board leader with internal credibility and authority is necessary to execute the task of overseeing and participating in the creation and implementation of the assessment process. The person most often considered appropriate to do so is the non-executive chair of the board, lead director, chair of a committee of the board, or another outside director with a high degree of trust and respect from his or her colleagues. External assistance may also be used.

Given the experience of boards that have begun to assess the effectiveness of the board and its individual directors in a regular, systematic and rigorous manner, there appear to be no insurmountable administrative reasons why boards should not perform effective evaluations of their activities and those of their members.

Table 4.2

Some Directors' Views on the Successful Use of Board and Director Assessments

Board Assessments:

"In simple form, it's self-governance. 'How do we make ourselves most effective?' is self-criticism. Boards are supposed to set the example. It's like asking yourself to do your annual performance review." (director)

"That's why it's so important to have a regular performance process, for everyone to see, with objective data. The better job the board does at a performance management system, the better it will detect performance problems and then have to deal with them. For example, 'Here are the five objectives that we have not accomplished.'" (director)

"[This company] evaluates board performance. As Chair of the Nominating and Corporate Governance Committee, I am making phone calls to all directors and spend about fifteen minutes with each of them. I have three questions. First, is the board still too large or should we move to fourteen? Second, should we evaluate individual directors and can we? And third, what are the strategic planning responsibilities of the board?" (director)

"When we evaluate our own board, we use a survey . . . and I discuss with each board member how things can be improved. . . . For individual assessments, if the board member is new, we evaluate them after three years. The lead director and I talk to the individual. We have had one [difficult] situation ... and we had to work with them." (chair)

"There has been a substantial improvement . . . 75 percent attendance . . . tremendous increase in the last two or three years. We had thirty-two directors, versus twelve at [Company ABC], thirteen to fourteen at [Company DEF] and seventeen here. So you notice [when someone doesn't participate]. There has been an improvement in the operation of the board and in the participation and preparedness of directors." (director)

"Here is my contribution of what should be assessed of each director. First is time, including attendance at board meetings. [The chairman] thinks it should be 85 percent attendance. I think it should be 90 percent. We don't have a formalized attendance policy, but we have asked directors to leave who have had attendance problems. Second is the quality of thought expressed at the board, including strategy, competitiveness, success of the company, hiring of management and policy. Third is the capacity to assist the company directly, both in terms of experience and the corporation's endeavours beyond board meetings. We have asked directors to evaluate themselves. We put the evaluations in a report and they go to the corporate governance committee and to the board—the corporate governance committee in detail and the board in summary report. The questionnaire is open-ended and evaluates directors on their contributions and how they can improve." (lead director)

Director Assessments:

"For peer appraisals, I know these are very sensitive...*primus inter pares*. We're all equal and no one is above being subjected [to an appraisal]. I find a disconnect between management and a ceremonial board. Certain things work and certain things don't. If you apply it to management, apply it to the board. I'd like directors to leave the room with the same ulcers I have. This might reach the point of full-time directors, which is fine so long as there's a charter of expectations." (chairman and CEO)

"The peer appraisal was effective for one director. He said to the board, 'I realize no one wants me on this board.' But he stayed and his performance increased significantly." (CEO)

"We're in the second round now. Everybody was being nice the first time, which is not atypical. It's interesting to get a more valid, accurate assessment." (CEO)

"Directors are uncomfortable being critical of their colleagues. It's okay for management to be evaluated, but there's ego and fear for directors being judged by their fellows. My own view is that this can be done so that it is tasteful, thoughtful and rigorous. Sacking underperforming directors is the stick. Some positives are that assessing other directors is not necessarily not of value—it can enhance director performance. You can identify individual performance that can be corrected." (chair of governance committee)

Continued

"The corporate governance committee has credibility and does the director evaluation. Each member opines on each director. The chairman [of the committee] has a chat with each director. It's better that he does it than I because it doesn't make sense for the CEO to do it. . . . For the board assessment, [the secretary] sends out a questionnaire and he sees the results. I see the results if the directors okay it. [The secretary] compiles the results to the governance committee, which in turn sends the results to the board. . . . I never see these. Some feedback was 'not enough strategy at the board level, ' for example, and starting committees at 9:00 rather than 10:00." (chair and CEO)

"There are self-assessments that just go to the files—a questionnaire every two years about the board and information. The results are collated. I'm not there." (CEO)

"The problem is that the information isn't acted upon, other than the individual director initiative—where you stand in relation to the average. Directors aren't acting upon the data. There's no 360-degree mechanism for feedback." (director)

BEST BOARD PRACTICES AND ASSESSMENTS: GOOD OR BAD THEY ARE HERE TO STAY

Boards of directors are under attack. Regulators, investors, shareholders, the media and the public are demanding that they perform better—that they be changed—and it is certain that change will come. And yet even as change is being demanded, very little is known about the manner in which directors are fulfilling their duties and how boards actually work.

While no one would deny that it is probably useful for the various exchanges to require listed companies to engage in "board assessments," the major force leading to more and better assessments in the future will not be so much exchange or commission rules or regulation, but recognition on the part of chairs, nominating committees and eventually shareholders that boards cannot be constructed to maximize shareholder returns without knowledge of how boards and directors meet and complete their basic responsibilities. And to obtain that knowledge there must be both board and director assessments.

Anyone contemplating joining a board, as well as members of the boards of companies with progressive leadership, should accept the fact that assessment of their performance is certain to become a regular occurrence. The days of the non-accountable director and board are clearly coming to an end.

THE TRADITIONAL BOARD: THE TRIUMPH OF STRUCTURE

For the time being we cannot establish a cause-and-effect relationship between corporate governance and corporate performance. As long as we do not show that a relationship exists between the two, the principles of corporate governance, in the best of cases, will be the object of polite attention or, perhaps more often, the subject of generalized skepticism.

—R. J. Daniels and R. Morck, eds.,[1]
Corporate Decision-Making in Canada

Our overall conclusion is that the typical structural indicators of corporate governance used in academic research and institutional rating services have a very limited ability to explain managerial decisions and firm valuation. These negative results imply either that corporate governance is of modest importance, or the available indicators of corporate governance are not especially useful."

—David F. Larcker, Scott A. Richardson & Irem Tuna,[2]
"Does Corporate Governance Really Matter,"

One of the interesting characteristics of corporate governance—a characteristic that makes it almost unique—is that by and large its quality is judged not on the basis of results but rather on the basis of form. Study after study has stated, without much evidence, that an effective

---

1. R. J. Daniels and R. Morck, eds., *Corporate Decision-Making in Canada* (Calgary: U. Calgary Press, 1995), 658.
2. "Does Corporate Governance Really Matter," by David F. Larcker, Scott A. Richardson & Irem Tuna, The Wharton School, University of Pennsylvania, June 9, 2004, as reported in *The Australian Financial* Review, July 2, 2004, in an article entitled "Directors best for governance outcomes."

board may be defined as one with appropriate board leadership, composition and size. Such a definition leads to some paradoxical situations: *e.g.*, Berkshire Hathaway, Warren Buffett's company, which has had the highest rate of return in history for shareholders, has not by this definition been effectively governed. For many years the board consisted primarily of Buffett, his friends and his relatives.

The Buffett paradox, however, may be easily explained. The host of rules and regulations concerning corporate governance enacted as a result of various studies and reports have not been adopted primarily to improve corporate performance, when performance is measured in terms of rate of return on investment. Rather, they have been put in place to provide the maximum possible protection for investors by assuring that the monitoring of management by directors is effective, and that there is in place a set of widely understood laws, rules and regulations within which corporations must operate. No one should be astonished that few if any correlations have been found between most of the regulations enacted with respect to corporate governance and the improvement of individual corporate performance. The rules are not designed to make corporations more efficient.

WHY THE EMPHASIS ON MONITORING?

There are a variety of reasons why regulators have placed so much of their attention on the monitoring side of corporate governance. By far the most important is that in order to grow and expand, corporations are constantly raising equity funds in capital markets from the investing public. Indeed, well-functioning capital markets are an essential condition for the successful operation of the free market capitalist system. If people are to invest their funds, they must be confident that markets are functioning fairly—that there is no insider trading, that boards of directors and corporate executives are operating honestly, that earnings are reported accurately, that the accounting is correct, and that there is complete and full information reported to everyone in a timely manner.

The achievement of these goals is sought in two ways: first, through laws and regulations establishing the general environment within which corporations operate, and second, through the careful monitoring of the activities of corporations by their boards of directors. To assure that the second line of control is properly fulfilled, public policy and regulations with respect to governance have been largely directed at requiring what is deemed to be the appropriate board structure for overseeing the activities of a corporation in its shareholders' interests. It is the fervent hope (often in vain) of regulators and legislators that these actions will prevent corporate failures and investor losses because of inappropriate or illegal governance activities.

In order to assure that the monitoring role of boards of directors is done properly, by the beginning of the twenty-first century regulators almost universally recommended that there be a larger percentage of outside than inside directors on every board; that the offices of chair of the board and chief executive officer of the company be held by two people rather than one; and that the size of the board be maintained at a relatively small number, possibly eight to twelve.

As a result of the adoption by trading exchanges and regulators of rules, codes and regulations supporting these recommendations (even though some are voluntary), there has been a great movement among corporations to structure boards according to the above criteria. Indeed, it has become almost customary for boards to accommodate the rules. Form continues to triumph over function.

THE RUSH TO OUTSIDE DIRECTORS

During the past decade, it has become the custom in various jurisdictions for regulators to classify directors as "unrelated" versus "related" (Canada), "independent" versus "non-independent" (United States, Australia, New Zealand) or "executive" versus "non-executive" (United Kingdom), and to recommend that the majority of directors be outsiders. For example, a portion of the second Toronto Stock Exchange corporate governance guideline states "the board of directors of every corporation should be constituted with a majority of individuals who qualify as unrelated directors. An unrelated director is a director who is independent of management and is free from any interest and any business or other relationship that could, or could reasonably be perceived to, materially interfere with the director's ability to act with a view to the best interests of the corporation, other than interests and relationships arising from shareholding. A related director is a director who is not an unrelated director. . . ."[3] Other stock exchanges have similar guidelines applying to boards and board committees.[4] The placing of a specific director into one of the categories is usually done by the corporations themselves, and the correctness of their judgment can be assessed from an analysis of readily available public information about directors.

Since a major part of corporate governance, broadly defined, is to provide oversight of the operations of management—the monitoring function—the rationale of having outside directors is obvious. It is simply assumed that if a director is independent, he or she is somehow better able to keep a check on management. On the other hand, it is similarly assumed that if a director is not independent, he or she can less likely be trusted to act in the best interest of the corporation and to fulfill his or her fiduciary duties. Thus, it is argued that if the majority of directors on the board are independent, the board will be more objective in monitoring the actions of management and supporting the role of stakeholders and minority groups than if the board consists mainly of directors who have some particular relationship with the company. And this may be true. However, an examination of the internal workings of boards indicates that director independence may be more a state of mind than a definable function and depends largely on the individual director involved and the *behaviour* of that director inside a boardroom (see Chapter 8).

A second reason for the emphasis on independence is that among corporate governance scholars and regulators, there has been a large amount of interest and discussion of "agency theory."[5] According to this theory, the interests of the shareholders and the managers of a corporation are not the same. The former want the maximization

---

3. The Toronto Stock Exchange Committee on Corporate Governance in Canada, "Report: 'Where Were the Directors?' Guidelines for Improved Corporate Governance in Canada," Guideline 2.
4. The New York Stock Exchange Corporate Accountability and Listing Standards Committee, *Report of the NYSE Corporate Accountability and Listing Standards Committee* (New York: New York Exchange, June 6, 2002).
5. There is a large body of literature about agency theory and its application to corporate governance. Possibly the most significant paper in giving the theory prominence is Michael C. Jensen, "Agency Costs of Free Cash Flow, Corporate Finance and Takeovers," *Papers and Proceedings of the American Economic Association* (May 1986).

of shareholder value, whereas the latter, who are the agents of the shareholders, are much more interested in maximizing their own wealth through high salaries, bonuses, options and expenditure on personal needs. It is the role of the board of directors to control these "agency costs" in the interests of the shareholders, and it is assumed that directors who are totally independent of the management are better able to do this than those who are in some way beholden to it. It may well be that the writings of the proponents of this theory have had some impact on the thinking of regulators—an example of academic research actually having some influence on policy.[6]

In its most extreme form, proponents of the agency theory of corporate governance do not believe that any board of directors is actually able to exert the extent of control over management that is desired in a well-functioning economy, and because of this fundamental flaw they argue that in the future, proportionately, there will be fewer and fewer public, widely held corporations as more and more corporations are taken private by dominant shareholders who are unwilling to pay outrageously high agency costs.[7]

A third reason for the view that a board fulfills its functions more effectively if it is made up of a majority of independent directors may be based simply on ordinary common sense that such ought to be the case. It seems only reasonable to regulate board membership to the extent of assuring that people with unmanageable, fundamental conflicts of interest be barred.

Defining independence is a very difficult task. Some directors[8] simply believe that it is a question of "resources," that persons are independent directors if they do not need the fees they receive for serving on the board and can walk away at any time they disagree with something. Others believe that if they have no dealings whatsoever with the organization—that they receive no compensation from the company other than their director fees—they are totally independent.

---

6. The principles underlying the theory were spelled out by Berle and Means' *The Modern Corporation and Private Property* in 1932 and the book had enormous impact on regulators at the time the Securities and Exchange Commission was created in the United States and for the next half century.

7. Michael Jensen, "Eclipse of the Public Corporation," *Harvard Business Review* (May–June 1979).

8. It is important to remember that these are the observations gleaned from interviewing almost two hundred active directors, regulators and advisers (vast majority were directors). No attempt was made to sample a population so as to permit generalizations from the replies.

Still others believe that directors owning shares guarantees independence—it aligns their interests with those of the shareholders—whereas others, particularly directors in companies with a controlling shareholder, believe that owning shares compromises independence since they view their task as representing the shareholders holding a minority interest in the company. Finally, many directors believe that the greatest cause of compromise is the social relationships between directors and managers outside of the boardroom. And many thoughtful directors believe that independence is primarily a state of mind.

Has the move to require boards to have a majority of outside directors led to more effective monitoring of companies? As noted before, it is impossible to prove a negative. The regulations may have kept many unscrupulous people off boards and therefore, because of the regulations, corporations in total may have performed better than they would have if there were no regulations. Who knows? What *is* known is that, from time to time, existing regulations have not prevented a large wave of corporate failures. Indeed, many of the corporations that failed at the turn of the twenty-first century had, by structure standards, exemplary board governance. Enron, WorldCom, Adelphia and many other notorious corporations that failed at that time had boards made up of a majority of outside directors.

While a relation between "the number of outside directors" and "board failure" is not proven, available studies show that director independence and board structure are not significant factors in determining levels of corporate performance. There is absolutely no persuasive evidence linking board structure—and specifically board and director independence—to the financial success of firms. So far as the literature on board independence is concerned, "[n]early two decades of research find little evidence that board independence enhances board effectiveness. Some studies have, however, found a negative effect."[9] And so far as the literature on director independence is concerned, "[t]he most important predictor of director effectiveness is not independence, but strategic experience that matches the company's needs."[10]

9. J. D. Westphal, "Second Thoughts," 6.
10. *Ibid.*, 8.

As well as the difficulties in defining independence, the problem is complicated by the fact that there is a substantial difference of opinion among the directors interviewed for this study about the importance of having a number of independent directors on a board. Some believe that it is essential to assure effective decision-making; to give credibility to the board, particularly in the area of corporate governance; to provide independent advice to committees, particularly the audit committee; and to stand up to strong management. At the same time, many believe that guidelines far from guarantee that a board will be independent.

Table 5.1

Some Directors' Views on Various Aspects of Independence

"There are two aspects to independence. First, you need to be financially independent. You don't need the money to live. This allows you room to maneuver. Second, you don't need to enhance your own reputation by being on the board." (director)

"Directors should be well paid, but the board should be something they can walk away from. They should not be financially dependent on boards as their main source of a living." (director)

"Ego and pay. You should not be a director if you need the pay or can't dissociate the decision from your pecuniary interests." (director)

"Very few people would say, 'Here's the way it should be done. The fee they get is worth something. . . . ' [Former politician X] does not have a ' _____ you' bank account." (director)

"We need [directors] with no fear, who don't need the job . . . [who say] 'no, no, no, do this, then do this and then do this.'" (director)

"You think twice before you rock the boat because we like being there . . . I'm guilty of this too . . . the reputation it brings . . . We can't have too many guys like this." (director)

"Independence is a state of mind. You can be independent and conflicted and you can be not conflicted and dependent." (former regulator)

Continued

"If you don't have conflicts, then you don't have paradigms for judgment. It takes you a long time to get there. . . . Conflicts of interest are multiple interests. They have to be managed. A layperson board has no corporate experience and is not conflicted. Conflicts really mean increased information. It means you can solve the problem and act responsibly. But you can't eliminate all conflicts. Proper governance therefore is the paradox of managing conflicts. They are worse in some industries than in others. A lot of conflicts are created by regulators who don't think things through rather than by [board members]." (shareholder)

"Social interaction can compromise you." (director)

"Independent directors should own shares and their money should be on the line in a meaningful way." (shareholder)

"Give them DSUs [deferred share units] not beer money or money for their wife's fur coats or for the house. . . . Complete DSUs, 100 percent, so they can't be bought. DSUs force them to be independent. It focuses your mind to do what's right." (director)

"Do you think I'm a better director because I have ten thousand shares in my safe? No. Will I be more effective? No. Will I be more forceful? No. I don't think share ownership makes for more effective directors. There's no one single thing. It's a matter of perception. Good directors don't act any differently." (director)

"[It is] more difficult to construct a board [that] is independent of management, if there is a controlling shareholder and, in particular, if the controlling shareholder is management." (director)

"The . . . guidelines are like describing hockey by describing the rink. You can fit all of the guidelines but have a terrible board." (director)

"You have independent directors for external credibility." (director)

"It's the big names. They don't mean a hell of a lot except they look good on the listed records." (chair)

"Watch out for [politicians] who 'rent their names.' Look at [former politician X] at [Company ABC], [former politician Y] at [Company DEF], who got in over his head, and [former politician Z] at [Company GHI]. . . .

[Former politician Y] for instance can't even read a P&L statement. They are 'enthusiastic amateurs.' Government is not governance." (director)

"Who are your truly independent directors? [Former politician X], for example? He belongs in the Kingston Pen [prison]. We have inept boards and indifferent [citizens]. They deserve each other." (director)

"We're not doing this to get a good board. We're doing this to satisfy the [stock exchange]. . . . The[y] told us we needed more independent directors. I'm not sure whether he'll be an effective director." (management)

"For appointments to the board, you're dealing with a limited number of directors and it's limited to the business sector. It happens all the time. Good people focus on the position rather than on the skill sets." (director)

"[The chair] asked [a high-profile U.S. director] to join the board after meeting him in a taxicab." (corporate secretary)

Despite all the evidence, regulators in the United States and Canada continue to focus their regulatory efforts on director independence. For example, the Sarbanes-Oxley legislation and New York Stock Exchange corporate governance guidelines are basically built around the concept that changing structural independence will improve board operations. Given the limited amount that is known about how boards operate and a general feeling that there must be something good about independence, it is understandable that the trading exchanges should have such guidelines. However, given the fact that the evidence now available does not show any direct relationship between independence, however defined, and effective corporate governance, when effective governance is defined in terms of corporate financial performance, it may be time for a refocusing of the regulations regarding "independence" from rules about relationships to assessments of competencies and behavioural characteristics of individual directors.

THE SEPARATION OF THE POSITIONS OF CHAIR AND CHIEF EXECUTIVE OFFICER

The most controversial of the recommendations on structure is the requirement, or at least recommendation, that the positions of chair and chief executive officer be separated.[11] The debate on this question is an old one. There are those who argue that combining the two makes great business sense since the CEO knows, or certainly should know, the manner in which the business is operating and the industry in which it is positioned, and is assumed to be totally immersed full-time in making the business a success for the shareholders. A separate chair, on the other hand, is usually part time, may not know the business and the industry (or if he is the former CEO of the firm, as is often the case, may be becoming out of date), may have a tendency to interfere in the operations of the enterprise and may not have the energy or time to devote to the needs of the company. The majority of the FORTUNE 500 companies in the United States in the early 2000s were more convinced with the arguments for combining the two positions and, therefore, had the offices combined.

The powerful argument against combining the two positions—and the argument that most regulators, policy-makers and academics advance—is that the jobs are fundamentally different. The CEO is appointed to run the company; the chair is appointed to run the board. It is argued that as long as the board of directors has the responsibility of appointing (and firing) the CEO and monitoring the activities of the enterprise, it must have a leader that is different from the person whose performance it is assessing. Moreover, directors must have someone to whom they can take their concerns who is not actively involved in the problems with which they wish to deal. Indeed, it is often argued by effective directors that there should always be some "creative tension" in the boardroom between the board and the CEO. Such creative tension cannot be managed; it can hardly exist when the CEO and the chair are the same person. And finally, the issues that some board members believe should be discussed at board meetings may be substantially different from those that the CEO wishes discussed. Since the latter normally prepares the agendas for the meetings, it can be very difficult for board members to get their matters on the agenda when the CEO and chair positions are held by the same person.

11. The separation of the positions of CEO and chair is discussed in a number of contexts throughout the book. It was clearly one of the most important questions on the minds of directors and management.

For all the above reasons, it has become the conventional wisdom that for effective governance the two positions should be split. In some cases, attempts have been made to retain the advantages inherent in having the two positions occupied by one person by appointing a "lead director" or "presiding director" (less common) of the board. This person functions as a spokesperson for the directors whenever it is apparent that the position of a director or directors is not receiving sufficient attention from the CEO/chair. The evidence of whether splitting the roles makes any difference in terms of the corporation's monitoring of board activities is mixed; the evidence that it impacts "corporate performance" is more definite—there is none that shows that it makes much difference.

At best, the results seem to be contextual, *i.e.*, they depend upon the particular circumstances of the enterprise. The fact is "many if not most of the highest profile [corporate] scandals in the US and Europe (e.g., Enron, Worldcom, Vivendi, Adecco, Royal Ahold, ABB, Manesmann, Deutsche Telecom) involved firms that had separated the CEO and chairman roles, but the split hardly prevented subsequent scandals. Accordingly there is no research that has established a link between the split leadership roles and firm performance."[12]

THE SIZE OF THE BOARD

The average board of directors is declining in size.[13] There are many reasons for this, but probably the most important is that boards are becoming more functional and less decorative. For years, membership on many boards was as much a matter of prestige within the business community as it was a serious business obligation. In the 1950s, for example, boards of Canadian financial institutions— banks, trust companies and insurance firms—were very large, occasionally exceeding fifty members. The banks believed that they needed representation from all sections of the country where they operated and representation from every economic segment of the economy in which they lent money. In addition, they seemed to

---

12. Jeffrey Sonnenfeld, "Good Governance," 109.
13. See, for example, the annual survey by Patrick O'Callaghan and Associates and Korn/Ferry International, spanning from 1995 (at page 14) through to 2003 (at pages 38–39).

think it wise to have a representative of the British aristocracy on their boards, presumably to add class to the gathering. As recently as 1970, one of the authors was told by a director that "when I was elected to the board of the Royal Bank I considered it the equivalent of being knighted."

Table 5.2

Some Directors' Views on Changes in Board Structure

"[W]e had a board of [over fifty directors]. Today we have less than twenty and are moving to fifteen. We're getting small. And we have only two inside directors. . . . A board size of twelve to fifteen is ideal for decision-making." (chair and CEO)

"With board downsizing we are smaller and more effective boards. Ten to twelve directors is optimal—directors fully committed and intellectually able to carry the load." (regulator)

"I wish we had a smaller board. My style is more direct, one-on-one. . . . Take [Company ABC], for example. You have a development of strategy that's harder with a bigger board." (chair and CEO)

"We've gone from fifty . . . directors down to seventeen. I think it's a bit too small given the work and committees. Twenty to twenty-two would be an ideal size." (lead director)

"There needs to be delegation to the Audit Committee, delegation to committees. Relationships and length of tenure matter too much. Going over the annual report or a press release, line by line, should not be on the agenda. The culture is too ingrained. How do you loosen it up? You need twenty-five-year-olds from e-business. . . . It's always been done that way. It's too open, a too-heavy use of the board. They're clerical issues. And strategic sessions are operational rather than strategic. . . . These issues should be pushed down. Management should be pushed to use the board strategically. [One director] is always into operations and splitting hairs." (director)

"We want to make more effective use of committees. The CEO will have to get used to this, and be there when asked. This has been the greatest

corporate governance change—the need to delegate control to committees. The chairman should be a regular member. The chairman should be
the preferred role because he should be on all the committees that the
CEO and president is not." (chair)

In as much as bank boards were controlled and managed by the
chief executive officers, there was no need to be concerned about
the efficiency of board meetings and the capacity of boards to make
decisions. Directors were, as so eloquently described by Irving Olds,
"like parsley on fish—decorative but useless." Over time, as the
function of the boards changed from being almost symbolic to practical, there was a need for a change in size. After all, it was difficult
for a fifty-member board to make any decisions, let alone competent ones. And so Canadian bank boards have been reduced in size
to make them more efficient, and what has been true for banks
appears to be true of boards in general.

Another reason for the decline in size of boards has been the
increase in the definition, both through law and regulation, of the
responsibilities and duties of directors. Boards want to be certain that
they are fulfilling all these obligations, and with a smaller, more structured size, they are better able to do so. There was a general feeling on
the part of directors interviewed for this study that the most effective
size for a board was from ten to fifteen. As was pointed out, "with a
smaller group of twelve to thirteen to fourteen the dynamics are easier. You have a real interchange of ideas and it is not a show."
Moreover, with the rapid rise in director fees, the costs of a large board
are now being assessed against the possible benefits, and in many cases
the conclusion has been that the costs far exceed the benefits.

As well, it appears that it is becoming somewhat more difficult
to recruit new directors. The number of boards to which an individual CEO belongs has been in continual decline during the past few
years, primarily because boards of directors are limiting the number
of boards they will permit their CEO to join. In an increasingly
competitive world, it is assumed that the CEO should devote the
great bulk of his or her attention to managing the company of

which he or she is head. In addition, the increase in litigation and directors' liability are making many well-qualified people more cautious about joining boards. And, with the increase in global business, boards often need some directors from a foreign country, and it is difficult to recruit such people because of the time commitments they must make when they join a board.

There is, however, the feeling among some board members that the downward trend in size may be becoming somewhat overdone given the number of committees that need to be staffed and the smaller time commitment that many directors have available to spend on boards.[14]

THE IMPACT OF STRUCTURE ON BOARD PERFORMANCE

Although the implicit, and in many cases explicit, claims that codes and regulations designed to improve corporate governance through changing the structure of boards have been designed primarily to eliminate fraud and conflict and to modify the power of management, there has been a considerable effort on the part of various groups to determine whether the recommended changes have had any major impact on corporate financial performance. Indeed, a substantial research industry has sprung up, dedicated to determining the relationship, if any, between mandatory or voluntary changes in internal corporate governance and the performance of firms. Investment advisers want to know if a causal relationship exists between internal board governance and corporate financial performance so they can make intelligent choices among companies when making investment decisions. Scholars wonder if firms that follow sound governance practices, as defined by their structure, can raise capital at a lower cost than firms that do not. And practising directors, chairs and nominating committees want to know the optimum structure for a board so that they may nominate for election the most appropriate directors.

---

14. See, for example, P. O'Callaghan *et al.*, "Special Report: Is There a Shortage of Qualified Directors?," p. 14, where "time demands" was the number one answer to the question "Why do you feel Canadian boards are facing a shortage of qualified directors?"

The Semi-Popular Research

Probably the best-known popular research on the topic are the McKinsey Global Opinion surveys.[15] The first was undertaken in 2000 and was updated two years later. It covered about two hundred institutional investors and found that about 80 percent of the respondents would pay a premium for good corporate governance, which was defined primarily in terms of board structure. The amount that would be paid varied from country to country depending on the amount of capital market regulation that existed in a particular country, presumably on the heroic assumption that the greater the amount of regulation, the lower the amount of risk. In Russia, the premium was high; in Canada and the United States, it was much lower. However, there was neither follow-up of the studies to see if people actually invested according to the findings, nor analysis of the impact of specific changes in board structure, such as increasing the number of outside directors on performance.[16] These were, after all, opinion studies, and it is hard to believe that chief executive officers of major institutional investment firms, surveyed by a major consulting firm, would not support the proposition that good corporate governance is preferable to poor.

Probably the most often quoted studies are those of CalPERS,[17] which basically measure the amount of improvement in the performance of a company's shares after CalPERS selected it as an example of poor governance and publicly raised questions about the value of investing in it. The rate of improvement in performance of these focused-on companies, which is attributed to better governance as a result of changes in structure, has been astonishingly high. A 1997 report showed that the companies that CalPERS focused on in the five years after they were first identified outperformed other companies in their group, as measured by relative change in share prices, by 23 percent, compared to underperforming them by 89 percent in the

---

15. P. Coombes and M. Watson, "2000, 2002 Global Investor Opinion Survey," *McKinsey Quarterly* 4:74 (2000).

16. Colin Melvin, "The Value of Corporate Governance: A Brief Review of the Evidence for a Link Between Corporate Governance and Investment," (London: Hermes Pension Management Ltd., July 2003): 4. This short paper provides a relatively good bibliography on the topic.

17. M. P. Smith, "Shareholder Activism by Institutional Investors: Evidence from CalPERS," *Journal of Finance* 51:1 (1996), p. 227 *et seq.*

five years before they were identified.[18] However, other studies indicate that the degree of improvement is almost totally related to the extent "that they have potential to respond to investor pressure . . . [this would suggest that] . . . the most significant factor linking corporate governance and company performance is likely to be the process of active ownership, rather than the fact of companies compliance with extant codes."[19]

All this material, plus a good number of other related studies, has been gathered together and used by private organizations to provide advice to investors about the quality of governance and implicitly its impact on rates of return, and to corporate boards with a low rating on governance that are looking for ways of improving themselves. Institutional Shareholder Services, Inc.[20] and Governance Metrics International,[21] two such companies, both have developed methods for measuring and assessing corporate governance performance, primarily through weighting various structural factors—number of outside directors, separation of the chief executive officer and chair tasks and so on. Through applying their formula to various boards, they claim to provide an indication of the probable effectiveness of the governance, and to make recommendations of how it may be changed.

Professor Sonnenfeld has been particularly critical of the professional private companies claiming that they can demonstrate a relationship between structural governance and corporate financial performance. He writes "in research I have been doing with Sanjay Bhagat at Colorado and Dick Wittink of Yale on 1500 public companies we are finding no support for a relationship between structural dimensions of board governance and company performance."[22]

---

18. Colin Melvin, "The Value of Corporate Governance."
19. *Ibid.*
20. Lawrence D. Brown and Marcus L. Caylor, "The Correlation between Corporate Governance and Company Performance," a research study commissioned by Institutional Shareholder Services, Inc., 2004.
21. See, for example, "GMI Releases Global Governance Ratings: Improvements Seen but Governance Risks Remain," press release, February 9, 2004, New York.
22. Jeffrey Sonnenfeld, "Good Governance," 109. Sonnenfeld goes on to address the "myths" of age, split CEO/board chairman, director equity, former CEO, independent board, "outmoded standards: attendance, size and others" and concludes with a discussion on "the missing ingredient: the human side of governance." He writes (at page 109): "The ratings services evaluate the corporate governance of firms by mixing together empirically based standards and the myths and clichés of "the Street." Further, "They perpetuate unfounded myths and clichés by downgrading firms for such reasons as failing to have a retirement age for directors and failing to separate the chairman and CEO roles."

Moreover, he argues in another earlier article that no significant correlation exists between, on the one hand, such things as director independence, age of directors, the degree of equity held by directors, the presence of ex-CEOs on boards and a host of other commonly held "myths," and, on the other hand, board effectiveness or corporate performance.[23]

Of course, Sonnenfeld is correct. The age of a director, tenure on a board, number of shares a director owns, strict attendance measures, number of other boards on which a director serves, formal independence standards *etc.* may have precious little to do with whether a particular director is effective or not within a boardroom. These types of metrics are relatively easy to measure. A problem with such metrics is that what can be readily measured may matter less in determining good corporate governance than the competency and behavioural characteristics of the board members. Indeed, the central thrust of this book is that it is substance not structure that is the most important factor in determining the performance of the board.

Unfortunately, pioneering as they are, none of these semi-academic studies offer any conclusive evidence of a major relationship between corporate structure and corporate performance. The fact is that for every article claiming a positive causal relationship between some aspect of corporate governance, as defined by structure, there is another claiming that no such relationship has been properly demonstrated.

THE ACADEMIC RESEARCH

One of the most oft-quoted pieces of academic research on the topic is a study by Milstein and MacAvoy that focuses on the relationship between board structure and corporate performance in large, widely held corporations. They use board independence as a proxy for an "active board," which is defined as a board that "met one of the following criteria: (a) had a non-executive chairman or lead director, (b) scheduled meetings of outside directors without management present, or (c) showed substantial adherence to the well-known General Motors guidelines for corporate governance."[24] They found that

---

23. J. Sonnenfeld, "What Makes Great Boards Great." See also *ibid.*
24. Ira Milstein and P. MacAvoy, "Active Boards of Directors and Performance of the Large Publicly Traded Corporations," *Columbia Law Journal* (June 1998): 1283–1322, as cited in Sonnenfeld, "Good Governance and the Misleading Myths of Bad Metrics."

well-governed companies (according to their definition) outperformed the not-well-governed by about 7 percent over a period of
five years when performance was measured in terms of changes in
share prices. However, it is impossible to tell from the study whether
the improvement in performance was, in fact, because of the changes
in governance or a consequence of other forces, such as substantial
changes in the marketplace.

Not astonishingly, with the great increase in interest in corporate
governance, the Academy of Management—probably the most
distinguished academic association interested in strategy and management—published in July 2003 a "Special Topic Forum on Corporate
Governance." In the report of the findings of the forum, entitled
"Corporate Governance: Decades of Dialogue and Data," it was
reported that "[w]ere independent governance clearly of superior benefit to shareholders, we would expect to see these results reflected in
the results of scholarly research. Such results, however, are not evident. . . . "[25] Other studies of the relationship between board size and
firm performance "provide no consensus about the direction of the
relationship"[26] and suggest that "there is no statistical evidence of a
relationship between corporate performance and proportion of outside directors on the board."[27] In addition, "[there has been a] failure
to consistently link the separate board leadership structure [i.e., the
separation of positions of chair and CEO] with enhanced firm performance."[28] And Sanjay Bhagat, Professor of Finance at the
University of Colorado, and Professor Bernard Black of the Stanford
Law School, write unequivocally that "in large public companies,

25. C. M. Daily, D. R. Dalton and A. A. Cannella, Jr., "Introduction to Special Topics Forum – Corporate
Governance: Decades of Dialogue and Data," *Academy of Management Review* 28:3 (July 2003): 374.
26. D. R. Dalton, C. M. Daily, J. L. Johnson and A. E. Ellstrand, "Number of Directors and Financial Performance:
A Meta-Analysis," *Academy of Management Journal* 42:6 (1999): 674.
27. B. Amoako-Adu and B. F. Smith in R. J. Daniels and R. Morck, eds., *Corporate Decision-Making in Canada*
(Calgary: University of Calgary Press, 1995), 413.
28. C. M. Daily and D. R. Dalton, "CEO and Board Chair Roles Held Jointly or Separately: Much Ado About
Nothing?" *Academy of Management Executive* 11:3 (1997): 19. Drs. Daily and Dalton also state (at page 17):
"Our finding that separate chairs are not characterized by higher levels of independence than their dual counterparts leads us to question under what circumstances board leadership structure is likely to matter and to ask where
the academic and practitioner communities should now direct their efforts." The authors of this book are of the
view that board leadership *effectiveness* (rather than structure) is where research efforts should be directed, namely, assessing the independence of mind, competencies and behaviours of board chairs and the impact of these three
variables on board decision-making effectiveness and, ultimately, shareholder wealth maximization. In short, it is
the "selection" of the chair of the board that matters, not the "separation" of roles of CEO and chair. See Chapter
9 and the discussion of Conductor- and Caretaker-Chairs.

there is no convincing evidence that greater board independence correlates with greater firm profitability or faster growth. In particular, there is no empirical support for current proposals that firms should have 'super-majority independent boards' with only one or two inside directors. To the contrary, there is some evidence that boards with super-majority independent boards are less profitable than other firms."[29]

Not everyone is impressed with this array of research. Indeed, one person interviewed for this book, a corporate governance scholar, was quite adamant that "the academic research is garbage, most of it." And such a position, although incorrect or certainly overstated, is understandable because it underscores one of the great difficulties in studying various relationships between boards of directors and corporate results: namely, that for every company that one can quote as an example demonstrating a positive correlation between good corporate governance, as defined by board structure, and good corporate financial performance, another that followed very good corporate governance practices can be found with a negative relationship. But nothing can be generalized from this fact. It certainly neither means that all companies with good corporate governance, as defined by structure, are likely to fail, nor that all companies with bad corporate governance are likely to succeed. Knowledge about corporate governance is not much advanced by quoting the experience of a few companies. The combination and permutations of boards that exist make it impossible to generalize much of value from a series of analysis of a limited number of individual boards.

Table 5.3

Some Academic Findings on Board Structure

"Although a host of theory-driven rationales suggest a relationship between board of directors size and firm performance, the literature provides no consensus about the direction of that relationship." (D. R.

Continued

29. Sanjay Bhagat and Bernard Black, "The Uncertain Relationship Between Board Composition and Board Performance," *Business Lawyer* 54 (1999): 921.

Dalton, C. M. Daily, J. L. Johnson and A. E. Ellstrand, "Number of Directors and Financial Performance: A Meta Analysis," *Academy of Management Journal* 42:6 [1999]: 674.)

"Board size is another issue for which there is no apparent consensus." . . . "This article has largely focused on board composition measures primarily because they represent the bulk of the empirical studies that have been conducted in the area of corporate governance." (J. L. Johnson, C. M. Daily and A. E. Ellstrand, "Boards of Directors: A Review and Research Agenda," *Journal of Management* 22:3 [1996]: 431.)

"[B]oth researchers and practitioners have focused largely on the conflicts of interest between managers and shareholders and on the conclusion that more independent oversight of management is better than less. Independent governance structures (*e.g.*, outsider-dominated boards, separation of the CEO and board chair positions) are both prescribed in agency theory and sought by shareholder activists. Were independent governance structures clearly of superior benefit to shareholders, we would expect to see these results reflected in the results of scholarly research. Such results, however, are not evident. (Schliefer and Vishny, 1997)." (C. M. Daily, D. R. Dalton and A. A. Cannella, Jr., "Introduction to Special Topic Forum—Corporate Governance: Decades of Dialogue and Data," *Academy of Management Review* 28:3 [2003]: 374.)

"Nearly two decades of research find little evidence that board independence enhances board effectiveness. Studies have, however, found a negative effect." (J. D. Westphal, "Second Thoughts On Board Independence: Why do so many demand board independence when it does so little good?" *The Corporate Board* 23:136 [September/October 2002]: 6.)

"The most important predictor of director effectiveness is not independence, but strategic experience that matches the company's needs. . . . Evidence that director experience is critical to board effectiveness is relatively new. However, evidence that board independence has neutral to negative effects on board effectiveness is not. The first research casting doubt on the value of board independence appeared in the late 1980s. Since then, not only have advocates of governance reform in the U.S. continued to focus on this issue, but the board independence mantra has spread to other countries, including Canada, the U.K. and Germany." (*Ibid.*, 8, 10.)

"Careful review of extant research addressing the relationships between board composition, board leadership structure, and firm financial performance demonstrates little consistency in results. In general, neither board composition nor board leadership structure has been consistently linked to firm financial performance. . . . These . . . provide little evidence of systemic governance structure/financial performance relationships." (D. R. Dalton, C. M. Daily, A. E. Ellstrand and J. L. Johnson, "Meta-Analytic Reviews of Board Composition, Leadership Structure and Financial Performance," *Strategic Management Journal* 19 [1998]: 260.)

"We question the need for such a policy [of 'separating the CEO and board chair positions']. This activity becomes even more questionable in light of the failure to consistently link the separate board leadership structure with enhanced firm performance." (C. M. Daily and D. R. Dalton, "CEO and Board Chair Roles Held Jointly or Separately: Much Ado About Nothing?" *Academy of Management Executive* 11:3 [1997]: 19.)

"So if following good-governance regulatory recipes doesn't produce good boards, what does? The key isn't structural, it's social. The most involved, diligent, value-added boards may or may not follow every recommendation in the good-governance handbook. What distinguishes exemplary boards is that they are robust, effective social systems." (J. A. Sonnenfeld, "What Makes Great Boards Great," *Harvard Business Review* 80:9 [2002]: 109.)

THE STRUCTURE BROUGHT BY REGULATION: SOME CONSEQUENCES

There is no doubt that the plethora of rules and regulations, some mandatory and others voluntary, enacted in the past decade, have led to a change in the structure of boards. More boards have been organized with a majority of outside directors; boards have become smaller; and some boards have split the position of chair and chief executive officer. The important question is "What differences did all these changes make in the governance of corporations?"

The most important consequence of the regulated board has been on board composition. It appears that many more outside directors have been appointed. As a result, one would expect that the way in which directors are recruited and the characteristics of the members of boards would have changed markedly over the past ten years. The evidence suggests that this may not be so.

For example, there does not appear to be much change in the number of women on boards. Opinions are very mixed, ranging from the belief that "every board desperately needs more women" to the position of one CEO that "[having a woman on the board] is a requirement that I have to meet so I meet it." While there is evidence that sexism and male chauvinism is not dead in the boardroom—"she likes skiing and sailing so she'll be a good board member"—by far the bigger concern is the availability of competent women directors and the high degree of recycling of women who are currently serving as directors. One senior male director remarked, in one of the author's corporate governance classes at the university that, "only twenty women in the country . . . are board-ready." One woman director pointed out, "once you're on a few, you get on others. You meet more people and if you are good you'll be invited on others."

As the number of women in senior management positions increases, many male directors interviewed for this study were of the view, rightly or wrongly, that the number of women on corporate boards would also increase. However, a female respondent, an advocate of women directors, offered a countering view. In the words of this senior woman business leader, "women are angry." They are angry, in particular in her view, because the figures for women on boards have tended to range, depending on the survey and the country, anywhere between 8 and 12 percent or so, and have been relatively constant over the last ten years. Despite the various platitude-type statements about the need for more women directors, little, according to many knowledgeable women, is changing. The qualitative data from this study tend to support what female directors suspect to be the case, namely, the director recruiting practices and candid views of their male counterparts remain relatively unchanged. (See Table 5.4.)

The general position of the directors on the boards that were studied was that the most sought-after directors are still experienced senior business executives, but there was a view that, as the number of boards on which active CEOs serve continues to decline, recruiting for directors must as a matter of necessity extend deeper within organizations and across the corporate sector to include people within professional service firms such as law, accounting and consulting and the academic and community sectors. The evidence, however, suggests that this broadening of the director pool has not yet occurred, or has not, as the quotes in Table 5.4 suggest, occurred at a rate with which some directors are comfortable.

Table 5.4

Some Directors' Views on Board Membership

"Directorship is an old man's game." (director)

"It's a WASP world, still. Look at the . . . Club." (director)

"Directors like to have more people like them, that went to the same university, club and have the same friends." (director)

"You do your due diligence but you take a directorship because a very senior member tells or asks you to do it. It's the old boy network." (director)

"There's a way WASPs respond to being recruited onto a board. They like the person making the request to drone on about how wonderful it would be to have them on the board and they never ask about money." (director)

"The worst thing is to bring someone on the board where they don't have the experience and can't make a contribution. So you need diversity and competence, diversity within context." (director)

"A board should have directors of different ages, sexes, experiences and backgrounds—diversity, as opposed to nest-feathering and interlocking directorships. Having a homogeneous board fosters an absence of imagination, like the earth is flat." (director)

"Directors should be part of the real world. . . . Being a director should not be a full-time job." (director)

Continued

"[Director X] and [Director Y] are bright guys, but what have they done? Have they had to meet payroll?" (director)

"Work at who the board members are. For your suppliers, investment banker or lawyer, if they are on your board, you will never be able to go to another law firm, investment banker or supplier. . . . Also your board should not be all active CEOs. . . . The skills of directors—financial, marketing, *etc.*—should reflect the company's situation and the industry." (chair)

"We have difficulty finding new directors for three reasons. First, the number of outside boards on which CEOs serve has decreased from 4.2 to 1.6. Now we're not looking at CEOs. Second, with globalization, you need [foreign directors]. But [it is] very difficult [to recruit] from Europe . . . and especially Asia, with the distance, culture and twice the travel time. Third, director liability [is making many people cautious] about joining boards. The responsibilities [in being a director] have gotten much greater." (director)

"Women are on the board because they wear dresses." (CEO)

"There are only twenty women in the country who are board-ready." (chair)

"Women, CFOs and senior partners. . . . They're useless. They don't know anything about the business." (director)

"Women are on the board, but if a guy was doing the job, and the job was fifth class, they wouldn't be on the board, but women are." (director)

"I must say she is very attractive, but perhaps my comment is better placed in the 1950s." (chair, during an all-male board meeting)

"Most boards favour current or past CEOs. Women are something like .5 percent CEOs. . . . Boards are looking for senior management experience and not that many women have senior management experience. It's a small number." (director)

"The pool of directors *is* big enough." (director recruiter)

"'Senior experienced CEO.' These criteria are male. They focus on line operating at senior levels, no corporate communications, law, accounting, consumer marketing. . . . You need to go lower in the ranks." (chair)

"I fit in because I knew everyone. Businesspeople don't like surprises. There are only 6 percent women [on boards] because they don't know the people. There is huge 'cronyism.'" (director)

"It's not getting any better for women on boards. The corporate culture is not changing. It's safe and uninteresting. . . . Men and women are different races." (director)

"They're not listening to me as a woman. What happens is that I make a point during one of my board meetings. Then, two or three comments later, a male director has the same point or idea. And you know what happens? He gets the credit!" (director)

"Comfort is not the problem. Discomfort is the problem. If I ask a question, management says 'where's the evidence?' We're treated as dimwits because we're women. It's a silencing factor—dub-like behaviour. We need to be even stronger. All the boards on which I sit have business-women and we're treated the same way. So, I think that, that is a risk. It's intimidating for people, brushed with the same discomfort, and that's a problem. You feel as though it's embarrassing if you ask a question. And so you ask fewer questions. So . . . its discomforting." (director)

"The CEO wants similar experiences. Women have to learn how to play that role. Sometimes I have said things too directly on boards. I have had to learn how to 'say' things. . . . I've always been the only female but I guess I grew up with men. They, men, that is, think and act differently. It takes men a while and they have to learn a language to add. It's bilingual-ism, 'male-female,' with enormous differences. The way you say something can be just as important as what you say because people cannot hear the message. It's the approach. You wouldn't wear shorts to a dinner party." (director)

"Women are very direct and open in their style. Old boys have a different style. As the number of women on boards grows, director style will change. This is a positive. It saves time." (director)

Many boards, apparently, have been able to find "independent directors" without markedly changing their recruiting efforts. A great deal of recuiting still appears to be done by many boards through the chair or chief executive officer canvassing incumbent directors about whom they know in the community or within the industry, who is well known and who can qualify as an "independent" director. Indeed, it appears that "reputation among peers" is used in many cases as a proxy for director independence, or at least how independent a particular nominee will be perceived to be by the regulators and the public. This has led, because of their high profile, to an increase in the appointment of ex-politicians to boards, with both favourable and unfavourable reactions from many board members.

In fact, the criteria of public reputation and acquaintanceship were, in several of the boards analyzed for this study, more important for obtaining board membership than independence and competence (see Table 5.4). Incumbent directors on the boards studied were, not unexpectedly, more comfortable in selecting candidate directors who were most similar to themselves, rather than strangers they did not know, regardless of how competent and appropriate the stranger might seem to be for board membership. As one shareholder pointed out to one of the authors when asked about a board, there really has been no change—the board is "a group, an elitist group that chooses their own, like . . . the Symphony."

The dominance of these two criteria in director selection—public reputation and acquaintanceship—means that candidates for board appointment apparently still largely come from the same social, political, economic and cultural background as they always have, that of incumbent directors. Therefore, it is not surprising that the boards of directors studied were composed largely of "older white males" with homogeneous backgrounds. There was, in general, little visible board diversity (*e.g.*, gender, race, age, profession, *etc.*). Nothing much has changed. Undoubtedly in certain cases, director preferences still lead in part to discriminatory practices within boardrooms, both in intent and in effect, most specifically with respect to women.

WHAT DOES IT ALL MEAN?

All the research, slim as it is, indicates that the structural characteristics of a board, *i.e.*, the number of outside directors, the number of independent directors, the separation of the position of chair and chief executive officer, the independence of directors, *et al.*, really make little or no difference in general board performance when performance is measured in terms of corporate financial performance. And there is no evidence to indicate that it matters, one way or another, in terms of the capacity of boards of directors to better perform their oversight duties.

In short, therefore, although the evidence is far from being conclusive, it appears that over the years the requirement that a majority of directors be independent, while nominally changing the structure of boards to more outside directors, has had little impact on the characteristic features of board members. In fact, there is some evidence—anecdotal, observational and otherwise—to suggest that it did not have much impact on creating actual independence within boards.

Moreover, since it is impossible to know what would have happened if the regulations had not been introduced, it is impossible to determine whether the regulations had any impact on increasing the degree of success of boards in monitoring corporate behaviour. It is known that some boards that followed the regulations religiously did not perform well for their shareholders. Nortel Networks is an outstanding example of a board that meticulously followed every guideline, but not once, not twice, but three times was involved in corporate financial reporting that did not meet appropriate standards. And there are many more such examples. It is not difficult to find a substantial number of companies who followed the guidelines, guidelines ostensibly designed to improve the monitoring of management, and still ran afoul of the regulations and laws.

Figure 5.1

Board Structure and Corporate Financial Performance

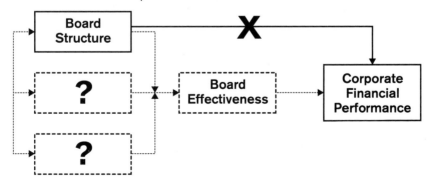

The same conclusion may be drawn with respect to the performance of firms where the positions of chair and chief executive officer were split. There is little hard empirical evidence that the change had any substantial impact on corporate financial performance.

And finally and most importantly, the evidence, again while still limited, clearly suggests that all the changes in regulations did nothing to increase shareholders' return on equity or increase the asset value of the corporation. No persuasive evidence can be found that having more outside directors, splitting the role of chair and CEO, or reducing the size of the board impacts directly on board performance when performance is measured in terms of corporate earnings. Although the evidence is far from clear, while regulating board structure may be a necessary condition for assuring that boards monitor the activities of the corporation effectively, it is probably a far less significant factor than board process in ensuring that boards operate effectively in the interests of their shareholders.

And yet we know little about board process. Indeed, it is it truly astonishing, given the enormous amount of work on corporate governance since the 1990s by a host of official commissions and advisory boards, as well as by academics and profit and not-for-profit research institutions, how little has actually been learned *about how boards actually function—what makes some more effective than others.* And yet learning "how boards work" could have tremendous practical significance for the governance of corporations. It could mean that chairs, nomination committees and directors, when putting together a board of directors or adding to an existing board, and regulators, when considering regulatory measures, would build better boards by concentrating on other things than structure.

THE EFFECTIVE BOARD: FUNCTION NOT FORM

At least as important are the human dynamics of boards as social systems where leadership character, individual values, decision making processes, conflict management, and strategic thinking will truly differentiate a firm's governance. Can fellow directors be trusted? Does management provide the full story? Is there enough time for advanced reading and full discussion of materials? Is dissent encouraged? Are people well prepared? Does management allow themselves to be vulnerable? How are board members kept accountable for their preparation and decisions? How is assessment conducted so board members can learn and improve?

—Jeffrey A. Sonnenfeld[1]
"Good Governance and the Misleading Myths of Bad Metrics"

Structure over substance: The committee noted that many boards did respond positively to the Report. There is concern, however, that the response of a number of corporations may have been more structural and more procedural than substantive. The Report contains guidelines which propose structures for governance systems which establish boards of directors independent of management . . . boards which implement the guidelines may achieve structural independence, but structuring boards in this way is only part of the answer. Boards must also function independently.

—"The State of Governance in Canada"
The TSX and Institute for Corporate Directors, 2001[2]

---

1. Sonnenfeld, Jeffrey A. "Good Governance and the Misleading Myths of Bad Metrics" *Academy of Management Executive* 18:1 (2004): 112.
2. The original 1994 Toronto Stock Exchange Committee on Corporate Governance in Canada reconvened in 2000, and on July 10, 2000, made this observation in a news release entitled "The State of Corporate Governance in Canada," under the subject heading "Structure Over Substance," on page 1.

The key to better corporate governance lies in the working relationships between boards and managers, in the social dynamics of board interaction, and in the competence, integrity and constructive involvement of individual directors.

—David A. Nadler
"Building Better Boards," *Harvard Business Review*[3]

Few public corporations are incorporated for the simple sake of establishing a company. They are created in the expectation that they will, within the bounds of law and acceptable social behaviour, earn money for their shareholders, either through paying a satisfactory rate of return on the shareholders' invested capital or increasing the asset value of the investment. And while it is true that boards of directors play a significant "oversight role" for the shareholders, few would disagree that the most important task of the board of directors is to assure that the corporation is operated so that "shareholder" value is, at the very least maintained, and generally increased. In short, an effective board *by definition* is one that preserves and increases shareholder value. If it does not, eventually it will be removed, and in the worst-case scenario the corporation will fail and the shareholders' assets will be wiped out.

The essential difference between an "effective board" and a "structured board" is that the "effective board" is evaluated in terms of how well it fulfills its goal of earning a strong rate of return for the shareholders. The "structured board" is measured not on its performance but on its form. Since the purpose of the corporation is to make money for its owners, in a manner consistent with the responsibilities owed to its other stakeholder groups, a necessary condition for effective corporate governance is that an "effective board of directors," not simply one based on structure, is in charge of the enterprise.[4] Consequently, the question that should be asked by shareholders, directors, regulators, chairs—anyone who is interested in modern corporate governance, is "What conditions are necessary to enable a board of directors to function in such a fashion that the corporation

3. Nadler, David A."Business Better Boards," *Harvard Business Review* 82:5 (2004): 102.
4. It is important to remember the hypothesis that how "effective boards," as defined in this book, are related positively to corporate performance is yet to be tested.

earns a satisfactory rate of return for its shareholders?" Or, in other words, "What are the characteristic features of an effective board?"

Most boards succeed, albeit to wildly varying degrees, in fulfilling the fiduciary, oversight, strategic and governance tasks for which they are responsible. But many do not. Unfortunately, there are few, if any, studies, and no models based on the actual observation of boards' internal activities that explain why this should be so—why some boards are very successful, some are moderately so and why some fail. In other words, there are no models that enable anyone to predict the prospects for a corporation on the basis of the manner in which its board operates.[5]

It should, however, be possible to create such a model—a model of board effectiveness—based on the conditions necessary to ensure better governance, when better governance is judged by the financial results of the enterprise. In short, a workable model of board effectiveness should help explain the relationship between corporate governance and corporate performance. If such a model existed, life would be much simpler for regulators, board chairs and directors. They would be able to tell whether or not a particular board was constituted and managed in a way to assure the successful fulfillment of its duties by simply comparing it to the model. Ideally, a board that had all the significant characteristic features of the model would function well; a board that did not, would not.

That said, the fate of a corporation is determined by many factors other than by the way it is governed. Exogenous forces outside of a company's control, such as a war, natural disasters, fraud, depressions, technological innovations, the sudden death of an outstanding executive, *etc.*, can lead to the demise of the best governed organization. Moreover, no model can guarantee that a board will always have sufficient information on which to make sound decisions, or indeed, that it will in fact never be wrong in its decision-making.[6] However, for the most part, corporations fail, or do not achieve their full potential because they are managed poorly, and they are usually managed

---

5. The purpose of building a model is to assist in the development of theory, and theory in turn permits the prediction of results.
6. Directors are protected by the "business judgment rule" from being sued for their mistakes, as long as they exercised proper business judgment when they undertook the action that turned out to be mistaken. See Chapter 1.

poorly because they are governed poorly. There is an old maxim that corporations do not fail, but boards do. Having knowledge of how boards function—how boards make decisions rather than how boards are structured—may well be the key to understanding the relationship between corporate governance and corporate performance.

SEARCHING FOR THE "BOARD EFFECTIVENESS MODEL"

The concept of the effective board is based on the proposition that a large part of corporate governance is about small group decision-making. The manner in which boards organize to, and actually do, make decisions may be described as "board process." It is a particularly fitting name since it captures precisely the central part of a board's activity—decision-making.

Traditionally, it has been believed that the capacity of a board to fulfill its obligations through making sound decisions has been based on one primary factor—the board's structure, which includes the board's composition.[7] Understanding board structure presumably has been a sufficient basis for making the recommendations and regulations necessary to ensure effective corporate governance. However, while board structure is a significant factor to consider in the establishment of an effective board, board structure, in and of itself, does not appear to be sufficient to ensure effective board performance, because structure does not take into consideration the competencies of individual directors (*Board Membership* in Figure 6.1) and the manner in which boards make decisions—possibly the most important thing that boards do (*Board Process* in Figure 6.1). Consequently, to have a full understanding of boards, a second and third element must be added—board membership and board process. The effectiveness of a board in meeting its obligations

---

7. "Board structure" traditionally refers to three items: (i) board leadership, *e.g.*, a non-executive chair *vs.* having the same person occupy the posts of chair and CEO (sometimes referred to as "CEO duality"); (ii) board composition, *e.g.*, the number and percentage of outside (or independent) directors versus inside directors; and (iii) board size. "Board composition refers to the distinction between inside and outside directors and is traditionally operationalized as the percentage of outside directors (*i.e.*, those not in the direct employ of the organization) on the board." in C. M. Daily and D. R. Dalton, "Board of Directors Leadership and Structure: Control and Performance Implications," *Entrepreneurship Theory and Practice* (Spring 1993): 69. Conversely, board "membership" as distinct from board "composition," as part of the board effectiveness model in this book, includes the competencies specific to an individual director him- or herself. See, for example, the Competency Matrix Analyses in Chapter 10.

depends, therefore, on three factors not one—1) board structure, 2) board membership and 3) board process.

Common sense alone, if nothing else, tells us that such things as:

1. the leadership qualities of the chair of the board,

2. the nature of the relationship between the board and management,

3. the operation of the board and its decision-making process,

4. the "human factors" in board decision-making, and

5. the "fit" among individual directors and how they relate to one another as a decision-making team

must be extremely important factors in determining how boards act. It is reasonable to assume, and the research suggests (see Chapter 7), that the behaviour of directors and the mix of *behavioural characteristics of directors have a major impact on the way in which directors make decisions and, by extension, on the effectiveness of the governance of the corporation.*

Figure 6.1
A Model of Board Effectiveness

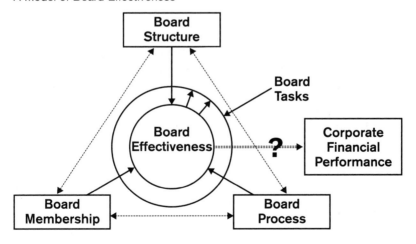

BOARD PROCESS

Boards of directors, like most groups, are made up of a diverse collection of individuals, many of whom have different behavioural patterns. Some directors, hopefully most, come to a board meeting fully aware of, and briefed about, the major decisions that the board must make, prepared to argue specific points with wit and wisdom. On the other hand, some directors do not speak at meetings or participate in the decision-making processes because they fear they will reveal a lack of knowledge about a topic and embarrass themselves in front of their peers. Others remain silent on an issue because they feel another director has already given an articulate expression of their point of view or they don't want to question the ideas and concepts of a perceived expert or challenge a major shareholder. And some simply do not participate because of lack of interest. And there are directors who act in exactly the opposite fashion—they speak without much knowledge, never worry about embarrassing themselves and are oblivious to the opinions of experts.

And what is true of directors individually is reflected in the actions of boards. Sometimes board decisions are the result of "group think" among directors.[8] Other times they are made because of a perceived need for consensus on an issue, the unwillingness of directors to seek out opinions contrary to those advanced by management, the fact that much time and money has gone into a particular course of action already (the sunk cost phenomena),[9] concern about public perception, or sheer desperation about what to do. In short, boards can be very ineffective, or conversely very effective, in their decision-making for any number of reasons.

In the course of their activities, boards make thousands of decisions. Some are routine and non-controversial, whereas others have major effects on the success and even the potential failure of a firm. Occasionally, major decisions are required as a result of forces over

---

8. "Groupthink" has been defined as occurring when "concurrence seeking of a cohesive group overrides a realistic appraisal of alternative courses of action." See I. L. Janis, "Groupthink," *Psychology Today* (November 1971). According to Janis, the eight symptoms of groupthink are invulnerability, rationality, morality, stereotypes, pressure, self-censorship, unanimity and mind guards.

9. The "sunk-cost phenomenon" is also termed as an escalating commitment to a losing course of action, or in the vernacular as "throwing good money after bad."

which the board has no direct control, but most decisions are made within the relatively stable conditions within which a business operates.

While decisions are influenced by the quantity and quality of information that boards have to work with, observations of twenty-one boards and committees at work in real time, experience on thirty-plus boards and interviews with nearly two hundred active directors suggests, as one would expect, that one of the most important factors in determining board performance, *i.e.*, in determining how decisions are made, is the manner in which directors interact with each other, or how they "fit" together and balance one another's personality, competency and behavioural type.[10]

An effective board of directors, like a cabinet in government, decides and speaks as a unit, collectively. And yet, individual directors often have strong differences of opinion about the correct course of action an organization should follow. It is reasonable to believe that to arrive at decisions all members can support, a board of directors should have a mix of directors with different behavioural characteristics involved in its decision-making process. Without such a mix, it is difficult, if not impossible, to have the full discussion of all the issues involved in making a decision on a complex matter. Just as the great economist Joseph Schumpeter argued that there must be "creative destruction" in the economy to make the capitalist system work, there must be "creative tension" in the boardroom to make boards work.

If directors are all the same, *i.e.*, they always support every proposal that management brings forward, it is unlikely that the debate will be vigorous. Conversely, if they are all constantly opposing the management, it is highly unlikely that effective decisions will be reached. Some routine decisions are made with minimal if any disagreement, and some only after vigorous, often lacerating, debate.

In a well-known case involving the sale of a company, one director was bitterly opposed to the terms and conditions of the sale recommended by management. Although all but one other member of the board accepted management's position, the dissenting director

10. For a summary of the methodology used to collect data while attending board meetings, see Appendix B.

fought the deal so vigorously within the boardroom that the terms of the deal were altered. While the sale did go through, one of the consequences of that director's action was that the shareholders of the selling company received a substantially higher price for their shares than the amount originally offered by the buyer.

The interesting point is that while the dissenting director originally received little or no support for his position—none of the other directors were prepared to vote against management's recommendation for selling the company when it was first brought to the board—it was because of a dissenting director's efforts that the shareholders received a substantially higher price for their shares. If all the members of the selling company's board had had the same or similar behavioural characteristics, the board would not have maximized shareholder value. There must be a balance among the decision-makers, *i.e.*, the directors, to assure that the board always thoroughly discusses all of the issues involved in deciding precisely what to do about the questions before it.

Table 6.1

Some Directors' Views of an Effective Board

"One of the most important roles is to set the tone and values held by the management team, who express to the organization what the board wants, the value systems and objectives. The way the board wants to respond to expectations and constituencies, especially with a new CEO. It's not just EPS [earnings per share]. The CEO has to have real values. The board should have clear expectations of the corporate management team regarding integrity, standards and the way the board wants the company run." (director)

"It's a balanced scorecard approach. Stakeholders are not independent interests. Managing one's stakeholders effectively contributes to creating shareholder value." (chair and CEO)

"Shareholders are still first, but watch for consumers, creditors, communities, governments. . . . Be careful about employees, but shareholders are first." (director)

> "'Board effectiveness?' We're trying to develop strict criteria. There's a lot out there. We look for common characteristics. Boards are getting smaller. Is the board involved in strategic planning? Does the board have effective committees? This is important. Do board members invest in the company? Is there an alignment of interests, in the broader marketplace beyond shareholders? Is there a separate chairman? But we're not too strong on this one. . . . Board process is difficult to do from the outside. Board process needs to generate value. It's difficult to get at it consistently so we use indirect processes." (shareholder-director)

Indeed, a board cannot work, that is, reach good decisions, unless there are directors who, through credibility, leadership and interpersonal and communication skills, are on occasion able to persuade other directors and management of their point of view or of a particular course of action. At the same time, a board cannot work unless there are directors who can find common themes within dissenting views and bring about a consensus.[11]

In short, the elusive notion of "group chemistry" is a significant factor in determining the effectiveness of the governance of an enterprise. And this is not astonishing. It is well-known that "winning teams" need to have "the right chemistry" where the directors and management support and respect each other. Unfortunately, while everyone knows that the right chemistry is essential for success, it is difficult to define, let alone create. As a great expert[12] from a field far removed from corporate governance has pointed out:

Chemistry is a funny thing. You fiddle with it at your peril. I can remember so well the way Glen Sather[13] dealt with it back in the 80s. He would bring 50 or 55 guys to the Oilers' camp and he'd make a speech. It would never be one of those GM speeches where they say 'Every job here is open.' Not Glen. He'd say, 'I'm not going to lie to you. There might be two jobs available here. Perhaps, only one. And everyone here brings something different to camp. I don't know at all which one of you it's going to

11. For a full discussion of the various categories for director classification, see Chapters 8 and 9.
12. Wayne Gretzky was, for many years, a superstar in the National Hockey League.
13. Glen Sather was general manager of the Edmonton Oilers, a very successful team in the National Hockey League.

be, but whoever it is it will be someone who fits in with the chemistry. I'm looking for a player to round out the equation.' That, in a nutshell, is about as good a description of chemistry as I know. It's something the New York Yankees have figured out and the Baltimore Orioles can't. Both spend about the same; only one is World Champion.[14]

Can this team chemistry analogy be extended to the boardroom? A good number of experienced directors and observers of the corporate scene seem to think so. One perceptive observer writes:

> It's difficult to tease out the factors that make one group of people an effective team and another, equally talented group of people a dysfunctional one; well-functioning, successful teams usually have a chemistry that can't be quantified. They seem to get into a virtuous cycle in which one good quality builds on another. Team members develop mutual respect; because they respect one another they develop trust; because they trust one another, they share difficult information; because they all have the same, reasonably complete information, they can challenge one another's conclusions coherently; because a spirited give-and-take becomes the norm, they learn to adjust their own interpretations in response to intelligent questions.[15]

Several of the directors interviewed for this study reported that creating the right chemistry was the most important factor in achieving board effectiveness.

Difficult as it is to create the chemistry, it appears that there are certain fundamental conditions that must be present in order for it to be achieved: mutual respect among directors and executives, openness in the exchange of information, trust, and robust and fulsome debate on issues. And it may also be that a mix of directors with various behavioural characteristics is a necessary condition for achieving the board chemistry that leads to effective decision-making.

14. Wayne Gretzky, "Don't Bet the Bank on Rich Rosters," *National Post* (April 1, 2000): A17.
15. Sonnenfeld, "What Makes Great Boards Great," 109.

Table 6.2

Some Directors' Views of the Importance of Board Process

"It's like building a hockey team, with different positions. So what's the optimum mix of people and skills?" (director)

"A board is chemistry, people. Corporate governance is organizational behaviour and creating an effective team." (director)

"With the wrong people it won't work. It's quality, competence and chemistry, relations that lead to the right decisions." (director)

"Boards are very unique. As individuals, they're powerless. As a group, they have enormous potential. . . . " (professional adviser)

"Groupthink is one of the greatest problems boards face." (director)

BOARD STRUCTURE AND BOARD MEMBERSHIP

The effective board, like the traditional structural board, must have as its foundation members who are independent, be of a workable size and have strong leadership (see Chapter 4). But it must have two additional features. It must be made up of members with the required competencies to assist in the solution of the specific problems facing the corporation and who can work together to make effective decisions. Without such a balance it is difficult, if not impossible, to have the interaction between and among fellow board members and management—to have the board process—that is essential for overall effective decision-making.

Unlike in a traditional board, the conditions for an effective board in terms of structure and membership—are *not* satisfied—by having directors who are independent, having a majority of outside directors and separating the position of chair and CEO. An effective board must not only be of a workable size, and under certain conditions have separation of the positions of chair and CEO, but also must have a set of directors who collectively have all the competencies required by the board to fulfill its duties; have the mix of behavioural characteristics that will lead to effective decision-making; and meet all the regulatory requirements of the jurisdiction within which the corporation is incorporated. This requires a well-developed process for not only selecting and appointing quality directors but an equally good process for removing them when they no longer meet the needs of the board.

COMPLIANCE AND THE "INDEPENDENCE PARADOX"

The last requirement, being certain that all the regulatory requirements are met, will normally require that some proportion of the board will meet some type of independence test. Interestingly, assuring that certain of the board members are independent is not as easy as it might at first appear to be. Obviously, conflicts arising from personal and family relationships, prior employment, being a member of a professional service provider or customer of the corporation, *etc.*, are easy to recognize and deal with. On the other hand, factors such as desire for continued membership on a board, availability of non-publicized consulting fees and/or stock options, and the pleasure that the enhanced profile of being a member of a particular board may bring are very difficult to detect. True independence is difficult to define, measure and regulate because much of what compromises independence can only be detected from direct observation and through questioning of board members who have served with the particular director.

In fact, observations in real time of some directors at board meetings did not always support the public perception or regulator's designation of a director's independence. In other words, while a director may be viewed and classified as independent, he or she may not necessarily behave independently within the boardroom.[16]

In the course of this study, there were observations of inside or related directors challenging the CEO, speaking their mind and voting independently despite being identified as having a conflict. There were also several occasions of supposedly independent (formally at least) directors saying very little, never challenging or providing opposing arguments to those presented by the CEO, or showing even a minimum of independence from management.

---

16. For additional discussion of the issues associated with independence, see Chapter 5.

Purely independent directors may not necessarily make the best or even better directors, primarily because they are so far removed from the corporation's industry or business that they really do not bring any new, informed and relevant perspective to the boardroom. They have been described as being "lily-whites."

COMPETENT DIRECTORS, STRATEGY AND SHAREHOLDER VALUE

If they are to make a significant contribution, directors on an effective board must have some understanding of the role and duties of the board in the corporation's governance, some specific competency with respect to understanding and contributing to the monitoring functions of the board, and specific competencies relating to the strategies that the company is following.

Generally speaking, effective directors know something about being a director. They have, or quickly attain, a basic knowledge of the principles of corporate governance and corporate law—the duty of care and the duty of loyalty, of the fiduciary duties of directors, *etc.* They are also aware of the monitoring responsibility of the board, both in terms of the specific tasks of attesting to the reliability of the financial statements and the need to assess the activities of the senior executive officers, and they may have some specific competencies to assist in these activities. For example, while all effective directors have a basic amount of financial literacy, given the significance of monitoring the corporation's financial activities, a chartered accountant may be selected for membership on the board. Directors are protected from making egregious errors in business judgment but not from mistakes in the reporting of the financial condition of the enterprise.

While competencies in general aspects of corporate governance and monitoring capabilities may be necessary conditions for being an effective director, they are not sufficient. In addition, the effective director must have specific competencies that contribute to, or compensate for the lack of, those competencies that a board must have to fulfill its strategic goals.

That this type of competency should be emphasized in seeking directors for "effective boards" is not surprising. Companies are organized for the purposes of producing and selling goods and services at a profit. In complex competitive markets, they are constantly developing strategies, ranging from the very complex in the large international companies to relatively simple in smaller organizations, and everywhere in between. In fulfilling their duties, a board of directors should be involved at a minimum in approving, and at the most in the developing of, the enterprise's strategies. Indeed, it is the formulation and implementation of effective strategies that leads to not only the unlocking of shareholder value but ultimately the success or failure of the firm.

The monitoring function of the board, exceedingly important as it is, is after all subject to endless regulations and laws. No such rules or regulations set any prescriptive parameters with respect to the "strategy function." The fulfillment of the monitoring function is basically a compliance problem, whereas the strategy role is a creative one. It may well be that working with the executives of the firm in the development of strategy is the most important task of members of the board. Choosing directors who have no interest in strategy is a mistake that must not be made when creating the effective board. It is an area from which the directors should never be excluded.[17]

THE EFFECTIVE BOARD: 1) STRUCTURE, 2) MEMBERSHIP AND 3) PROCESS

In short, in an effective board the directors work as a group decision-making team and directors must be selected who can make the most effective contribution to the work of the group.

Finding, retaining and maintaining the mix of directors with the necessary competencies and appropriate behavioural characteristics for an effective board is not easy. The capacity to do so depends on four factors:

1. having a complete inventory of the competencies and behavioural characteristics needed by the board to fulfill its functions;

---

17. See Chapter 10 for a full discussion of the relationship between strategy and competence.

2. having a complete inventory of the competencies and behavioural characteristics of existing board members;

3. having a well-developed process for recruiting directors to the board;

4. having an equally well-developed process for removing directors when they no longer meet the needs of the board.

In order for board membership to include a recruitment and tenure policy based on competence, as opposed to attrition, three actions are required: 1) an assessment of the qualities and performance standards of the board and of existing individual directors (the latter of which is estimated by directors interviewed for this study to happen effectively in only 5 percent of all boards); 2) the rigorous association of such data with continued tenure by directors; and 3) strong board leadership. Many of the boards observed for this study did not meet these three requirements.

Those that did were the ones with engaged nominating committees with strong chairs who reported to the full board and who were moving to having their nomination procedures "competency-based," as opposed to "representation-based." They treated the director nomination process very seriously, using director search firms, developing watch lists (which included a list of potential candidates for nomination to the board), conducting extensive interviews and reference checks. They developed "pre-candidate packages" for use by prospective directors, which included information on directors' and officers' insurance, liability matters, expected time requirements, extensive information about the company and the industry and any other information that a prospective director might require. Such an approach is a far cry from the traditional historical process of inviting a golfing companion of most of the directors to join the club.

Table 6.3

Some Directors' Views on Recruitment, Retirement and Balanced Competencies

"Board members feel as though they're entitled rather than that they've earned their directorship. And it ends due to age, which is to admit defeat. It's representative rather than competency-based. I've been at [Company ABC over two decades] and we haven't had the right people in the past five years. How do you change the culture, to be able to still recruit the kind of directors one wants and terminate the service of those you don't when it's what the corporation needs, rather than the individual? It's natural to have human expectations, but we need to raise the bar higher. We need to change the culture so that board service makes it unacceptable for any corporation to default when it comes to competencies." (director)

"The board should reflect the demands of the company at a point in time and be dynamic and flexible over time. Boards can get old and people can get stale. You need tenure limits, or link tenure to performance appraisals . . . or have an understanding of what it takes to stay on the board." (director)

"How many boards have an annual process and renewal based on not attendance but the relative contribution, currency, relevance and alignment of competencies with strategy?" (director)

"I'm convinced boards do succession planning by policy. The next step is to link effectiveness with tenure. We should rate and rank the people and set a threshold, for example, one bad director. Have green, yellow and red on competency dimensions. Two directors are red and that's unacceptable, and this is where the rubber hits the road. Does the lead director have the courage to invite the director to resign or not reappoint? People are not stepping up to this hard dialogue, generally. . . . Time is a-wasting." (professional adviser)

"I don't see the need for tenure. Both age 70 and tenure are mechanisms to deal with the issue of non-performers. Otherwise, why participate and have an age of 70? Really as a board it's a real loss [in losing effective directors because of a fixed retirement age] and others we couldn't wait and should strike them at age 66. Tenure is designed to avoid dealing with performance." (director)

"Is the lead director or chairman prepared to say to the individual, 'We want you to step down.'? I'm not sure boards really tackle this. [The CEO] says to me, 'Why's it so hard? I do it every day with executives. But I won't fight this battle.'" (lead director)

"The fuzzy _____ about lowering the retirement age, tenure—it all comes down, as non-executive chairman … you tap old Charlie, the non-performer, on the shoulder after you've talked to others, and say he has no time if he's young, or tell him 'don't stand for re-election.' So fire me if I'm not doing my job. Don't use tenure or retirement. They're excuses for non-performers. I've tapped Charlie on the shoulder. So it's a non-executive chairman, as board leader, who needs awareness, who has to start being explicit. That's where the power lies, not lead director. It's good, better, best." (chair)

"Very few chairs get rid of ineffective directors." (director)

"I can't remember one board, out of the twenty or so, that didn't have that problem and had to live with it. . . . I have had to fire three directors for cause—in two cases they objected. It's a common problem among all boards. If they say they don't have it, they're lying. . . . Europe, America, Asia . . . I'll believe it when I see it. You're reluctant to take on the unpleasant[ness] of getting rid of the nice man or lady, so you find ways to avoid. . . . The ones you want to get rid of—they wiggle and make it awkward." (director)

"In general, everybody on the board knows who is not performing. Over the years we spend a lot of time together. What you need is some leadership that is prepared to make hard calls. . . . " (director)

Boards following best practices had either formal or informal policies governing board tenure that included a combination of mandatory retirement age (common), tenure limits, change-in-principal-occupation rules, preferences regarding geographical location, and implicit or explicit limits on the number of boards on which the chief executive officer could serve. The rationale for these rules was simply to prevent inconsistent or arbitrary treatment of individual directors.

A disadvantage of specialized replacement policies is that they often result in unintended consequences. An effective director who falls afoul of a policy (*e.g.*, reaching age seventy, at which time retirement is compulsory) has to leave the board, whereas a non-performing director who falls within the scope of a policy can stay. For example, many of the boards included in this study had non-performing directors who were allowed to stay, simply because it was not worth the effort and embarrassment of removing them, when, by rule, in a year or two (or more), they would have to retire. In the strong boards, that was not the case. When a director no longer met the needs of the board, arrangements were made for his or her replacement.

The selection process should not be driven by independence or the need for unrelated directors, although the conditions relating to these items in the corporation's operating jurisdiction must be met. Rather, on effective boards, it is driven by the competency and behavioural characteristics that are needed to assure that the board is organized in such a fashion that it is capable of making sound decisions that lead to a higher level of corporate performance. Choices are made to assure that possibly the most important function in corporate governance—board process—operates well.

WHAT DOES ALL THIS MEAN?

The model of an effective board has been constructed from an examination of how boards work—the forces that impact on its decision-making processes—and not on how boards are structured. While it is impossible at this stage of knowledge about corporate governance to draw a definitive conclusion, it does appear that board process may be more important than board structure in determining board effectiveness. If this turns out to be the case, as some evidence suggests, it may well be possible to determine a relationship between board effectiveness and corporate financial performance.

In short, a board of directors constructed according to the model of board effectiveness should more likely than not be successful at accomplishing the tasks assigned to it, and therefore should be able to achieve appropriate corporate financial returns for its shareholders. We do not know if this is true, but it is reasonable to assume that it may be.[18]

While the model of an effective board may seem somewhat complicated, in reality it is not. It is based on the fact that in the final analysis, it is the decisions of the board of directors that largely determine corporate performance, and that while the manner in which boards make decisions depends upon many factors, in the end it is the specific competencies and behavioural characteristics of the directors and how they interact with each other that is the ultimate determinant of effective decision-making. This conclusion is only useful if it is possible to classify directors by their behavioural characteristics. It is this critical question that is examined in the following chapters.

---

18. By coincidence, there is one report on corporate governance and corporate performance ("magazine study") that contains a number of the same boards of directors that were examined for this study. The study cannot be identified due to confidentiality concerns in this study. Of the boards in common to both studies, those that were ranked highly in the magazine study most closely approximated the model of board effectiveness of this study (see Chapter 6). Those boards that were not ranked highly least approximated the model of board effectiveness from this study.

In comparing the make-up of the effective boards to the non-effective boards, those boards that were highly-ranked appeared to have on them a balance of directors who most closely resembled directors classified as Change Agents, Consensus-Builders, Counsellors, Challengers and Conductors—a possible indication that the mix of behavioural characteristics of directors has an impact on board performance. (These director behaviour types will be descibed fully in Chapter 8 and 9.) Similarly, directors who most closely resembled Controllers, Conformists, Cheerleaders, Critics and Caretakers were members of those boards that the magazine study ranked at a lower level of effective governance. In other words, the effective boards and non-effective boards, as defined by the magazine study, appeared to closely approximate the ideal effective and ineffective boards and director behaviour types as defined by this study. This very limited analysis is, of course, far from conclusive, but it is a positive indication suggesting that creating boards along the lines recommended in this book may indeed lead to superior corporate governance and corporate financial returns.

CHAPTER 7

EFFECTIVE DIRECTORS FOR EFFECTIVE BOARDS: PUTTING THEM TOGETHER

For board dynamics, how do you create a team when there are only four to six meetings a year? How do you develop rapport?

—Director

Boards are a social science. You need to be an anthropologist. For example, you have twelve strong people but collectively the board fails because of poor interaction between and among them all—group dynamics.

—Director

[T]he board needs to work as a team. It's a group of individuals working together and being compatible.... It's easy to talk about having a good board but difficult to make happen.

—Director

Almost all writing about boards of directors is totally impersonal. Unless a scandal of considerable proportion is involved, most stories about corporate activities report that the "board of directors" decided to do something or other. Boards are treated as an anonymous group of invisible, powerful people who are almost impervious to outside pressures or interference. Seldom in a news story are members of a board of directors identified by name. Indeed, few shareholders know the names of the directors of the companies they own.

And what is true for the press and the public is also true for much of the analytical writing about boards. In even the most serious discussions of corporate governance, boards are treated as more or less homogeneous groups of people who may be further identified as either "independent" or "executive" board members. Except in the annual reports of companies, which have limited public circulation, or the announcement of the appointment of an individual to a board, one seldom sees much about individuals in the context of any discussion of the board.

While this general anonymity of directors is understandable, given the generally low level of interest in directors in comparison with politicians, entertainers and professional athletes, it is also unfortunate because it unconsciously, if not consciously, implies that the competencies and behavioural characteristics of individuals who are members of the board of a company are not very important. And yet these two features of a person, excepting the basic ones of honesty and fairness, may well be the most important factors in determining the overall effectiveness of a board of directors.

Boards of directors are *small decision-making groups,* who, in the final analysis, collectively determine, through the decisions that they make, the fate of a corporation. A board is not some amorphous entity that functions independently of its members. It is a group of people who have individual prejudices and views, behavioural patterns and cultural backgrounds. Whether a board works well and makes good decisions, or is dysfunctional and makes poor ones, depends largely on the manner in which board members work together. This in turn depends, to a considerable degree, upon the combination of behavioural characteristics of the various directors on the board. Finding that combination is the key to the unknown element in board effectiveness—board process—or to give it a generic term—board processes.[1] As in most things, in the last analysis, the fate of a corporation depends on people.

1. This is unknown but not unsuspected. For years, observers of corporate governance have made the point that the decision-making of the board of directors is what drives the corporation. At the same time, it has been generally conceded that it would be impossible to find out much about the process given the great difficulties in learning how boards make decisions.

EFFECTIVE DIRECTORS AND EFFECTIVE BOARDS

As outlined in the previous chapter, an effective board depends upon the existence of appropriate board structure, board membership and board process. The characteristic features of the first of these three factors are well known. The second—board membership, including the role of competency in the selection of directors—was canvassed in the preceding chapter and is thoroughly explored in Chapter 10. It is the third—board process—that has been previously overlooked and needs to be investigated. It may well be the most important one of all for it refers to the way in which boards make decisions, clearly one of the most significant parts of board operations.

Since decisions are made by people, it is the people on the board—the directors and their behavioural characteristics, plus the manner in which they interact among themselves—who determine the decision-making process. Obviously, therefore, board effectiveness is deeply linked to the behavioural characteristics of the directors. The interaction between individual board members and board effectiveness is shown in Figure 7.1.

Figure 7.1
The Interrelationship Between Board and Director Effectiveness

Board effectiveness (BE) depends on board structure (BS) + board membership (BM) + board process (BP).

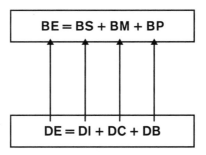

BE = BS + BM + BP

DE = DI + DC + DB

Director effectiveness (DE) depends on director independence (DI) + director competence (DC) + director behaviour (DB).

DIRECTOR EFFECTIVENESS

Three factors determine whether a person will be an effective director on an effective board—1) his or her independence of mind, 2) his or her competencies and 3) his or her behavioural characteristics. As indicated in Figure 7.1, each factor is related to some part of the model for board effectiveness—director independence is related to board structure; director competence to board membership; and director behaviour to board process.

A good deal is known about the necessary qualities required of board members with respect to the question of independence.[2] Less is known about the competencies that directors must have to be effective on a board. And almost nothing is known about the behavioural characteristics of directors. This omission is critical inasmuch as it is the combination of directors with different behavioural characteristics that creates the "board chemistry" that assures effective board processes. And it is the success or failure of board processes that is a major factor in determining the board's effectiveness.

In order to create an effective board, therefore, in addition to knowing the independence and competencies of individual directors, it is essential to know their behavioural characteristics so that the chemistry, which is so essential for effective decision-making, may develop.[3] Whether the board makes good decisions or bad, as measured by the corporation's financial performance, may well depend on how individual directors work together to determine how the company, in the broadest terms, is managed in the interests of the shareholders.

BEHAVIOURAL CHARACTERISTICS AND THE EFFECTIVE DIRECTOR

Anyone who has ever been a member of any group charged with making decisions knows that there are many differences in the way in which members act—some are aggressive, others passive; some are always prepared for a meeting, others never; some are anxious to find solutions to problems, others will use any pretense to delay

2. See Chapters 4 and 5.
3. The "chemistry" of the board drives the decision-making process and chemistry is all about people. See Chapter 6.

a decision. After several meetings, the perceptive observer can usually predict the manner in which a person will respond to a particular type of question or situation.

Boards of directors are no different than any other small groups, but because they meet in private, all that is known about the manner in which they make decisions is based on the revelations and reminiscences of individual board members who may have served on a dozen or so boards[4] and the war-stories that come out after titanic board struggles, successes or failures. Historically, there have never been sufficient data available to answer the question "Are there behavioural features of directors at board meetings that can be identified and classified that impact on their decision-making capacity?"

Table 7.1

Some Directors' Views on the Behaviour of Their Peers

"It's incumbent on you to fit in. I have built relations with co-directors. The first year should be learning the dynamics of the board and it's incumbent to make some kind of contribution because when the tough circumstances arise, you'll just be a listener." (director)

"Young members need to be counselled on how to raise issues but are afraid to raise them at the meeting. You have a tendency to act alike, depending on the board, like trained seals. It takes courage, but you can do it without being offensive. It could be media training, asking questions without getting personal." (director)

"Orientation tells you about the company, not how you should behave." (director)

"How do you not be abrasive, [but still be] independent and helpful?" (director)

"You have to pursue and have probing questions without being disruptive. . . . How to be elegant but responsible. . . . " (director)

Continued

4. In recent years, a number of directors have written books about their board experiences that provide valuable insights into board activities. Since they were written by participants in the boards' activities themselves and are not based on across-the-board observation and analysis, while valuable, they differ markedly from a study conducted by an independent researcher.

> "Directors need to disagree without being disagreeable." (director)
>
> "We need to look at behavioural aspects of competencies—whether people behave in a certain way." (professional adviser)
>
> "Hours have been spent on how to fit . . . the soft [skills] must be in." (director)
>
> "We should incorporate behaviour into the performance discussion." (director)
>
> "One issue is consistency of directors. A lower-quality director can ask the wrong question and gum up the works. You can add up the mistakes, in other words. Their motivation is good. This is true for inexperienced directors, such as those who are young, or those that don't completely understand their governance roles, such as catching up off-line. The lowest common denominator is about eight to ten years on the board, before which things can get bogged down. Take the stock option plan, for instance. This has to do with director maturity, or 'emotional intelligence.' It's the committee chairman's responsibility to use different degrees of tact." (manager, director)

Between 1998 and 2003[5], a systematic study—based on carefully developed research criteria and protocols—was undertaken by Dr. Leblanc to collect the data to answer this critical question—perhaps the most critical of all for a true understanding of corporate governance. The premise of the study was that it would be possible to attain access to board and committee meetings to observe directors in action in real time; that an effective research protocol could be developed that would enable the data gathered from observing board meetings to be analyzed and classified in a useful fashion; and that conclusions could be drawn about behaviour of directors from 1) observations of their actions in the boardroom and 2) carefully conducted interviews that would permit the development of useful hypotheses about the way in which the behaviour characteristics of individual directors influence the decision-making capabilities of boards.

5. Since the formal study was completed, information has been collected from additional private sector boards.

It is well known that psychologists and psychiatrists, although they are not certain that they have a complete explanation of why a person acts in a particular fashion, do know quite a lot about human behaviour. They know that individuals tend to behave in certain ways; *i.e.*, through time individuals show, for one reason or another, certain patterns of behaviour,[6] and indeed they know that the behaviour of an individual to a considerable degree can be predicted, *i.e.*, under the same or similar circumstances, an individual is likely to behave in a similar fashion. Taken together, a person's behavioural characteristics reflect what is generally classified as an individual's personality, that is, a person who is shy and withdrawn may typically be classified as an introvert while someone who is outgoing in their behaviour may be considered as an extrovert.[7]

Obviously in this study of directors in action, no attempt was made to conduct controlled psychological experiments to determine specifically how a corporate director acted in response to a set of stimuli or how the actions of two directors differed in the face of similar circumstances. No attempt was made to define in any way the personalities of various directors, or why they acted the way they did. Nor was an attempt made to sample the director or board population in a random fashion in order to generalize from a sample to a larger population. In fact, the researcher began the study with no preconceived notions regarding director behavioural characteristics.[8]

What was done was to:

1. observe and carefully record the actions and outwardly visible behaviour of directors during board and committee meetings;

---

6. See, for example, Parts One and Two, including Chapter 8 (group influence), in David G. Myers, *Social Psychology*, 7th ed. (New York: McGraw-Hill, 2002) and "Interpersonal Decisions" and "Organizational and Group Decisions" within Lee Roy Beach, *The Psychology of Decision Making* (Thousand Oaks, CA: Sage, 1997).

7. See, for example, Eysenck's theory of Extraversion-Introversion, in Jerry M. Burger, *Personality*, 5th ed. (Belmont, CA: Wadsworth/Thomson, 2000), 254–256.

8. Directors were observed in action in board and/or committee meetings of twenty-one organizations—eleven corporations, four government controlled enterprises and six not-for-profit organizations. As anticipated from the hypothesis that there are inherent within individuals fundamental behaviour characteristics which they manifest as directors in the same way regardless of the type of group organization they are serving, similar behaviour characteristics were observed in all three groups, *i.e.*, there were directors in all three types of organizations who ranked high on the persuasiveness scale (see below) and there were directors who ranked low; directors who ranked low on dissent and directors who ranked high; and so on.

2. interview approximately two hundred active directors about the behavioural characteristics of their colleagues in the boardroom;

3. distill and carefully analyze the data according to the qualitative methodology used for this study, addressing concerns of trustworthiness, reliability and validity of the data (see Appendix B); and

4. draw on the experience gained from attending several hundred board meetings

to determine if individual behaviour characteristics of directors could be identified that influenced the collective decision-making capabilities of boards of directors.

On the basis of the data, it was concluded that it could be hypothesized that there were three behavioural characteristics of directors that had a major impact on the decision-making capabilities of boards.

THE BASIC BEHAVIOURAL CHARACTERISTICS OF DIRECTORS

PERSUASIVE / NON-PERSUASIVE

First, and by far the most important factor in determining a director's influence on a decision in the boardroom, is the degree of a director's persuasiveness. Some directors, because of their persuasiveness, actually drove the decision-making process. Persuasiveness, in turn, was not primarily a function of articulateness and debating skills, but appeared to be strongly based on the credibility that a director had with his or her colleagues. Credibility, of course, cannot be observed. However, in the process of observing the degree of persuasiveness of directors in action, it was clear that experience, knowledge, length of association with the board, external reputation and record of reliability in assessing previous board problems—all conditions for credibility—were important in determining the extent of persuasiveness of directors. Without credibility, no amount of oratorical capabilities seemed to be able to persuade a board to take a certain action. At the same time, the lack of ability to present one's case effectively was a definite liability in terms of a director being able to influence the "decision-making process." The ability to persuade is perhaps the most important of all director characteristics in determining an individual board member's effectiveness in the decision-making process.

DISSENT/CONSENSUS

A second important factor in determining the impact of a director on the decision-making process is the degree to which a director is known by his or her colleagues to dissent or agree about issues. Some directors, regardless of the issue involved and the presentations made, always found a reason to disagree or agree with a recommended action. As soon as a fellow director could predict with reasonable accuracy how a director would react on every issue because he or she always reacted that way, the director lost his or her influence on the decision-making process.

INDIVIDUAL/COLLECTIVE

Finally, a third factor influencing the individual impact of a director on decision-making is the degree to which a director appears to act alone, without much discussion with other board members, in arriving at his or her position regarding an issue. A board is a collegial organization; decisions are made after considerable discussion and debate. To the extent that directors did not join in or participate actively in the decision-making process, that is, in the give-and-take discussion among fellow board members about the merits or demerits of specific positions, it was observed that they lost some influence, and if they seemed to take an unalterable, individualistic position on an issue, regardless of the discussion, they lost all their influence.

BOARD MEMBERS AS DECISION-MAKERS

On the basis of the data accumulated for this study, directors were placed on scales ranging from "low" to "high," according to the degree to which they appeared to display these characteristics. In other words, taken together, the scales reflect the extent to which a director was persuasive / non-persuasive; inclined to dissent or move for a consensus; acted alone or with the group (see Figure 7.2 on page 166). The positioning on the scale was not determined by the quality of the decisions eventually made about particular issues, but rather by the data collected from observations and interviews about directors' contribution to board decision-making.

Because of the number of decisions made by the number of directors on the number of boards that were studied in real time, it was theoretically possible for there to have been an endless number of permutations and combinations of directors and decision-making characteristics. However, the observed facts did not support the possibility. In reality it was relatively easy, based on the data generated by the observations and interviews, to conclude that these basic behavioural characteristics in the board room—1) persuasiveness versus non-persuasiveness, 2) the tendency to dissent or work for consensus, and 3) preference for working alone rather than in the group—were the fundamental behavioural characteristics determining the effectiveness of an individual director in board decision-making. It was observed that directors by and large possessed these behavioural characteristics with respect to decision-making in a consistent fashion across meetings and over time.

Not all directors ranked high on all three scales and not all ranked low. All types of combinations, based on the above three scales, were observed. For example, there were directors who were very non-persuasive who placed much closer to "dissent" than "consensus" on the "dissent/consensus" scale. And there were directors constantly in the midst of discussion with their fellow directors, who placed close to "collective" on the "collective/individual" scale and who placed close to "persuasive" on the "persuasive/non-persuasive" scale who were quite capable of persuading directors to follow a particular course of action. And there were some directors who worked alone in arriving at a decision and, therefore, ranked very close to "individual" on the "individual/collective" scale and who were very persuasive who also had a major impact on decision-making. Others directors who ranked close to "individual" on the "individual/collective" scale, yet lacked persuasive capability with their colleagues had little or no influence in the decision-making process.

On the basis of where individual directors were plotted on the three scales, it was possible to divide directors into two groups—those who, through their behaviour, contributed in a positive fashion to the decision-making capacity of the board and those who did not. Or, to put it in the vernacular, those who contributed to creating the "positive chemistry" among directors so essential to effective decision-making in the boardroom and those who did not. The former—those who worked together to arrive at decisions after thoughtful discussion and debate were designated as "functional" directors; those who did not were labeled "dysfunctional."

Functional directors ranked high in their ability to persuade fellow directors to accept their point of view and worked constructively with their fellow directors in seeking effective decisions for perplexing problems. And while some were closer to the "dissent" than the "collective" end of the scale, or "individual" or "collective" end of the scale, or vice versa, these directors had in common a capacity to work with their fellow directors in hammering out, through give-and-take discussion, a decision that the majority of the board could support.

Conversely, dysfunctional directors lacked the combination of behavioural characteristics that led to positive decision-making on the part of the board. They did not contribute positively to the board decision-making process. They did not make the team more effective and their presence on a board assured that the much sought after, but so elusive chemistry, essential for effective board process, would not be present. They ranked low on the persuasiveness scale and, regardless of how their outward behaviour manifested itself—either individually or collectively—or by dissenting or agreeing—they did so in such a fashion as to impair the overall dynamic within the boardroom.

An individual director's classification—behavioural type—was occasionally observed to change. However, for the most part, directors tended to display the same behavioural characteristics across time and circumstances. Directors who were not very persuasive in one circumstance did not appear to be persuasive in another. Similarly, directors who were observed, and considered by their colleagues, to operate as "lone wolves" in one meeting appeared to act the same way in others. Directors who were observed to have the practice of always disagreeing appeared to be always disagreeable, a characteristic that was confirmed by interviews with their peers. Strong board chairs were observed and viewed by board colleagues to be consistently effective across time and circumstances. Similarly, weak chairs were not all of a sudden observed or viewed by peers to be effective at another board meeting. In short, 1) a director's observed behaviour, together with 2) other directors' views on their behaviour, appeared to be remarkably consistent across time and governance situations.[9]

Figure 7.2
The Five Functional and Five Dysfunctional Director Behavioural Types

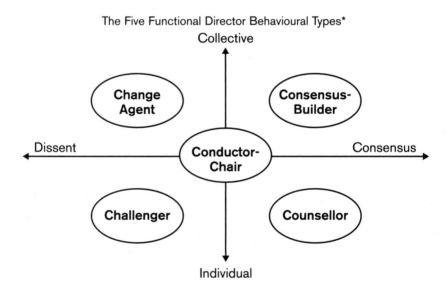

The Five Functional Director Behavioural Types*

*All functional directors rank high on the "persuasiveness" scale.

9. See, for example, "The Trait Approach" within Jerry M. Burger, *Personality*, and the discussion concerning the consistency of traits within Ziva Kunda, *Social Cognition: Making Sense of People* (Cambridge, Mass.: The MIT Press, 2001), 415–450. In the more popular press, see also Otto Kroeger, Janet M. Thuesen and Hile Rutledge, *Type Talk at Work: How the 16 Personality Types Determine Your Success on the Job* (New York: Random House, 2002).

The Five Dysfunctional Director Behavioural Types*

Collective

Controller

Conformist

Dissent — Caretaker-Chair — Consensus

Critic

Cheerleader

Individual

*All dysfunctional directors rank low on the "persuasiveness" scale.

SKILLS, APTITUDES AND CAPABILITIES: THEY DIFFER AMONG DIRECTORS

THE TEN TYPES OF DIRECTORS

At the same time as directors were being studied to determine the three basic behavioural characteristics, it was observed that directors manifested these behavioural characteristics in a variety of ways. This is not, of course, astonishing, given the background and experiences of the wide range of people who serve on boards. Directors are after all individual human beings and like all human beings, they have many different qualities. Every director brings to the board skills, aptitudes and capabilities that come from his or her life experiences, education and training. Some prefer to decide only on the basis of solid facts and past experiences; others cannot be bothered with too much detail. Some are very analytical and objective about issues; others are subjective and empathetic. Some can only work within well-structured and organized statements of a problem, while others are quite willing to look "outside the box." Some are constantly wishing to change things, whereas others fear change. Some constantly criticize while others are continually optimistic. Some are constantly working to bring about solutions, whereas others are determined to avoid them. Some enjoy being on a board; others dislike it.

A total of ten types of directors were identified. The characteristic features of each type are outlined in detail in Chapter 8.

Inasmuch as many directors, through the course of the interviews used similar nomenclature when describing the actions of their fellow directors, it seemed only sensible when classifying director types to use the terms and references that directors themselves used to identify how directors performed in the boardroom. For example, the comments were made over and over that so-and-so "criticized all the time" and that so-and-so was a "consensus builder," or so-and-so tried to "control everything," whereas someone else was nothing more than a "cheerleader" and that the board chair "conducted" a meeting with skill. The names used for the eight director types are Change Agents, Consensus-Builders, Counsellors, Challengers, Controllers, Cheerleaders, Conformists and Critics—and for the two chair types, Conductors and Caretakers.

Since classification of a director as a certain type incorporates the director's education, experiences and habits, the boundaries among the types tend to blur, *e.g.*, Change Agents may at times become Challengers, and Challengers may become—if for some reason they begin to act increasingly more intemperately—Critics. At the same time, Critics may become Challengers, if for some reason their tone, style and technique of questioning management and interacting with fellow directors changes. And so, no one director ever fits a "type" perfectly. Directors can rarely be classified as either/or with complete precision.

The directors who were classified by type, of course, were the same directors who were observed and interviewed and identified according to their basic behavioural characteristics (see page 166). It was found that their was a close relationship between behavioural characteristics and the classification types. Indeed, it was possible to identify five of the types as "functional directors" and five as "dysfunctional." The five functional, *i.e.*, those that contributed to effective decision-making by the board were basically Challengers,

Change Agents, Consensus-Builders, Counsellors and Conductors. The five dysfunctional directors were Critics, Controllers, Cheerleaders, Conformists and Caretakers.

DO BEHAVIOURAL CHARACTERISTICS MATTER?

When building a board, it is essential to choose only functional directors—directors who have the fundamental behavioural characteristics that lead to good decision-making in a group. This does not mean that every director has to rank "high" on every scale. Few boards, for example, are effective without Change Agents or Challengers, who basically are inclined more towards dissent than consensus. A board made up entirely of Consensus-Builders would never get anything done. And choosing directors who have great competencies in some particular function is worthless in creating an effective board if those directors, plus the ones they are joining on the board, do not have the mix of behavioural characteristics necessary to work as a group in arriving at decisions.

Do the behavioural characteristics of directors have an impact on decision-making? When behaviour is broadly defined, the answer, of course, is "yes." Does it follow automatically that chairs, nominating committees, directors, shareholders, search firms, *etc.*, should place more emphasis on behavioural characteristics when selecting or recommending new directors? Again the answer appears to be a reasonably confident "yes."

It should be noted, however, that this is a pioneering qualitative study. The observations, particularly in the area of director behaviour and board decision-making, cannot be generalized, and some of the methodologies used can be quarreled with. On the other hand, there does seem to be sufficient evidence to suggest that it is an area of study that is worthy of continuation, particularly when the major objective of such work is to discover the nature of the unknown link between board governance and corporate performance.

SELECTING THE RIGHT MIX OF DIRECTORS

It is clear that there are still serious issues associated with the independence of directors on boards and some concerns about competencies. It is not improbable that sound management and a new approach to regulations can overcome the problems that independence and difficulties in assessing the competencies on the part of directors create. However, obtaining the appropriate mix of behavioural characteristics among directors on a board may not be as easily resolved. It will, as a minimum, require a new approach to director selection to do so.

In regulatory practices, directors are listed as "unrelated" versus "related" (Canada), "independent" versus "dependent" (the United States, Australia and New Zealand) or "executive" versus "non-executive"(United Kingdom). Such classification schemes, while perhaps useful for building a board for monitoring purposes, are irrelevant to building a board that has the major task of making difficult decisions to assure the future well-being of the corporation. And, they provide no indication whatsoever as to how a board should be composed to increase the corporation's wealth for the shareholders.

It may well be very difficult to identify, let alone recruit as board members, people with the unique combinations of behavioural characteristics essential for the creation of the "effective board." However, to the extent it is done, it should lead to the creation of a board that can make decisions effectively. When the decision-makers, that is, the directors, also have among them all the competencies (see Chapter 10) and the independence necessary to define and execute the strategic needs of a company, it may be hypothesized that all the necessary and sufficient conditions for corporate success are fulfilled. Recognizing the importance of putting together a board with the appropriate behavioural characteristics of individual directors may well be the first step in relating corporate governance to corporate performance. The next step is to identify the behavioural characteristics and competencies of existing and potential directors, to match them to the strategy of the company, and to put in place a recruiting program for assembling directors, and, if necessary, removing some existing directors. When these tasks are completed, a board will meet all the requirements of an effective board. How they can be accomplished is the topic of the following chapters.

THE DIRECTOR BEHAVIOURAL TYPES

My fundamental belief is that I can run a better corporation with highly skilled directors—not yes-men—who have a strong sense of obligation rather than a sense of cheerleading, agreeing with every thing management does. Too many boards define directors as stewards. I see them as change managers, agents, ones who change the company.

—Chair and CEO

Directors need to disagree without being disagreeable—how to ask the questions. It's human nature. You need to go below one level. Asking the question, and then the second and third question, so you're stuck! It's board process but with the psychology, we're programmed from birth.

—Director

Good boards are really good when they ask the questions and raise the issues that the CEO, for whatever reasons, isn't addressing or addressing adequately. Good boards act as boards. They recognize that they are not management—that their major responsibility is to make sure management is effectively running the company. Good boards save CEOs from their own weakness.

—Director

The search for individual directors with various behavioural characteristics is driven by the belief that a combination of directors with different behavioural characteristics will lead to a more effective decision-making process by the board.[1] However, it should not be forgotten that the board of directors acts as an entity, that it is in fact a team and that every team member must follow certain fundamental rules if the team is to be successful. This is as true of a board of directors as it is of any group. It means, in the most elementary sense, that all the "best practices" of effective board operations must be met. Members of effective boards attend meetings regularly, read all the material sent to them in advance of a meeting and come well-prepared to discuss the issues on the agenda. They share a common set of ethical standards from which their views on various issues are shaped and the group operates as a "well-functioning social system in which members trust and challenge one another and engage directly with senior managers on critical issues facing the corporation."[2] Through time and experience, the "effective board" will learn to respond as a group to crisis, will alter its operating style to meet new challenges and basically will be able to deal with the changing issues that come before a board. In time an "effective board" develops a "culture" of its own. To use the words of one director, a board develops a "sense of self."

Although one of the crucial factors in determining the selection of directors is their decision-making characteristics, it is important to remember that classification categories, particularly those for human beings acting to fulfill responsibilities under sometimes difficult circumstances, are not set in stone. In certain specific situations, because of a number of unique conditions, a director may well behave differently than what might be his or her normal fashion. Under the stress of a takeover, for example, a usually uninvolved member of a board

---

1. The classification of directors according to their behaviour "types" has been driven completely by the data obtained from observing boards in action, interviews with directors and experience in boardrooms. As outlined in the appendices, the method for this study was qualitative in nature. Emphasis was directed to ensuring that the information collected accurately reflected what was going on in the boardroom and what the interviewees were communicating. See Appendix B and references to reliability and validity (which were not necessary steps within a qualitative study but nonetheless incorporated).

2. Wayne F. Cascio, "Board Governance: A Social System Perspective" *Academy of Management Review* 18:1 (February, 2004): 97.

may bring forward some outstanding ideas for dealing with the situation, and a previous leader may not be as effective as one might have anticipated. However, for the most part, directors studied for this book tended to exhibit quite similar behavioural decision-making characteristics across time and circumstances, as judged by observing 1) their outward behaviours in and outside of board meetings, 2) how their colleagues assessed these behaviours, and 3) how directors reflected on their own behaviours.

Directors may, because of additional education, training, new work experiences, new associations—or even carelessness in attending to their own behaviours, *e.g.*, defaulting from a functional to dysfunctional type, exhibit new and different behaviours that lead to their being classified as a new behavioural type. However, the evidence supports the proposition that basically 1) directors may be identified by their decision-making characteristics, 2) these behavioural characteristics are a good predictor of future activity, and 3) obtaining and maintaining the appropriate mix of behavioural characteristics of directors is a necessary condition for assuring effective board processes.

Table 8.1

Functional and Dysfunctional Directors

Functional Directors	Dysfunctional Directors
Conductor-Chairs (see Chapter 9)[3]	Caretaker-Chairs (see Chapter 9)
Change Agents	Controllers
Consensus-Builders	Conformists
Counsellors	Cheerleaders
Challengers	Critics

THE FUNCTIONAL DIRECTORS

CHANGE AGENTS

Change Agents are among the most important type of all board members. They are catalysts for bringing about fundamental change

---

3. Because of their unique responsibilities, the responsibilities and characteristics of chairs are examined in Chapter 9.

(for example, replacing the CEO, fighting a takeover, developing a new strategy) when they perceive that change is needed. They think broadly about the future directions in which the company should go and may well have a tinge of an over-optimistic style.

Change Agents are not necessarily the first to propose a major change, but during board deliberations or in conversation with other directors, they quickly pick up on dissenting points of view and are prepared to step up to the plate and act as a champion for an alternative approach or course of action to that proposed by management. Their goal, once they are convinced that "the change" is necessary for the good of the company, is to bring it about in a transparent and inclusive manner. They want to ensure that the change is not simply talked about but that it takes place and that they provide the leadership and make the tough decisions, unpopular as they may be with management and other directors, to get the change made.

Experienced Change Agents often gauge support for their position or ask questions before meetings in an effort to assure that there is a broad discussion of the issues that they raise. They are very aware of the manner in which they behave—it is not random—because they know that if they are to be successful, they must adeptly manage their approach to supporting issues of dissent and to questioning management. They realize that how they operate determines whether they will be successful in making the changes they want. They have a high degree of credibility with other board members, are typically very persuasive and are able to work closely with dissenting directors. In this respect, as advocates or champions of change, Change Agents are invaluable in overcoming issues of groupthink. Externally, they act as connectors, linking and liaising with independent advisers and other third parties to gain the information and expertise necessary in order to bring about change. A Change Agent functions well as a lead or presiding director.

Retired CEOs, who have had success in running major enterprises, particularly when they have been involved in takeovers and divestitures, make excellent Change Agents.

Table 8.2

Some Directors' Views About, and Actions of, Change Agents

"I fired three CEOs. I was the instigator. I put it on the table. [The board members] festered and were living with the rotten guy for two or three years, and that's just dumb. You get hardened." (chair)

"At the [Company ABC] board, an _____ looked like a nice guy but he was a punk kid. He took over from the founder. Of the two . . . he was the worst. I went to the shareholders and said, 'Get rid of him or I'm off the board.' I wanted him fired from the organization, not the board. We could only do this at the annual meeting. I polled the board and they agreed. . . . The board was also of the view that they didn't want the founder. The board was factionalized but we became unified after we fired them both." (director)

"The CFO from [Company ABC] was under forty. I came on the board shortly after they had picked him to be president and CEO. He didn't perform, so we fired him. We then went to the outside. There was some dissent on the board in transferring power to a completely new individual who was new on the job. The mental pressure on this new hire of running a five-billion-dollar company got to him. This was one of my toughest issues as a director. Anyway, the pressure got to him. He was in tears and he [had] a nervous breakdown. It was an unpleasant board situation and we had to replace him as CEO. That was six years ago. We lived through it. Good corporate governance prevailed. The board made the decision and was led by outside directors. . . . The most difficult area for a board is the choice of leadership, particularly when succession involves an incumbent who has been there for a long period of time. The choice of leadership is the most difficult decision for a board. We're doing succession planning tonight, two years ahead of time." (chair)

"It's also human nature, the dynamics of a board. I've seen the situation where one-on-one directors are of the opinion that the CEO is not performing, but all support the CEO in the meeting. CEOs are high risk, high pay. Boards don't understand that they don't need justification to fire the CEO. You don't need documents. . . . The company was tanking. We were putting off the inevitable." (director)

"We avoid things. And so the board must ask or get the CEO to think of things he doesn't normally want to do, or is disposed to do. In the end it saves him or her." (director)

QUESTIONS TO IDENTIFY CHANGE AGENTS*

- Can you provide examples where this director read the sentiments of his fellow directors, put an issue on the table that the board for some reason was reluctant to discuss and, in doing so, lent collective support to it and its legitimacy?
- Describe the behaviours that this director uses in bridging the gap between a point of dissent, the need to discuss a point, and the need for the board to come to consensus over an issue.
- Has this director ever had to lend support to a vital question posed by another director and, in doing so, caused a discussion to ensue?
- Provide examples where this director was instrumental in initiating change at the board level that might not have happened if not for this director. Does this director work well under stress? In a crisis?
- Does this director have the intellectual capacity to cope with complex strategic change and the collective credibility and persuasiveness with board colleagues and management to assist in leading the change?
- Describe how this director's behaviours came to bear when the board was tackling an extremely complex problem.
- What is the director's relationship with the CEO? To other directors?
- What is the director's behaviour during executive sessions? Does he chair such sessions? If the CEO were to step down tomorrow, would this director be the one the board chooses to run the company on an interim basis? Why?

*A series of questions is provided to assist in the identification (and possibly recruitment, in the case of functional director types) of each of the eight director types discussed in this chapter. Questions are also provided in Chapter 9 to assist in the recruitment of Conductor-Chairs and identification of Caretaker-Chairs. Many of these questions are based on actual board situations observed for this study and individual director interviews.

CONSENSUS-BUILDERS

In the boardrooms of active boards, where directors are involved in fulfilling their duties, there is always some creative tension between the board and management, and sometimes between various groups on the board. The Consensus-Builder acts as a conciliator among the groups and is as equally valuable to a board in disarming and resolving conflict as the Change Agent is in getting change. The phrases common to Consensus-Builders during board meetings are "I didn't mean to cut you off," "To pick up on [Director X's] question," "If you could perhaps please refresh my memory," "Going back to [Director Y's] question" and so on.

Consensus-Builders have superior conflict-resolution skills. They get along well with almost all board members and have no apparent rough edges to their personality. They often use tasteful humour to make colleagues feel at ease and they have the respect of directors and management, as well as of directors on other boards. A Consensus-Builder is often a more senior member of the board, used to operating in an environment where building a consensus is a necessary condition for getting things done.

Consensus-Builders use their interpersonal and communication skills to rally dissenting directors to a particular position. Most importantly, they are usually able to prevent differences of opinion from escalating into major disputes. Consensus-Builders' relaxed but effective style is usually so great that they may be asked by directors on other boards for advice regarding their internal decision-making difficulties.

The chief negative feature of many Consensus-Builders, however, is that they may not recognize a problem and/or have the intestinal fortitude to push an important issue to a conclusion until it may be too late for effective decision-making. They are often used to "briefing notes" and so approach issues from a very high (policy) level of analysis. They may not read the details and minutiae of board binders thoroughly.

If a board is populated by too many Consensus-Builders, a situation may evolve into a crisis before it is identified as being potentially serious. If no one is present to recognize a problem and initiate dissent and add collective support to the dissent, a simple matter may become a real problem. Once a crisis occurs, a Consensus-Builder is usually slow to react without the prompting of a Change Agent. A board made up primarily of Consensus-Builders will never be "effective."

Former senior politicians are usually exceptionally able Consensus-Builders. They are "polished" and "smooth" and have, from long practice in the political arena, the skills to bring competing sides together. Moreover, once their careers in politics are over, they may not be difficult to recruit.

Table 8.3

Some Directors' Views About, and Actions of, Consensus-Builders
"Some people thought it might be . . . but perhaps I'm wrong about that and it can work. But we'll have to come back to that and make a decision." (chair)
"I don't want to vote but we need consensus.... Let's walk a middle road. . . . Do I have support? . . . Have we reached consensus? Okay, everybody?" (chair)
"Directors like [former politician X] or [former politician Y] can resolve a conflict before it gets to the board. . . . [Former politician X] is good at disarming conflict." (director)
"It was autocratic at [where I was previously] . . . 'you will do it.' At [this board], you can't do this. We operate by consensus. . . . Nothing has gone to the board without the president and the chairman thinking it was the right thing to do. If it should go to the board, it goes. . . . In the process for selecting board members, at [Company ABC] and [Company DEF], I would not recommend to the board someone the president . . . was not comfortable with." (chair)

QUESTIONS TO IDENTIFY CONSENSUS-BUILDERS

- Provide tangible examples of how this director has bridged the gap between dissenting sides of issues during a board meeting or outside of a board meeting.

- Is this director well-liked, respected by all directors and management?
- Will this director work offline, resolving and disarming conflict? How so?
- Does this director use humour strategically? How so?
- How does this director deal with fellow directors, particularly those who may have less-than-optimal behavioural characteristics?
- What other specific skills and examples can you provide of this director's ability to resolve conflict? Be very specific, outlining the steps the director took to resolve the conflict and bridge the gap between competing sides of a complex issue.
- Has this director ever regretted not speaking up when he or she should have?
- Has this director's past occupation been in government?

COUNSELLORS

Counsellors have strong persuasive skills, high credibility and have the ability to work individually with a variety of people, both inside and outside the company. Counsellors have many one-on-one meetings, lunches and telephone discussions with interested parties and their personal and preferred style is to work out problems behind the scenes. They may not speak a great deal at board meetings and may have less-than-perfect attendance records,[4] but their input, although not always highly visible, is nonetheless very important.

Counsellors play four important roles on the board. First, they are a coach—a trusted person to whom the CEO, a family member, e.g., sibling, etc., or other directors can turn for wise counsel or "grooming" on a one-on-one basis. Second, they serve as external connectors, linking management with outside contacts that they have developed. Their one-on-one negotiation skills may be so good that they may even assist in resolving an issue on behalf of the company. Third, they have a good understanding of policy issues that are outside the normal operations of the enterprise—issues of social change

---

4. However, "poor attendance [chronically] almost always means poor performance." (director)

179

or political developments that could have an enormous impact on the company. Fourth, Counsellors often play the role of adviser or mentor to new board members. They are the directors newly-elected board members can turn to when they are uncertain about a particular policy, the board's role in decision-making, their own performance, and so on.

Retired CEOs, board chairs, and academics and lawyers, if they have extensive business experience, often make effective Counsellors. Experienced political leaders may also make effective Counsellors.

Table 8.4

Some Directors' Views About, and Actions of, Counsellors

"I tell the CEO, 'Listen, I don't want your job. I don't want to run this place!' I like working with people and seeing successes. I ask the CEO, 'How do I add value to what you're doing?' . . . I need to direct my energies and understanding." (director)

"Corporate governance is often subtle, for example, what happens off-line at the directors' dinner, with a heads-up. Because of the problem of overcoming group dynamics, often you save the best advice for the CEO in a private meeting." (chair and CEO)

"What happens outside the board meeting is important. For example, directors should have lunch with the CEO once a quarter." (former regulator)

"Not all the directors speak always. It depends on their style. Some like one-on-ones behind the scenes." (director)

"We have two or three directors who speak and when they do they're listened to, with much of this offline. This can be very meaningful." (director)

"A lot of work is done behind the scenes to make sure everybody is on board. I liken the board meetings to a Greek opera: 'Everybody knows the outcome but it's a tragedy along the way.'" (management)

"It's what goes on inside and outside the meeting. [Director X], [Director Y], [Director Z] and I speak the most in the meeting. We discuss the larger issues outside the meeting, or before the meeting. All the time there is dialogue before the board meeting." (executive director)

"Things don't necessarily happen in the board meeting. I read the pre-mail in advance so I can pick up the phone and bring a concern to the committee, the chairman or management in advance of the board meeting. It's better to go one-on-one with an individual—so directors are not uninformed—which is far more effective than blindsiding. That's been my experience." (director)

"We have one director from [the Far East]. He comes to meetings three times a year at most, because it's so strenuous to travel, and given his time. . . . but he's our man in the Far East. It's important to be well-connected in foreign countries." (management)

"[Former politician X] provides a sense of politics, policy and public opinion—the hot connections." (lead director)

"If we desperately needed to see the Prime Minister that morning [former politician X] could do it and that's of value, even if he doesn't crack a book." (CEO)

"I asked one or two old boys to be a mentor for me. I went to them and they gave me a lot of good advice." (director)

"I am more like your senior Counsellor . . . behind the scenes, speaking in private, where you can phone me." (director)

QUESTIONS TO IDENTIFY COUNSELLORS

- Who are this director's external contacts? If a member of management needs to see someone, are this director's contacts able to be leveraged so as to ensure that this happens?
- Does this director work behind-the-scenes effectively?
- What are this director's negotiating skills?
- If the board were in a crisis, what role would this director play?
- What type of advice does this director provide offline (*e.g.,* phone, lunches, *etc.*) to the CEO? To fellow directors?

- Can this director work on a potentially contentious issue before it reaches the board?
- Explain how this director has brokered a situation that was unexpected, or perhaps dealt with a negotiation very effectively.
- Has this director ever been described as a mentor or a coach? To another director or to the CEO? Explain.

CHALLENGERS

Challengers are invaluable members of a board. Their role is to ask the tough questions, to speak up and challenge management and on occasion other directors. Experienced challengers are always very well-prepared about the issues on which they are seeking information and operate on the assumption that, if directors do not ask the right questions, they will never get the correct answers.

When questioning management, Challengers are direct and fair, unlike their poisonous counterparts, Critics. Their questions are almost always well-thought-out and they seldom speak impulsively without being sure of the position and the facts. They use the appropriate tone and style in their questioning, but at the same time their questions are searching, always causing the CEO, CFO and other members of management to think very carefully before answering. Their interjections at board meetings are substantive, made at the right time in the dialogue, and Challengers are judicious in terms of the use of boardtime. Challengers have credibility both with their board colleagues and with management.

Usually Challengers' questions are specific, but sometimes they are open-ended to initiate discussion on a particular topic. In order to ask the important questions, they must have solid information, something to which they are always entitled from management, so they are constantly seeking information. Challengers have the analytical ability to assess and understand detail and are quick studies. They will read and digest the board and committee materials and will grasp the implications of various decisions very quickly.

A major negative trait of Challengers is that sometimes they try to "micromanage," intruding on management's day-to-day responsibilities. A second is that they may default into becoming a Critic (see below) if they are not vigilant at controlling the tone and approach of their questioning.

Challengers see themselves as the loyal opposition to the management and as guardians of the rights of shareholders. It is essential that someone on every board fulfill this role. Because of the nature of their occupation, which includes preparation, skilful cross-examination and attention to detail, professional advisers (*e.g.*, lawyers, accountants and consultants) and academics are often very effective Challengers.

Table 8.5

> Some Directors' Views About, and Actions of, Challengers
>
> "A board is a prisoner of the information available to it." (director)
>
> "It's very easy for directors to be overwhelmed, shy, afraid or brainwashed. . . . He didn't speak up and say, 'What the _____ is this guy talking about?' It takes a lot to challenge an expert with jargon, rapidly, because it's a race against the clock. . . . [Director X] said, 'Go back, I don't understand.' So my advice to younger directors is don't pretend you understand. Maintain a critical sense. . . . If directors of Enron asked good questions about limited partnerships, special purpose entities, it wouldn't have come to [bankruptcy], and they pretended they understood but they didn't. For example, [Director Y] is one of the best directors in [the country]. He asks very tough questions. He would have said, 'You run the company—I don't—so if you want to go ahead and do this, go ahead.' But only a fool would. If he asks three tough questions, you walk away from the meeting and say, 'He's got a hell of a good point!' After cross-examining you, [Director Y] always finishes the interview with 'You have the information and I'll support you.'" (CEO and director)
>
> "You need to get the right information on fewer pages, not a management brain dump. How to get the right information given the time demands on directors is critical." (director)
>
> "So I say, 'What exactly is the issue, and what exactly do directors need to know?' Huge amounts of paper make me suspicious, as management [can] snow you with quantity. . . . " (director)

Continued

"With information flow, the quality of managerial presentations to the board is generally an area of significant opportunity. . . . No one complains. . . . For the management team, the board engages in a willing suspension of disbelief." (director)

"You need the will to challenge constructively, and that takes five years, and fifty percent of directors never actually develop it and that's a broad range of directors. To be more specific, they hide behind other directors." (director)

"My greatest strength is my greatest weakness, and that is challenging. Being provocative is not my goal. I need to maintain balance. It's important that [a Challenger not become a Critic]." (director)

"Be strong enough to put it on the table. Being the nice guy doesn't work anymore. The liquid lunches are over and you take a risk. If you can't stand the heat, get out of the kitchen. But we're still uncomfortable in asking the tough questions." (director)

"Directors need to ask the right questions. 'Are you satisfied?' is a terrible question for a director to ask of management. There are open and closed-ended questions. I spent three hours once with [a renowned criminal lawyer] discussing the rules of evidence and how to ask questions. What you want to ask as a board member are direct and precise questions rather than leading questions." (former regulator)

"You need a question 'kit' and know how to read [management's] answer. And here's the answer you get and then here's the second and third question. And then management gets caught." (director)

QUESTIONS TO IDENTIFY CHALLENGERS

- How extensively does this director prepare for meetings?
- Describe the tone, words and timing of a typical question that this director poses to management. Be very specific and provide at least three examples.
- Give an example of the content of the director's question and especially the approach.
- Is it obvious to you that this director's presence on the board is invaluable, even if just to challenge management? Explain.

- Is this director a quick study, learning the key success factors within a business or industry without necessarily being from the sector?
- Explain this director's views on the informational needs of the board.
- Does this director have the respect of his peers and management? Explain.
- Has this director ever had to rephrase a critical question in order to rehabilitate the credibility of another director who asked the question in an improper manner?
- Is this director known for asking the second and third penetrating questions, at the right time, and in the right tone? Explain with concrete examples.

THE DYSFUNCTIONAL DIRECTORS

Unfortunately, but not astonishingly, all directors are not competent to fulfill their duties and responsibilities. There are many reasons for this—sometimes they do not age well; often they are appointed to a board without the qualifications to do the job well; many times they are selected because of their acquaintance with existing board members; occasionally they are appointed simply to meet the "independence" recommendations of regulators and stock exchanges; or they may be appointed because they are well-known for their activities in other areas—politics or entertainment—and it is felt that their "celebrity status" might be helpful to the company. The reasons for such appointments are endless and the results are often unfortunate. These dysfunctional directors, like the functional, differ in various ways and may be characterized and classified according to those differences.

CONTROLLERS

The Controller-Directors are very dissatisfied members of the board.[5] They are incapable of accepting any position that is first presented and register their dissent without necessarily putting forth an alternative,

---

5. The material referring to "Controllers" is about directors with behavioural characteristics, traits and aptitudes that lead them to behave in a controlling fashion. For a discussion of the impact of "control ownership" on board decision-making, please see Chapter 2.

well-thought-out resolution of the issue. They revel in dissent and contribute negatively to effective board process by often indicating that they are simply trying to focus discussion on an issue, when their goal is to be certain that all directors eventually come to the same conclusion that they have. A Controller appears to have the need to create the perception that he or she played a major part in any decision that is finally reached. It is not unheard of for a Controller to interrupt directors in mid-sentence to bring up irrelevant material simply to block good discussion and generally to disrupt meetings.

A Controller's ability to influence board process—which may occur when the board is made up of dysfunctional directors, who lack the ability to provide a countervailing force sufficient to neutralize either the Controller or the faction he or she leads—makes him or her a very dangerous threat to board effectiveness. Indeed, if the CEO is a Controller and the board is weak, corporate governance as a broad exercise in collective decision-making simply does not exist.

Many (perhaps most) CEOs have at least some tendencies towards control, as demonstrated by the fact that they have the drive to achieve the top position within an organization. It is, therefore, somewhat natural for Controller-CEOs to undertake, consciously or subconsciously, management of the board. This type of domination and manipulation can be either subtle or outrageous—CEOs were observed both flattering directors who were quite incompetent and pounding on the board-table during meetings and berating fellow directors. Strangely, sometimes such CEOs are extraordinarily effective in the short run, although ultimately their actions are very costly to the company.

Domination of a board by a Controller-CEO is particularly harmful if he or she has the ability—through skill, tact, humour or anger—to address but nonetheless marginalize individual directors' and the board's concerns. The goal of the Controller-CEO, ultimately, is not only to manage the board, but to make directors believe his or her version of reality, in an effort not only to stultify dissent, but to lull the entire board into a collective sense of believing that everything is fine when in reality it is not. The consequences can be very harmful to shareholder interests. Earnings and values may eventually decline to the point where institutional shareholders demand changes in the board—or in the very worst of circumstances, the company fails.

When there is a controlling shareholder who is also a Controller-CEO, and the board is populated by dysfunctional director types, put there by—and beholden to—the controlling shareholder, "board effectiveness" simply does not exist.

Table 8.6

Some Directors' Views about, and Actions of, Controller-CEOs

"[The chair and CEO] is a control freak." (director)

"[The CEO] is manipulative." (director)

"The CEO must be willing to share power. If it's withheld, he has to go." (chair)

"He was a pillager and raper and the board was led up the creek. He was a frightening individual. The issue was that no one would ask this guy a question . . . because it was rude to ask. It was scary. He was finally fired but he should have been fired a year-and-a-half earlier. . . . " (director)

"[The CEO] was not as open as he should have been. . . . I think we all learned some expensive lessons. . . . " (director)

"The posture of the CEO is more important than the effectiveness of the chairman." (director)

"The governance question here is whether the CEO has a relationship with the board [in which] he or she feels the board's input is useful. If not, there will be little moving forward." (director)

"A strong-performing CEO will naturally take advantage of [a] weak board." (chair)

"It's very tough for a board to deal with a high-performing CEO who is also greedy." (director)

Continued

> "If you don't like it, don't argue with me, get rid of me or resign." (CEO)
>
> "Moved, seconded, approved, fine." (CEO, during a board meeting, without looking up from his board binder)
>
> "For the bank mergers, the question is 'Where was the board?'" (director)
>
> "Oh, were there any questions on that? What else do I have to tell you about? . . . My time is sort of running out. One other thing. . . . " (chairman and CEO, who spoke during the majority of the board meeting)

QUESTIONS TO IDENTIFY CONTROLLERS

- How does the director exert influence over fellow directors, *e.g.,* control information or the agenda?
- Does the director interrupt other directors? Cut them off? How often, during a typical meeting?
- Is the director (if he is CEO) averse to executive sessions wherein he is asked to leave the room?
- Is the director especially concerned about being involved in recruiting new directors?
- Does the director have a majority of the voting shares (Controller-Shareholder)?
- Has the director ever made decisions unilaterally or with minimal board input, decisions which you thought should have been more collective in nature or made by the whole board?
- Is the director concerned when other directors wish to contact a certain member(s) of management directly?
- Does the director limit your exposure to outside advisers?
- Is the director averse to board, committee or individual assessments?
- Is the director limiting other directors' exposure to other members of management, either in presentations to the board or more informally, *e.g.,* board dinners?

A SPECIAL NOTE ON CONTROLLING-CEOS

A CEO's behavioural characteristics are often critical to, if not highly determinative of, board effectiveness. If the CEO is a Change Agent, Consensus-Builder, or Counsellor, and a champion of corporate governance, the likelihood of the board being effective is quite high. On the other hand, if the CEO is a dysfunctional director who uses knowledge, information and resources to control or manage a board and individual directors, the possibilities for board effectiveness are greatly diminished.

Table 8.7

Questions for Directors to Assess Whether a CEO is a Controller

1. How does the CEO work with the non-executive chair and committee chairs to keep them fully informed on significant or material activities and initiatives intended to advance the interests of the company?

2. Does the CEO try to influence or "control," even in a subtle fashion, inside or outside of meetings, information, reporting, communication, agenda-setting, *etc.*, provided to the board or its committees, regardless of formal governance guidelines and charters?

3. Does the CEO seek to use the board as a strategic asset and bring strategies to the boardroom before they are a "polished crystal ball"? Is the CEO candid, telling the "whole story" to the board, bringing forward key issues early in time?

4. Is the CEO willing to be "vulnerable" in front of the board and allow his or her direct reports to have this type of exposure as well?

5. What are the CEO's views of executive or "in-camera" sessions of non-management directors? Are executive sessions between the CEO (no direct reports) and the board candid and productive? Does the CEO welcome or attempt to influence executive sessions between external advisers and the board/committees, absent management?

6. How does the CEO welcome or influence access by the board to his or her direct reports? How does the CEO affect or influence the relationship between the chair of the board or committee chairs and the

---

Continued

corporate secretary? Between the audit committee chair and the CFO? The general counsel? Between committees and other key executives, *e.g.*, the chief risk officer, internal audit, *etc.*?

7. What are the behavioural "postures" of the CEO's direct reports? Is there an open and candid relationship between them and committees of the board to whom they may report? Does the CEO influence or allow dysfunctional relationships or behaviours to continue in any way?

8. Does there exist mutual trust and respect between the CEO and the board during board meetings? Overall, does the CEO, as demonstrated by his or her behaviour, contribute to a healthy dialogue during board meetings? Is the CEO open and receptive to constructive criticism from directors?

9. Does the CEO ensure that the board of directors and committees are provided with the staff support, external advisers and information they require? Does the CEO welcome board and committee retention of external advisors and continuing development opportunities and orientation for directors?

10. How does the CEO react to discussions during board meetings about ethical business standards and behaviour throughout the company and in its business dealings?

CONFORMISTS

Conformists are non-performing, cooperating directors who support the status quo. They seldom prepare for, or take part in, any serious discussion of issues facing the board. Although they have limited credibility in the eyes of their colleagues, they are normally well-liked and respected by their colleagues, not for their current work as board members, but because of some past successes or relationships.

While fellow directors know that the Conformists make no contribution to the board or to the company, they are all reluctant to recommend their removal simply because Conformists never cause any problems and basically are "nice people"—good members of the club who had noteworthy accomplishments in the past, perhaps as a chief executive officer or a politician.

This explains a Conformist's longevity. While Conformists' currency and contacts are now largely stale, they are using their reputation, *e.g.*, "renting their name," as one director put it, with fellow directors—or tactfully leveraging a relationship with a significant shareholder, *e.g.*, a controlling shareholder or a key customer—to retain their board appointment(s).

When Conformists speak seriously, which is seldom, they usually repeat the same mantra that directors and management have heard before. They may be a humorous embarrassment to their colleagues, *e.g.*, falling asleep at a board meeting. They may sit with their binders unopened or facing the wrong direction, bantering aimlessly with their colleagues who happens to sit to their right or left. Conformists are basically nice, social, predictable, highly ineffective directors. They are free-riders, standard "per diem" directors, who rarely rock the boat, and are always compliant, and can be counted on to vote with the majority.

Table 8.8

Some Directors' Views About, and Actions of, Conformists

"Don't rock the boat. Play the game." (director)

"[Director X] can't [function] because of a [health condition]. . . . [Director Y] hasn't said much for ten years but he's on the board because he was a member of [the regulator]. He initially brought a lot of information on what it's like to deal with certain regulators. He had them in bed. It was staying alive in those days. Now he doesn't play that big of a role. . . . He always would show up." (director)

"He's a golfing buddy of the Prime Minister." (chair, when asked about a director who fell asleep during a board meeting)

"[Director X] is a good guy but normally doesn't say anything." (director, when asked why one of his colleagues sat silent in front of his unopened binder during an entire board meeting)

"[Director X] is probably ready for retirement." (director, when asked why one of her colleagues sat silent with his arms folded and was not

Continued

following along in his binder during a board meeting)

"Non-performance happens for three reasons. One, the director is too busy. Two, the director lacks the experience. And three, the director is lazy." (chair)

"I chair that committee, I think." (high-profile, likeable director, who is on several boards and who, during a board meeting, could not remember whether he chaired a particular committee)

"How do you like interviewing us fat cats?" (director)

QUESTIONS TO IDENTIFY CONFORMISTS

- Could the director be described as "cooperative," working well and almost always in agreement with board decisions?
- Has the director ever actively dissented, either against management or fellow directors? Explain and be specific.
- Has the director formerly been in an occupation where he or she has had to exhibit skills of diplomacy or tact?
- What friends does the director have on the board or associated with the board? Are they in positions of power, capable of continuing to allow the director to serve?
- Why was this director originally asked to serve on the board?
- What is this director's view on board and director assessments? Has he or she ever expressed disapproval?
- Would the saying "decorative but useless" apply to this director? In other words, would you say that this director rarely rocks the boat?
- Do you think that this director is ready for retirement?
- Have you ever been surprised by this director actually preparing adequately for a board or committee meeting?
- Are the director's comments superficial, predictable ones that you have heard before?
- Is the director on the board because he or she represents a stakeholder group considered important by the board? Is this a "political" appointment in any way?

CHEERLEADERS

Cheerleaders are "enthusiastic amateurs." They consider their duty as board members to praise constantly the performance of fellow directors, the CEO, the chair of the board and every activity that the company undertakes. They attend all board meetings and can be counted on to be present at all company events. As a result of their lack of discrimination about anything associated with the company and its management, they lack credibility in the eyes of their fellow directors. Cheerleaders neither prepare for, nor participate in, board discussions, other than to praise management, and they are blithely unaware of the strategic issues facing the company.

Cheerleaders have the capacity to embarrass their fellow board members through making irrelevant remarks about the greatness of the company to outside, knowledgeable observers, and they have the capacity through their ignorance, over-exaggerations and lack of confidentiality to get the board into trouble. During board meetings, Cheerleaders make comments that often take the discussion off-track.

Cheerleaders bring an optimistic view to every situation and provide support to the CEO and management in difficult situations. The problem is that they show little or no judgment about issues and take the same position regardless of the situation, namely that as long as "X" is in charge, everything will work out. The only redeeming quality of a Cheerleader, if it can be called one, is that they are too predictable and can be counted on to always raise their hand on cue from the chair or other colleagues at voting time.

Whereas a Conformist is well-liked and skilled at leveraging his or her past accomplishments and relationships to remain on the board, the Cheerleader is not. The Cheerleader's currency and relationships have expired. At worst, Cheerleaders are regarded with contempt and considered somewhat obnoxious by other contributing, functional directors. At best, Cheerleaders' peers usually refer to them as "sleepers," "non-performers" or "ineffective directors."

Table 8.9

Some Directors' Views About, and Actions of, Cheerleaders

"You know after a period of time you've said all you can say and done all you can do and, after a period of years, you begin to start repeating yourself. The circumstances may change but your perspective on them doesn't very much." (director)

"At [Company ABC], they opened their binder at the table [for the first time]. I prepared it a month ahead so they could get it two weeks ahead of time. How do you form an opinion? It's a _____ joke!" (management)

"[Director X] was largely a Cheerleader . . . " (director)

"We have 'sleepers' on our board." (CEO)

"A key corporate governance question is doing something about the non-performers." (director)

"There are still board members who have not made one single, solitary point that was worthwhile. I don't understand why they are still there." (director)

QUESTIONS TO IDENTIFY CHEERLEADERS

- Why was this director originally asked to serve on the board?
- Does the director agree with most if not all board decisions?
- Is the director overextended in any way, or sitting on too many boards?
- How long has the director been retired from active executive or professional service? Has he or she kept current?
- Has the director ever embarrassed the company in any way, or demonstrated a lack of judgment?
- How is the director regarded by board colleagues and management?
- At meetings, how does the director participate? Does the director have his or her full mind on the strategic issues facing the company?
- Does the director contribute meaningfully and knowledgeably to board discussions?

- Does the director have adequate external contacts and associations to assist the company or management? Did he or she at one time? Or are the director's external linkages stale? Explain.
- Is the director opposed to board and director assessments?

CRITICS

The Critic criticizes and complains. He or she is frequently critical of the way management presents information to the board and is highly critical of board processes and of the management in general. The Critic also is inclined to criticize fellow directors, often behind the scenes in a manipulative sort of way, engaging in subtle but not undetected gamesmanship. The Critic lacks the "constructive" component of being constructively critical.

The Critic has only limited credibility with fellow directors. The Critic's style tends to be abrasive, particularly in the tone in which they ask questions, and in some cases Critics are confrontational. Critics choose words so accusatorily—e.g., the management is "self-serving" and is "misleading" the board—that they may at times be asked to apologize for their behaviour. There is a tendency for Critics to be somewhat "over the top" in their assessment of situations. Their certainty and directness has a very negative impact on the chemistry of the board.

Usually after a Critic poses a question, in his or her own inimitable style, an awkward few seconds of silence follow. Other board members hesitate to support this director (unlike a Challenger), or to even comment on the question posed. Critics take the discussion of issues off-track at inopportune moments, and they are particularly disruptive when they dissent on personal and philosophical grounds. When this happens, sides develop and positions harden, with a vocal minority on one side, the rest of the board on the other, and the Critic in the middle of it all. Over time, however, Critics' tactics become evident to sophisticated directors, and the Critics become marginalized by colleagues.

Critics have not developed the persuasive skills and techniques in dissenting that the Challengers or Change Agents have, or if they have, they choose not to use them. They simply go too far, all the time. Critics are considered at best a nuisance by their fellow board members and at worse manipulative or "sneaky."

For a Critic to become a Challenger, the Critic needs to:

1. change the tone and style in which the Critic questions management and dialogues with other directors;

2. speak more judiciously during board meetings;

3. choose the words that the Critic uses very, very carefully; and

4. be very conscious of how his or her actions and behaviours are perceived by colleagues and management.

Critics are very difficult to remove from a board. If the Critic is pushed to resign, in his or her opinion, "the board is wrong" and "I am the only director who is right." The Critic may adamantly refuse to go. Despite this, Critics, if they cannot control their behaviour (most cannot), are a negative, poisonous influence in the boardroom and should be removed from the board as fast as possible, regardless of the difficulties in doing so.

Table 8.10

Some Directors' Views About, and Actions of, Critics

"[Director X] used to ask prickly questions, but now his edge is gone and his style has changed. It's been good for board members and a contribution to board effectiveness overall. . . . It was just a shift." (CEO)

"It's very important not to have sons of _____ on your board." (director)

"There's a fine line between dissent and _____ . . . . I met more _____ in the last four years than in the previous thirty. . . . Yes, you want dissent on your board but you don't need an official opposition." (director)

"I'm the wicked witch of the west. It's not a tactic, but I speak up and don't feel restrained." (director)

"You must conduct yourself to be a constructive critic. Both are impor-tant, 'constructive' as well as 'critic.'" (director)

"[Director X]'s an absolute _____ ." (CEO)

"Where they're destructive is when the board member philosophically is opposed to the objectives or strategy of the company and tries to bring in his own perspective. I recall one incident where someone stepped off a board. Either you're on the team or resign." (director)

"Pick the time where you hang in and be ugly and for others you save it till later. You have a limited number of shots." (director)

"I already gave him one heart attack." (director)

"The mistake I made is the way in which I tried to get full information. . . . A friend . . . was appointed head of the . . . Committee. . . . I felt . . . [inappropriate words] . . . pressure. . . . I made the mistake and said [an inappropriate choice of words]. . . board members went to . . . asked for an apology . . . wanted to sue. . . . It was the words I used. . . . I was alleged to have implied . . . " (director)

"I was very critical of the information that management provided us with, and said so during the board meeting." (director)

"A comment I made—it was agreed with—but I shouldn't have said it out loud. . . . " (director)

"I eventually was asked to leave the board. No one would listen to me, but I was right." (director)

"I brought a book to the board meeting. I needed to have something to read as no one would talk to me." (director)

QUESTIONS TO IDENTIFY CRITICS

- What is the content, frequency and tone of this director's questions? Be specific, especially in regard to the approach of the questions.
- What is management's view of this director?

- Is the director frequently critical of information provided to the board?
- Does the director make the right choice of words in his or her questions?
- Have the director's emails or other communications ever offended someone?
- Is the director ever negative towards other directors or management in any non-constructive way? In other words, is the director not *constructively* critical?
- Has the director ever been accused of micromanaging or moving into management's territory? Provide examples.
- Has the director ever offended a member of management, or a fellow director, in a personal way?
- Has this director ever breached board protocol or norms in any way?
- Does this director have the respect of his or her peers? Of management?
- Have "sneaky" or harsher words ever been used to describe this director?

BEHAVIOURAL CHARACTERISTICS AND EFFECTIVE BOARD PROCESSES

Traditionally, two factors have primarily determined the selection of directors to boards—the requirements of regulators and stock exchanges for a particular board structure and the comfort of the existing directors. The result of such an approach to director selection has led to the "marginalization of directors" as important players in the governance of corporations. Despite that, by law, directors have all the power to monitor the activities of the enterprise, in reality they have, in many, many cases, exercised relatively little for the variety of reasons discussed in this book.

When regulating and constructing boards, it is important to recognize that boards are, above all, small decision-making bodies. To be effective, they must be made up of a group of people with the distinct behavioural characteristics that will allow them to work effectively as a team. Presumably, if they have an efficient process for making decisions, they will perform their monitoring and strategy responsibilities effectively. And, if the board is effective, it is reasonable to expect that the corporation will be more efficient and will earn satisfactory rates of return on the capital invested by the shareholders.

While there has not been sufficient research to prove the above statement, the possibility it is true is sufficiently high to encourage anyone associated with building a board—chairs of boards, chairs of nominating committees, directors themselves—to consider the behavioural characteristics of the individuals, and the way those characteristics fit with the individual behavioural characteristics of existing board members, when they are making their recommendations for additions or deletions to a board.

Moreover, regulatory agencies and other groups involved in establishing the framework of governance within which boards operate may find it worthwhile to consider that the mix of behavioural characteristics and the skills, aptitudes and capabilities of directors within boards are equally as important, if not more important, than some of the traditional structural regulations in assuring that corporations are governed in the best interests of all the shareholders.

A Special Type of Director: The Chair of the Board

Key phrases for a successful chair: Perhaps we might consider . . . That's a different point of view from the ones we've heard so far. . . . What if we were to . . . What about looking at it this way. . . . Have you thought of . . . We may want to develop a variety of options. . . . It sounds as if . . . What I think I heard you say . . . Let me try to confirm my understanding. . .

—Chair of a Board

One of the biggest mistakes that boards can make is not insisting that problems be faced, or not recognizing the problems. CEOs may be in denial, and boards may be in denial too, but boards should never be in denial.

—Director

There is no more significant factor in determining effective board governance than the leadership qualities of the chair. The chair of the board is not like other directors. The chair is *primus inter pares*—he or she is first among equals.[1] Chairs have the same responsibilities and the same legal obligations as all directors, but, in addition, they have the responsibility of running the board—of managing its operations.[2]

---

1. The phrase *"primus inter pares"*—first among equals—was developed with the evolution of parliamentary democracy. The leading minister in the cabinet eventually became known as the first minister or prime minister.
2. The position of chair is one of the most widely studied functions associated with corporate governance. See, for example, Sir Adrian Cadbury, *Corporate Governance and Chairmanship* (Oxford: Clarendon Press, 2002).

Not all directors can be effective chairs, but every effective board has one. Board leadership is a critical and determinative predictor of board process and overall board effectiveness. Functional boards have strong chairs; dysfunctional boards have weak ones. Strong chairs may be classified as "Conductors"; weak chairs are "Caretakers."

WHY CHAIRS MATTER

Every observation, every interview, every experience involved in this study reinforces the oft-stated proposition that the chair of the board has enormous influence over the manner in which the board operates. Indeed, in the view of many directors, the chair of the board determines the effectiveness of the board's deliberation simply by assuring that the mechanics of the board's operations are correct.[3]

The chair, along with the CEO, controls the agenda, and an effective chair makes certain that not only are the major issues of management brought forward for discussion, but also other issues that are of concern to the directors are as well. Moreover, and most importantly, the chair realizes that it is absolutely imperative that directors receive the proper information about every item on the agenda in a timely fashion and easily comprehended form.

Competent chairs encourage directors to ask penetrating questions about all the issues that are of relevance to the well-being of the enterprise. If chairs sense any feeling among directors that they are not fully satisfied with the quality or sufficiency of the information they are receiving from management, which is required in order to make an informed decision about a matter before the board, strong chairs always make sure that no decision is reached until all directors are completely satisfied. Sometimes they may simply postpone the decision until a later date; other times they may take a strong lead in the discussion by asking open-ended questions that pave the way for further questioning on the part of board members. Most importantly, by constantly developing an environment within the boardroom where "give-and-take" questioning is the common

3. For an illustration of a position description for a chair, see Chapter 4.

practice, wide-ranging and complete discussion about issues becomes the norm. Good directors and good chairs know that it is possible to disagree about an issue without being disagreeable and that sometimes pressing for more information saves the board from making premature decisions that may have major negative consequences for the company. Effective chairs make certain that no director is ever marginalized; indeed, if they sense that some directors are unhappy about a situation, they may go as far as contacting them outside of the boardroom in order to ensure that they are brought into, and kept in, the decision-making loop. One of the greatest deterrents to effective board operations is group think,[4] and good chairs know that one of the ways to minimize this phenomenon is through establishing a culture of questioning and debate within the boardroom.

SOME CRITICAL TASKS FOR THE CHAIR OF THE BOARD

Assessment of, and Relations With, the CEO

A major, if not *the* major, task of the board is to hire and at times fire the chief executive officer. Obviously, if one person holds both positions, and there is no lead director, it is very difficult for directors to act. But even when the positions are split, many directors believe that the decision to remove (or to re-appoint) the CEO, for one reason or another, is not well handled. Often directors do not want to be disloyal to the management, particularly if the CEO they are replacing is the one who invited them on the board in the first place; quite often directors are personal friends of the CEO and his or her family, and most directors believe that one of the functions of a good board is to support management. Moreover, in some (many) boards, there are no rigorous, formal processes for CEO evaluation and so many directors are reluctant to take the dramatic action of firing the CEO because of an intuitive feeling that he or she should be removed. If a company is not doing well, it may because of factors

4. For a discussion of the problems associated with "groupthink," see Chapter 6.

that are far beyond the CEO's control. Dismissing the CEO is in many respects an act of last resort for many directors.

Effective chairs provide the leadership board members need in dealing with any problems they may have with the CEO. They constantly exchange views and ideas with all the directors; they discuss how the management is operating the corporation and how progressive chairs implement CEO assessments so that they can work with the directors on the basis of solid information about performance rather than by guess and innuendo. Strong independent chairs are able to assess the discontent among the directors, evaluate the reasons for it, and if convinced that a change is needed, lead the action involved in dismissing the CEO.

PREVENTING BOARD DENIAL

Even in the best companies things do not always go well. Crises do develop. The CEO and part of the management team may be killed in an accident; serious fraud may be discovered; a downturn in the market may put pressure on bank borrowings; an expensive acquisition may not earn sufficient funds to carry its costs; a predator may make an unfriendly bid for the takeover of the company and so on. Well-run experienced boards usually know how to deal with such issues. However, there is a huge—usually fatal— problem if, in response to the crisis, both the board of directors and the senior management deny that there is a major problem. No one likes to hear bad news, particularly when it is so bad that it may cause the failure of the enterprise and place the directors in personal jeopardy because of some type of litigation. Crises can occur for many reasons, but a reaction of denial by the board is almost always the result of weak board leadership and poor board practices in general. Needless to say, effective chairs, by inculcating into the board sound decision-making practices, can do much to avoid the "denial syndrome" when a crisis occurs. If everything goes wrong and management and the board are forced to face the reality of a disastrous situation, the presence of an extraordinarily able chair is often the difference between the success and failure of the company.

Table 9.1

Two Views on Board Denial

"Directors usually see their job as supporting management. How often do directors really question management? We don't like bad news and we ignore or deny. The denial syndrome is universal and cross-cultural. What should directors do? You want factual information, good up-to-date information, on the issues raised. You want an orderly flow of good information during good times–this regime needs to be in place. You need to interpret and cross-examine management on the subject. This will be interpreted as disloyalty by the CEO. If there's no history of questioning management, that's a problem. You want to meet the regulator or auditors, with and without management in the room. 'In one month?' . . . No, the time to deal with it is now. You have escalating intensity and decreasing time. Management telling the board 'we don't know what to do to fix it' is happening more now." (former regulator)

"For instance, [at Company ABC] . . . analysts say the competition has 8 or 9 percent operating margins, but we have three percent, magically, when we should have ten percent operating margins. So pigs fly, right? Well that's tough, but what gives directors the ability? It's the kids on Bay and Wall Street making two-million bucks a year that get all that matters and compare to management's view and say ' _____ .' So, yeah, boards become active, but active when it's too late. . . . " (chair)

DEALING WITH NON-PERFORMING DIRECTORS

As there is increased recognition that the mix of director behavioural characteristics and competencies are probably the most important factors in determining the decision-making capabilities of the board, good chairs know that they must constantly monitor their directors and take action to remove those who no longer add value to the enterprise. There are few things so debilitating to directors as working with non-functional directors. So strong chairs, in the interests of maintaining "good chemistry" among the directors, work diligently to remove and replace the non-performing ones. However, as is the case with the CEO, for many reasons it is not always an easy task to accomplish.

Through the years, directors have played such a minor, almost purely ceremonial role, in the activities of many companies that there has grown up what can be thought of as a sense of entitlement among many directors—a sense that once they are elected to a board they can stay on until retirement age regardless of their performance. For years, directors had no real accountability to anyone other than the management of the enterprise, and so the concept of resignation because of poor performance has never been something that has dominated directors' thinking. In the face of such a culture, a chair needs to be very skilful to obtain the resignations that he or she needs. One of the most effective methods, or at least a less painful way of doing so, is by having, as part of the board's by-laws or governance guidelines, an accepted formal method for assessing board and director performance and for removing non-performing directors. Without such a program in place, removing long-serving, incompetent directors is almost impossible. Obviously it is important that nominating committees and board members rally around and support the chair's decisions once such a call is made.

Table 9.2

Some Directors' Views on the Importance of Chairs

"How chairs get selected . . . is the biggest corporate governance problem. It's the most hidden process. So much of the leadership and capabilities of the chairman affect[s] the board and this is so misunderstood and non-transparent." (director)

"The right chairman creates the right atmosphere. With the wrong chairman, it's completely different." (director)

"Generally chairmen are responsible for getting the dissent out, resolving it, and for supporting the majority." (director)

"The chair adjusts the chemistry." (director)

"A chair should move things forward by consensus. Once you know the facts and directors' points of view, you go one-on-one first. It's time consuming." (chair and CEO)

"Most board issues shouldn't have dissent. . . . If there is dissent, it's emotional and everybody needs an opportunity to be heard. The chair shouldn't try to force a decision at that point unless it's life or death, but most decisions aren't that way. Where there is often dissent is when management brings something to the board by surprise and the role of the chairman is important here. Preliminary things should have happened to move it forward, such as further information. Dissent might happen when you don't have all the facts or things are premature. Dissent can also be handled between meetings, person-to-person or over the phone. The chairman may also want to get the board member together with management." (chair)

"The chairman has to be emotionally and intellectually prepared to say he will leave if he is not comfortable with something. The board should not be his life. Like a judge, a chairman should be independent." (chair)

"There is not enough thought at the senior-most board level on how to run a good board. There is no thought given to the structure, mandate and rewarding of the board so that it's most effective. . . . Rarely will you find a chairman who brings someone on who will disagree with him or challenge him. This is fundamentally wrong in my opinion." (director)

WHO MAKES FOR A GOOD CHAIR?

From observation of boards in action and interviews with two hundred directors—including interviewing many of the best chairs as recognized by their peers, and observing them in action in board meetings—plus an examination of the literature on corporate governance, it is clear that chairs may be divided into two major classes: Conductors and Caretakers.

A necessary condition for successful operation of the board is that it have a Conductor-Chair. Such chairs are usually Change Agents, Consensus-Builders or Counsellors. Sometimes a Challenger, a functional director, is appointed chair, but usually Challengers find themselves more suited to perform as an integral part of the decision-making process of the board, rather than as a leader of the board. Non-functional directors never serve effectively as Conductor-Chairs.

Caretaker-Chairs, who are usually dysfunctional directors—Controllers, Critics, Conformists or Cheerleaders—simply do not have the credibility among their fellow directors to serve as effective chairs. Caretaker-Chairs tend to be distant and non-performing, or controlling and disruptive. They cannot manage interpersonal conflict or dissent nor can they work towards consensus, and they usually cannot establish effective working relationships and credibility with colleagues, the CEO or the management team.

Whenever a dysfunctional director is serving as a chair, it is often because he or she has been put in the position by the major shareholder—an individual owner who want something for a son or daughter to do, or a parent company that wants to give someone who no longer has a major function at headquarters a position with a title of some significance. In such cases, the chair, and for that matter the board, in the last analysis have really little to do with the running of the company—the critical decisions are made by the major shareholder. If the company is widely held and has a Caretaker-Chair, it is usually because the board is ineffective or for some historical reasons. In the final analysis, the reality is quite simple: Conductor-Chairs reflect and cause strong, engaged and effective boards. Caretaker-Chairs reflect and perpetuate weak and ineffective boards.

THE TWO TYPES OF CHAIRS

CONDUCTOR-CHAIRS

Conductor-Chairs relate very well to management, have a keen interest in good governance and serve at the hub of all important board activity. They understand group and individual dynamics and possess remarkable leadership skills, both inside and outside the boardroom. They relate exceptionally well to the CEO (if a non-executive chair), committee chairs and other directors. They lead the setting of the agenda, run meetings effectively, moderate discussion appropriately, manage dissent, work towards consensus and, most importantly, set the tone and culture for effective corporate governance.

Conductor-Chairs exhibit flexibility in involving other director behavioural types—Change Agents, Consensus-Builders, Counsellors or Challengers—depending on the situation, in the decision-making activity of the board. During board meetings, they have the skill (an elite number of Conductor-Chairs have perfected this almost to an art-form) to call on these director-types at different times during the meeting, in order to maximize the full decision-making effectiveness of the board and utilize the panoply of competencies and behaviours of the full director bench. Effective Conductor-Chairs seem to have an internal barometer, always seeming to tell them when they need to intervene in a discussion, when to be flexible and when not to.

Specifically, at board meetings, when a difficult decision must be made, the views of Change Agents, Consensus-Builders, Counsellors and Challengers may all come into play. A Challenger, for example, may challenge fellow directors about their perceptions and assumptions, based on his or her specific competency in an area where that of the CEO or other directors may be lacking. The Challenger, unlike the Critic, will be very persuasive because of the Challenger's skills, tone, background and competency but, most importantly, because a Challenger by nature *does* challenge— he or she will be opposing some idea probably advanced by management. A second Challenger may lend support to the first Challenger's position, and will also have the competencies, tone and approach required to be persuasive. A Change Agent may agree to meet personally with outsiders who are experts on the issue and, for the moment, will support the Challenger's position. A Counsellor, however, may give positive encouragement to the Conductor-Chair (who may also be the CEO) to press on with the original idea to which the Challenger has objected, but to modify it to meet some of the objections. The Consensus-Builder may start working to bridge the views expressed by seeking common ground, linking positions and forging consensus among directors with different opinions. The Conductor-Chair must handle all this discussion in a controlled and effective manner. A key for effective decision-making is the Conductor-Chair's ability to *conduct*, that is, to listen and skilfully manage all the director behaviour types and then obtain unanimous agreement on the issue. It is not always an easy thing to do.

Table 9.3

Some Directors' Views of Conductor-Chairs in Action

"A skilful chair, therefore, is a referee, moderator, and smoothly slips in his own views. They bring a sense of discipline to the discussion. They cut people off nicely and set a time limit to the agenda." (management)

"I talk to [the CEO] three to four times a day, in real time, as well as with other senior officers. . . . Ideally the CEO should not be the chairman. There should not be an adversarial relationship, though. The CEO makes the company work, not the chairman. The chairman a) should make a difference, and b) should be sort of a watchdog. He should be involved, but not too involved. It's a very difficult line. For example, I would never tell an officer what they should do. Normally, I will give advice if asked, and even in that case I am very careful, for example, not to give advice to officers on how to deal with one another. I would suggest bringing points up with other people." (chair)

"A good chairman produces a healthy dialogue. Management's position is expressed and the board is open to question management over the position taken and why or why not other positions weren't taken. It should be a true discussion as opposed to management justifying their position or board members advancing their own opinion based on their experiences but not the current discussion." (chair)

"It's up to the chairman of the board to give certain people time [during the board meeting] based on the subject matter rather than the people." (chair)

"There are different levels and planes. You can be talking about the same thing using different lenses. The chairman tries to get the discussion in the ballpark." (chair)

QUESTIONS TO IDENTIFY CONDUCTOR-CHAIRS

- Is this director one of the most effective chairs you have known? Why? What specific competencies and behaviours does this director bring to bear?
- If the CEO position is a separate position on some of the boards on which this director sits, explain the nature of this chair's relationship with CEOs, especially those CEOs who are Controllers.

- Provide examples of how, during a meeting, the chair was able to bridge the gap between dissent and consensus among those directors who function collectively and individually.
- Explain how the chair excels at managing issues during meetings by relying on the competencies and behaviours of other directors.
- Is this chair effective outside as well as inside of meetings? How so?
- Explain the chair's role in committee oversight, agenda creation, the informational needs of the board, and in his or her relations with other directors.
- If this chair also occupies the role of CEO, explain why and how he or she is effective at managing the inherent conflict of interest in occupying both roles.
- How does the chair ensure a productive relationship with the rest of the management team?
- Give three specific examples that occurred when, without the chair, a board meeting would have deteriorated, including what the chair did or did not do that was vital to ensuring effective decision-making.
- Would this chair subject himself/herself to an annual assessment by the rest of the board? Has it happened? Was the chair receptive to constructive criticism?

A Conductor-Chair may inherit a board that contains a number of dysfunctional directors. This is particularly true when he or she has been put in place by a controlling shareholder—usually a parent company—and told to "clean up the mess." The first act of the new chair is to introduce guidelines for all directors if they are not already in place, by preparing position descriptions for directors, for committees, for committee chairs and for him or herself as chair. The new chair may be fortunate enough to have come from a parent company where such guidelines are in place and so they can be introduced as part of the overall governance pattern of the entire company. If not, he or she must introduce them carefully, indicating that he or she needs them simply to get really well-oriented to the company. After the introduction of expected performance standards, it is only a matter of time before it is logical to measure the activities of the board members against the expectations of the company. When those expectations are not fulfilled, the chair can begin the process of counselling the delinquent performer(s) off the board.

CARETAKER-CHAIRS

A Caretaker-Chair is an ineffective chair of a board, and recognized as such by other directors. They usually are Cheerleaders, Critics, Conformists or Controllers whose defining characteristic is lack of leadership ability. They all fail as chairs but they fail for different reasons.

Cheerleader and Conformist Caretaker-Chairs are under-controlling, do not say much, or very little if anything during board meetings, do not manage interpersonal conflict and dissent, and do not know how to work towards consensus or how to run a board meeting effectively. They are unable to establish effective working relationships with fellow directors, the CEO or the management team, primarily because they have little credibility. In such situations, boards are very poorly managed and some individual member of the board with a strong personality—probably a Challenger or Change Agent, or a Controller-CEO—takes it over. Lines of authority are ignored, the chief executive officers do not know to whom they are really reporting, directors are derelict in fulfilling their duties, committees are ineffective, and corporate governance in any real sense of the word does not exist.

On the other hand, Controller and Critic Caretaker-Chairs are exactly the opposite. They use the power inherent in being chair in a negative manner. They govern by skilful intimidation and manipulation of board members. They carefully monitor the flow of information needed to understand what is going on in the organization, and directors who seek additional information are treated with contempt. Decisions are forced through, not on the basis of careful analysis and debate, but on the basis of personal relationships that may have nothing to do with the situation.

When there is a Caretaker-Chair who holds the position, as they usually do, because of some relationship to the majority shareholder, the board quickly realizes that it has little or no control over the destiny of the company. If the Caretaker-Chair decides to grow the company—not an unusual situation since Caretaker-Chairs with the behavioural characteristics of a Controller often appear to have a considerable amount of hubris—there is nothing the board can do. If they oppose a proposal, the Caretaker-Chair simply uses his connections to have the directors removed; if they support the proposal on the basis of the Caretaker-Chair's decision, their support is irrelevant since they will never have sufficient information on which to make a decision, even if they were asked. So in this situation the board of directors is effectively useless.

Given the powerlessness of a board with a Caretaker-Chair, some directors may attempt to renew the board by recruiting a new Conductor-Chair from outside its own membership. It is something that is not easy to do. Indeed, it may seem easier to work (and to hope) such that the incumbent chair may be trained to become more effective. While this self-development may happen, it is highly unlikely. The fact is, with a Caretaker-Chair, the board is dysfunctional. The company will not prosper, the board members will not fulfill their duties of care to their shareholders, the corporation will probably be targeted for a takeover, or the board will be marked for removal by institutional investors. The future of the company is bleak.

Boards with Caretaker-Chairs should not have been accepted by shareholders in the past. They will not be tolerated in the future.

Table 9.4

Some Directors' Views of Caretaker-Chairs in Action

"That board meeting was terrible and it is all the chair's fault. He just sat there and let the discussion go on and on and on with no closure on any of the key issues facing the company. . . . There really should be a . . . course out there on how to chair a proper board meeting–Robert's Rules of Order or something. It's getting ridiculous." (director)

"[The chair's] problem is that he doesn't do anything and he can't run a board meeting." (CEO)

Continued

"We went out of our way to hire . . . [the non-executive chairman] because of his credibility. He's well-paid but completely useless. . . . He's disgusting, greedy and outrageous and other board members agree. . . . " (director)

"The board has lost control because of the weak chair and that weakness is 'chair-think.'" (director)

"I take [my] marching orders from [the CEO]." (lead director)

"[The chair] should speak up more often. I know he knows what's going on. He should feel more comfortable offering us his view. He assumes people will speak up and he's encouraging us to speak. . . . He shouldn't worry about sway or influence—he does not control our thoughts." (director)

"[The chair] doesn't speak up when he should and run the meeting." (director)

"Look at the successes for non-executive chairmen. . . . We should pick someone who has the requisite skills already, versus training on the job. . . . Not just the time and availability, but the skill set that the job requires. We should recruit chairmen of boards with this in mind." (director)

"There should be a special course for how to be a chairman. Training for chairmen. The right chairman creates the right atmosphere. With the wrong chairman, it's completely different." (director)

"There should be a _____ ing course for chairmen to take on how to run a _____ ing board meeting." (frustrated director)

QUESTIONS TO IDENTIFY CARETAKER-CHAIRS

- Explain how this chair runs board meetings. Have other directors been frustrated by the chair's inability to run a successful board meeting? Gain proper discussion and/or closure on key issues? Be specific.
- Does the chair have trouble managing dissent?
- What is your view of the chair's competencies, knowledge of the business and use of governance best practices?

- Is the chair vulnerable to being influenced or controlled by the CEO in any way, even subtly? By another director or group of directors? By a controlling shareholder?
- Can you identify examples of poor leadership exhibited by the chair?
- Do directors have confidence in the chair? If not, why not? Be specific.
- How long has the chair been in this position? Has chair-fatigue set in?
- How does the chair relate to members of management and other directors?
- Provide an example(s) of a board meeting where the chair has lost control.
- Why do you think this chair is non-performing?
- Has this chair ever resisted being assessed by other directors, either formally or informally?
- Does the chair believe in good governance?
- Overall, do you think this board would be more effective with a different chair?

IT IS THE "SELECTION" OF CHAIR, NOT THE "SEPARATION" OF CHAIR AND CEO, THAT COUNTS

In many corporations, especially those in the United States, one person holds both the chair and the chief executive officer positions. There is considerable dispute among directors as to whether or not this is a good thing (see Table 9.5). However, there is little dispute about the issue among many regulators of boards (particularly in the United Kingdom, Canada, Australia and New Zealand); they all believe that the two positions should be separated, due to the inherent conflict of interest, *i.e.*, the CEO runs the company, the chair runs the board and the CEO is accountable *to* the board. And yet, despite all of this, none of the empirical evidence (see Chapter 5) supports definitively, even persuasively, that 1) having a separate non-executive chair enhances board effectiveness, and 2) having a non-executive chair enhances corporate financial performance.

The *Blue Ribbon Commission Report on Board Leadership*, of the National Institute of Directors, advocates "not one or two leaders, but a 'system of leadership.'"[5] The Report's Co-Chairs, Drs. Jay Lorsch and David Nadler, "view leadership as a complex issue. [Their] perspective is that the requirements for leadership in boards are changing, but that structural solutions alone do not help boards become more effective in their primary purpose of ensuring the long-term health of the enterprise on behalf of stakeholders, including shareholders."[6]

The data for this book support this Commission's position. The observations and information collected and analyzed suggest that it matters less whether the chair is formally executive, non-executive and/or holds the post of CEO, *i.e.*, the "separation of roles." Despite the inherent conflict, what matters more—indeed the most important conditions necessary to assure overall board effectiveness—are the independence of mind, competencies and behavioural characteristics of the person or persons holding the leadership positions.

CAN A CARETAKER-CHAIR BECOME A CONDUCTOR-CHAIR?

There exists skepticism about the ability of a Caretaker-Chair to *become* a Conductor-Chair. The fact is that weak chairs who do not know of their leadership flaws, or worse yet, know but do not want to change or improve their leadership capabilities, regardless of what their colleagues on the board think, clearly cannot be changed. However, if the board feels that the chair can change and the chair is amenable to change, it may be possible to make an incompetent chair into a competent one. With constructive suggestions for competency enhancement, better leadership techniques and the like, there is often ample room for improvement for those chairs who desire growth and development.

The assumption is often made by institutional shareholders, regulators, the media and the public that they cannot determine from outside the boardroom the leadership effectiveness of the chair of the board, *i.e.*, whether a particular board has a Conductor-Chair

---

5. The Report was released by the NACD (National Association of Corporate Directors), Washington, DC, October 2004. The Commission's Co-Chairs were Professor Jay W. Lorsch and Dr. David A. Nadler. See page 3 of the Report. The Report sets out sample position descriptions for the non-executive chair, CEO and lead director, and suggests that "leaders should be evaluated regularly." (page 5)

6. *Ibid.* at page 4.

or a Caretaker-Chair. This is not the case. With the proper questioning, it is possible to obtain a balanced view of the effectiveness of the chair. However, the right questions need to be asked in order to obtain the correct answers.

Basically those questions are:

1. Does a position description exist for the chair of the board? Is it disclosed to shareholders? If not, why not?

2. Is the chair of the board assessed on a regular basis by all directors on the fulfillment of the terms of this position description? If not, why not?

3. Do the results of this assessment inform whether or not the chair continues as chair, *i.e.*, is chair succession planning (including committee chairs) based on whether or not the chair fulfills the job effectively? This means that a poor assessment(s) would result in a chair stepping down as chair. The selection of the new chair should not necessarily be based on the most senior director, or the chair of a particular committee, but rather should be based on the person on the board (or an external candidate) who can most ably fulfill the position description, in the collective business judgment of the board; and lastly

4. Does the chair's remuneration reflect the responsibilities involved in effectively fulfilling the position description?

Table 9.5

Some Directors' Views on Splitting the Positions of Chair and Chief Executive Officer

"Board leadership is important, whether or not it's a non-executive chairman or CEO and chairman." (CEO)

"In addition, the board chairman assumes the formal responsibility of board governance—clear job description and duties, formal reviews,

Continued

criteria and needs for director . . . recruitment, and formal review of the CEO." (chair)

"The chair should be a separate position. . . . Absolute power corrupts." (director)

"I'm a big believer in a non-executive chairman. The problem if it's both is that the CEO is proposing and disposing. Sometimes you don't know when to go to the board. You're not hiding but managing the agenda. I don't want the blame. [The chair]'s a disinterested outsider as opposed to me. The most precious thing I have is the board's confidence." (CEO)

"A non-executive chair should be 1) either the subject area of an expert—me, for example—and therefore there's a huge danger in inappropriately intruding upon management, or 2) not be an expert and be at the control of the CEO. It's impossible to argue with the correctness of it. If you don't trust the CEO, get rid of him. A terrific chairman will not compensate for a charlatan CEO because he doesn't know enough. If, alternatively, he knows too much, this can be dangerous as well. In the end, there are different seasons and times and both kinds [of models] can and do work well." (chair and CEO)

"So far as the chair versus CEO is concerned, this is not an important question. It's theoretically legitimate but it's not a bridge to die on." (director)

"Chair versus CEO? You can have the opposites with both outstanding results. There are many different models of how to get things done successfully without following a script. It depends on the personalities, history and mix and you can't qualify this, so you need to leave something of discretion to the guys involved." (chair)

"A weakness is an outside chair who the CEO has put in. The board has lost control because of the weak chair and that weakness is 'chair-think.' With the lead director, you might have the same problem. You need a mechanism to deal with these problems directly." (chair)

"The chair should provide value-added advice, guidance and judgment for the CEO. If the chairman is working effectively, he is the one place where the CEO gets dispassionate advice. . . . So where do chairs go wrong? Frequently it's in high-visibility companies. The chair gets seduced. The chair begins to believe that they run the organization and want to speak on its behalf." (chair and CEO)

"I have no argument against splitting the roles [of chairman and CEO] constitutionally. None of the empirical evidence supports it though: a) you can manage it, and b) a non-executive chairman will not compensate for an incompetent CEO. Fabulous boards will not make for a fantastic company. But fantastic management with a weak board can generate strong financial performance. Shareholders live and die by the quality of management and the quality of the CEO. It's extremely dangerous if the board crosses that line." (chair and CEO)

"The chairman and CEO? Combined or split? We've done both at different times. It depends if both can work together or not. The board can decide according to the needs of the company and the board and type of personalities involved. [The non-executive chair] needs one week per board meeting." (corporate secretary)

"You need to tailor the situation [chair and CEO] to the people and personalities involved . . . the circumstances of the company and personalities of the company. In some situations, you might want both roles in one person or it doesn't matter." (CEO)

WHY WEAK CHAIRS ARE OUT AND STRONG CHAIRS MUST BE IN

The function of the chair is one of the most fully studied aspects of corporate governance. There is little in the findings of this study to dispute the general assessment of the important role of the chair found in previous studies, other than the view of many directors that the decision as to whether the positions of chair and CEO should be split is almost totally a question of context. Chairs must have leadership skills, the patience of Job and the sixth sense that leaders command in order to steer a board to effective decisions. It is a rare set of skills—not hard to identify, but difficult to find.

Throughout most of the twentieth century, the chairs of the boards of many (most) corporations were weak and ineffectual. And in companies which did reasonably well over time, where the roles of the chair and the chief executive officer were combined, the incumbent viewed the role of the chair as being somewhat subordinate to the role of the CEO.

Times have changed. For the many reasons outlined in this book, the role of the board of directors in the operation of a company is becoming much more significant, and with the increase in the role of the board comes a concomitant increase in the role of the chair. Indeed, a board cannot operate at its potential without an effective chair. Consequently, one of the critical tasks in searching for effective governance of a company is finding an effective chair.

The demand from regulators and shareholders for effective governance of corporations has grown remarkably. The experience with, and the effectiveness of, governance in the past is no longer acceptable as a suitable pattern for the future. One of the catalysts for this demand for change in corporate governance is greater understanding and acceptance of the following facts: a major condition for bringing about good corporate governance is recognition by effective, forward-looking boards that the choice of a person for the position of chair of the board is as critical as the choice of a chief executive officer.

"C-B-S-R"—How to Build a
Better Board

Corporate governance is not easy.

—Director

Corporate governance takes a ____ of amount of work, both for directors and management. It must be grounded in a strong, religious belief that it advances shareholder value. It should not be minimalist, or reactive, [but] proactive. Resources should be co-opted in a positive sense to be instruments of advancing corporate governance effectiveness, versus seeing corporate governance as the last pain in the ____ hurdle.

—Chair and CEO

Ever since the separation of ownership and control became a characteristic feature of the modern corporation, boards of directors have had two closely related but separate principal tasks. On the one hand, they are required, because of their duties to the corporation and its shareholders, to oversee the operations of the corporation in such a manner that the shareholders' investment in the enterprise is not only maintained but hopefully increased. On the other, they are expected to carefully monitor the activities of management to assure that the organization is operated in the best interests of the corporation, *i.e.*, the shareholders and the other stakeholders, and not the managers. These two goals are not in conflict, but over the years one

221

or the other seems to dominate thinking about corporate governance. In periods of irrational exuberance, emphasis is placed on the board's obligation to maximize shareholder value; in the aftermath of corporate failures, it quickly becomes the board's responsibility to monitor the activities of management more effectively.

It has long been the conventional wisdom that, if the structure of the board is appropriate (when "appropriate" is defined in terms of the number of outside directors, their degree of independence and the fact that the positions of chair and CEO are held by different persons) and effective accounting and reporting regulations are in place, the board should be able to fulfill these two duties. This is the premise upon which the selection of directors to boards and the enactment of codes and laws regulating corporations, arguably the most important economic entities in the nation, have been made for many decades.

The fact that corporate laws, codes and regulations have not always been adequate to prevent periodic failures among corporations is not necessarily a condemnation of their effectiveness—the situations might have been much worse if they did not exist. No regulations or rules can ever prevent fraudulent activity, nor should they be expected to do so. On balance, it is probable that regulations and codes have had some impact on improving the monitoring performance of boards of directors and on maintaining integrity in the capital markets, as the vast majority of boards of directors have followed the laws, rules and regulations to the best of their ability.

However, considerable evidence indicates that all the board structure rules and regulations that have been put in place, presumably to improve the monitoring capacities of boards of directors, have had little or no impact on the financial performance of corporations. And so, if it is true that form and structure have little or no impact on corporate performance, and yet achieving satisfactory rates of returns for the company is one of the major tasks of directors, how should boards be constructed so that, as well as performing monitoring activities effectively, they add value to the enterprise?

The answer is that no one knows for certain. However, analysis of the data collected for this book suggests that if boards are built around the three basic components that affect the manner in which boards makes decisions—1) the competency of directors, 2) the behavioural characteristics of directors (see Chapters 8 and 9), and 3) the strategy that the corporation is following—the decision-making processes of boards should be improved, and better decision-making should lead to better corporate financial performance.

Focusing on building boards to achieve high levels of corporate performance does not in any way minimize the important role that boards play in monitoring the activities of the enterprise. Indeed, the model designed to ensure that the corporation performs well, *i.e.*, there is a satisfactory rate of return for the shareholders, is also almost certain to ensure that the monitoring task is also done well. However, the opposite is not always true—effective monitoring may well take place by a board that is incapable of procuring adequate returns for the shareholders.

Responsible directors are interested in fulfilling both goals: monitoring the corporation effectively so that it is operated in the interests of all the stakeholders and earning a satisfactory rate of return for the shareholders. Fortunately, achieving both is not in any way in conflict. Adopting the model for building boards developed in this book may well be the most effective way of achieving both.

"C-B-S-R"—THE WAY TO BETTER BOARDS

Matching the competencies and behavioural characteristics of individual directors to the strategies followed by a company is the key to designing a better board. Following an effective director recruitment policy is the means of translating the design into reality.

Building a corporate board is a very complex task that may be divided into two major parts. First, there are certain characteristic features that all boards of directors should have. They should be made up of directors who collectively possess the specific competencies necessary to exercise sound judgment on the various issues that the company faces (the "C" in C-B-S-R), and who have the behavioural characteristics that lead to effective decision-making (the "B" in C-B-S-R).

Corporations are dynamic organizations that are always changing as the environment within which they operate changes.

Sometimes a change comes about because a company is proactive and implements a new idea to meet changing conditions, or sometimes a change is forced on a company, usually in the form of lost revenues or higher costs, because the management and directors did not recognize the impact that various forces outside of their direct control would have on its activities. Well-governed and well-managed organizations should have directors who are capable of recognizing and helping management to develop strategies for dealing with change (the "S" in C-B-S-R).

Because the business environment is always changing, boards are not "static" structures. The chair and members of a nominating committee, as members of the board, have the responsibility of approving the existing strategy of a firm and of constantly monitoring the manner in which the board is reacting to change. Consequently, as conditions and strategies change, the board members have the obligation of finding and recruiting directors whose competencies and behaviours can assist the board in dealing with new situations (the "R" in C-B-S-R).

Meeting and aligning all these varying needs—C: *competency*, B: *behaviour*, S: *strategy*, and R: *recruitment*—when building a board is somewhat like solving a simultaneous equation. This equation is unique for each corporate board because the competencies needed in a board vary from firm to firm, industry to industry and, to a considerable degree, depend on the strategies being followed by the firm. It may be relatively easy to find someone with the right competency and someone else with the appropriate behavioural characteristics. The challenge is to find someone with both. And the challenge is even greater when it is recognized that it is important to recommend for board appointment someone who can bring particular strengths to the implementation of the enterprise's strategy. Finding the three different appropriate characteristics in one person is not easy.

Needless to say, every chair of every nominating committee should search for functional directors, avoid like the plague dysfunctional director types and, of course, make every effort to replace non-performing directors with ones who perform.

ASSURING DIRECTOR COMPETENCE

A major condition for board success is the inclusion of directors with the competencies needed to assure the company can achieve its goals. Obviously, the competencies required by companies in different industries and at different stages in their development vary. For example, the range of competencies needed for a firm in the forest product industry is quite different from those for a firm in the financial services industry, which in turn differ from those for a company in retailing, or one in the high-tech sector. Moreover, no one director possesses all, or even most, of the full array of competencies necessary to meet the needs of a company. A director on the board of a pharmaceutical company may be exceptionally qualified in technology or science, but may not be financially literate, and one of his colleagues may know nothing about science but be a financial expert. In both cases, they are competent directors. The point is that the board, in its entirety, must have the range of required competencies, given the industry and strategic environment in which it operates, to deal with the various problems and opportunities that it faces in assuring the effective operation of the company.

The first step in determining that the board of directors collectively has the appropriate competencies to fulfill its responsibilities is the creation by the chair of the nominating committee, in consultation with the chair of the board and other directors, of a Director Competency Matrix Analysis. The Matrix (see Table 10.1 for four template samples, fictionalized characterizations of actual boards, modified and disguised to preserve confidentiality) simply outlines the competencies necessary for effectively understanding the factors leading to success or failure in the industry and the competencies of the directors currently serving on the board.

Such a Matrix is not difficult to create, although it must be developed with some degree of diplomacy. The competency of every existing director must be included and some directors may neither agree with the nature and degree of competency that they are assigned, nor agree with the competencies themselves. The process for competency identification and assessment, therefore, must be inclusive and constructive. If it is to be useful, it must include a candid assessment of each and every director.

While the board is always—implicitly or explicitly—assessing the competencies of the CEO, the point at which a Director Competency Matrix is being developed may be a good time, inasmuch as the CEO is a member of the board, to assure that a formal assessment of the CEO's competencies is made. Indeed, for competencies in which the CEO may not be particularly strong, the nominating committee can then ensure that a director or group of directors are brought on to the board who compensate for the CEO's deficiencies.

Identifying and recruiting directors with the appropriate competencies (the "C" in C-B-S-R) is not in any way meant to suggest that the board should micromanage the firm. Rather it is simply acknowledgement that no longer is it sufficient for a director simply to possess a generic competency such as "business judgment." Nor is it sufficient to have a competency assessment end at identifying certain directors as being "financially literate." To build a better board—a great board—a thorough assessment of director competencies must occur. Directors, to be effective, must bring to the board competency in areas that are of importance to that specific company with a specific strategy for doing well within the areas where they are competing. In short, creating a Director Competency Matrix Analysis is the first step in the development of an effective board.

> The required competencies are usually listed on the vertical axis and the current directors on the horizontal axis.

Table 10.1
Sample Director Competency Matrices for Four Industries

Director Competency Matrix for the Financial Services Industry

Competency	Director 1	Director 2	Director 3	Director 4	Director 5	Director 6	Director 7	Director 8	Director 9	Director 10	Director 11	Director 12
Financial Literacy												
Financial Expert												
Regulatory												
Technology												

Competency	Director 1	Director 2	Director 3	Director 4	Director 5	Director 6	Director 7	Director 8	Director 9	Director 10	Director 11	Director 12
Real Estate												
International												
Legal (privacy)												
Operating												
Risk Management												
Compliance, Controls												
Marketing, Consumer												
Strategic												
E-Commerce/Internet												
Compensation												
Human Resources												
Business												
Judgment												

Special (e.g., derivatives)

Director Competency Matrix for the Manufacturing Industry
(Pharmaceuticals)

Competency	Director 1	Director 2	Director 3	Director 4	Director 5	Director 6	Director 7	Director 8	Director 9	Director 10
Product Development										
Commercialization										
Chemistry/Biotechnology										
Technology										
Regulatory (approval process)										
Research (pure)										
Intellectual Property (patent)										
Operating										
Risk Management										
Legal (product liability)										
Research (applied)										
Strategic										
Consumer/Marketing										
Research and Development (general)										
Human Resources										
International (trade, generic drugs)										
Special (e.g., life cycle, compensation, etc.)										

Continued

Director Competency Matrix for the Natural Resources Industry
(Forest Products)

Competency	Director 1	Director 2	Director 3	Director 4	Director 5	Director 6	Director 7	Director 8	Director 9	Director 10
Heavy Industry										
Environmental										
Conservation										
Commodity/Cyclicality										
Corporate Finance										
International (markets)										
Manufacturing										
Engineering										
Operating (general or senior executive)										
Legal (product liability, risk)										
Financial Literacy										
Strategic (corporate)										
Consumer/ Marketing (integrated)										
Human Resources (compensation)										
Regulatory (tariffs, dumping)										
Special (e.g., acquisitions)										

Director Competency Matrix for the High-Technology Industry ("Dot-Com")

Competency	Director 1	Director 2	Director 3	Director 4	Director 5	Director 6	Director 7	Director 8
Governance								
Compensation (options)								
E-Commerce/Internet								
Taking Companies Public (e.g., IPOs)								
General Management (small, medium enterprise)								
Capital Access (e.g., angel, institutional investors)								
Industry (e.g., business-to-business)								
Privacy								
Strategic/Business Planning								
Financial Literacy (especially valuing IP)								
Productization of New Technology								
Senior Executive/Operating								

Competency	Director 1	Director 2	Director 3	Director 4	Director 5	Director 6	Director 7	Director 8
Public Co. Experience (*e.g.*, NASDAQ)								
Intellectual Property								
Marketing								
Special (*e.g.*, legal)								

Once the Director Competency Matrix Analysis is prepared, the gaps and mismatches between the board and the necessary competencies can be readily identified. With this information in hand, as the nominating committee searches for candidates for election to the board, it knows precisely the competencies for which it is looking, so candidates who may appear to be very good possibilities for appointment but who do not have the appropriate competencies can be quickly dropped.

When searching for new directors, the background information collected on prospective candidates must be more than name, age, address, education, current and past employment/accomplishments and area of professional interest, *e.g.*, a short bio. It must contain sufficient detail to permit the nominating committee to draw a precise conclusion as to how the candidates' competencies relate to the needs of the board. For example, the fact that a candidate may have had a very successful career as a chief executive officer of another organization may not mean that he or she has the particular competency needed for the board.

Moreover, the nominating committee must be careful, when searching for a candidate, that it does not use general phrases such as "CEO experience" as an acronym for leadership or executive experience. Not only is the CEO talent pool shrinking, as companies are restricting the number of boards they are permitting their CEOs to join, but using such a criterion has the effect of excluding from consideration direct reports to the CEO, many women and other non-CEO candidates who may be contemporary managers within large, complex organizations and possess the competencies that the board seeks. The nominating committee must have specific details in order to make a proper judgment about the competencies of a candidate.

DIRECTOR SEARCH FIRMS

In the process of searching for candidates, a nominating committee may decide to use the services of an outside director search firm. However, it is important to remember that it is a much more difficult task to assess the less tangible qualities of competency and director behaviour than it is simply to prepare a list of potential candidates on the basis of their general experience and their reputation in the community. Because of their knowledge of the board, individual directors, the company and the industry, directors from the board seeking new members may tease out this type of competency and behavioural information better than any outside service provider.

If a director search firm is used, the nominating committee must be strong and engaged in overseeing the criteria for the director search and, at the outset, require that the search firm, as part of its engagement, only identify candidates with the competencies and behaviours that the nominating committee wants. Because of their possible global contacts, reach and expertise, the search firm can assist in providing a wide pool of candidates, but the nominating committee members know the board—the search firm does not. The leadership driving the selection of candidates must come from the chair of the nominating committee.

In short, the recruitment process must be rigorous enough to give directors comfort that they have selected the right candidate(s) to fill the gap of competencies required for effective governance of the corporation, although he or she may not be known personally to a director on the board, or may not have a well-developed external profile.

ASSURING A BALANCE OF DIRECTOR BEHAVIOURAL TYPES

Attaining and maintaining the proper balance of director behavioural types is a necessary condition for developing, or continuing, a successful decision-making process on the board. Assuming that it is advantageous to have at least one of each of the functional director types on the board, in structuring a board the question arises as to what type of behavioural characteristics one should look for in the additional directors.

Obviously, to be certain that this goal is achieved, the chair of the nominating committee must have knowledge of the behavioural types within the current members of the board. As in the case for determining if the board has the proper competencies covered by the directors, the first step in assuring that the board has the proper mix of behavioural characteristics among its members is the construction of a simple Director Behaviour Matrix Analysis (see, *e.g.*, Table 10.2). Such an analysis indicates any missing types of director behavioural characteristics. The behavioural analysis must be sufficiently detailed to permit board members and candidates for board membership to be classified into one of the various behavioural types identified in Chapters 8 and 9.

It is more difficult for the nominating committee to create a Director Behaviour Matrix Analysis than it is to construct a Director Competency Matrix Analysis, simply because the chair of the nominating committee must classify current directors according to their various behavioural characteristics. In the process of doing so, it is more than likely that he or she will identify some dysfunctional directors who should be counselled off the board. However, this unpleasant difficulty should not stand in the way of the completion of the behaviour assessment process, as it is an essential part of the process of building a better board.

A Director Behaviour Matrix Analysis for a dysfunctional board, disguised and modified to preserve confidentiality, is provided in Table 10.2.

Table 10.2

A Director Behaviour Matrix Analysis for a Dysfunctional Board

Dysfunctional Board

Behaviour	Director 1	Director 2	Director 3	Director 4	Director 5	Director 6	Director 7	Director 8	Director 9
Conductor									
Change Agent									
Challenger									
Counsellor									
Consensus-Builder			✔						
Caretaker	✔								
Controller		✔							
Critic						✔			
Cheerleader					✔			✔	✔
Conformist				✔			✔		

It is especially important that the director selection process be thorough. It must be rigorous enough to comfort directors that they have selected the "right" candidate to fill the behaviour gap, despite the fact that this candidate may not be known personally to anyone on the board. And it should be sufficiently detailed so that, after thoughtful questioning of the candidate-director about the way he or she behaved in different scenarios, the nominating committee is able to classify the person as a Change Agent, Consensus-Builder, Counsellor, Challenger or Conductor (if the search is for someone to fill the position as chair). A number of sample questions that may be used in recruiting the five functional director types and in identifying the dysfunctional director types is provided in Chapter 8.

LINKING DIRECTOR COMPETENCY AND BEHAVIOUR

The Director Competency Matrix and Director Behaviour Matrix Analyses both are designed to determine the type or types of directors that are missing from a particular board, based on the interplay between the two Matrices. The goal of the nominating committee is to find candidates who have both the competencies needed to enable the board to make the judgments appropriate to fulfill the company's goals and the behavioural characteristics that will enable the board to operate as an effective decision-making body.

A nominating committee may find, for example, that it needs a Challenger with financial literacy or a technical background, or a Change Agent with a marketing or consumer background, or a Consensus-Builder with strong global contacts. Finding someone with the required combination of behaviour and competency can be a very long and difficult task.

Figure 10.1 (to follow), modified to preserve confidentiality and based on an actual board of directors, is provided to illustrate the behavioural types of five directors on a particular board—a Challenger, a Change Agent, a Consensus-Builder, a Conductor-Chair and a Cheerleader—and their different competencies. This board, for historical reasons, will probably never have only functional directors, but will be a hybrid, always containing one or more dysfunctional directors. The goal, of course, is always to have only functional directors who have all the required competencies. The fictionalized board in Figure 10.1 is made up of functional directors who collectively meet all the requirements of C-B-S-R. The board in Table 10.2 consists of dysfunctional director behaviour types (the "B" portion of C-B-S-R) and lacks directors with the appropriate competencies, therefore failing both the "B" and "C" portion of C-B-S-R.

The Conductor-Chair-CEO of the board in Figure 10.1 came to the board with a very important and complex strategy that he wanted to execute. He was an exceedingly able chair who listened and who could effectively manage dissent and lead the board to effective decisions.

During an executive session with only the Conductor-Chair-CEO and the board, *i.e.*, no other officers were present, a Challenger-Director stated rather strongly that he did not agree with the CEO's proposed execution of the strategy. Indeed, he argued, based on his experience and his competencies (for which he had been originally recruited to the board), that the CEO would be making a "huge mistake" proceeding in the manner that he outlined to the board.

In the second or two of awkward silence that followed the Challenger-Director's comment, a Controller-CEO—in combination with a

---

Continued

Caretaker-Chair in particular—would have tactfully but skilfully marginalized and managed that Challenger-Director's dissent, making it the main issue before the board.

In this instance, however, the Conductor-Chair-CEO was silent and listened. He did so because he knew from a knowledge of the behavioural characteristics of the directors (as shown in Figure 10.1) that the Challenger-Director was dissenting as an individual, *i.e.*, that he lacked the collective, team skills that a Change Agent or Consensus-Builder had. He therefore was challenging on his own and might even be slightly marginalizing himself because his dissent was so individually centered.

In the seconds that followed the Challenger-Director's concern, a Change Agent-Director spoke up, supporting, on the basis of his competency for which he had been specially recruited, the Challenger-Director's point, but in such a way as to invite other Directors to offer their views. At the same time, however, the Change-Agent-Director also strongly disapproved of the way in which the CEO proposed to execute the strategy, and said so, but "less forcefully than [the Challenger-Director]." Indeed, the Change Agent-Director might never have spoken up had the Challenger-Director not initiated dissent to begin with.

There now existed a split board, and another awkward but longer silence followed. Management had advanced a strategy, with the board's approval, but now two Directors had strong reservations about its execution. The two Directors—a Challenger and a Change Agent—had voiced strong dissent over the CEO's proposed program, based on their individual competencies, which, for the topic under discussion, were greater than the CEO's.

This board had functional Directors sitting in key positions—Directors recruited for their specific competencies and behavioural characteristics, who now became involved in the decision-making process. For example, by using humour, persuasion and conflict resolution, the Consensus-Builder-Director was able to skillfully and diplomatically bridge the gap between where the Challenger and Change Agent-Directors were strategically, where the Conductor-Chair-CEO was originally, and where the Consensus-Director proposed that the board as a whole should be. In the dialogue that followed, with leadership from the Conductor-Chair-CEO, the board was able to forge a collective position that addressed the Challenger and Change-Agent's dissent, which resulted in a markedly different approach to the implementation of the strategy than the CEO had originally proposed at the outset of the board meeting. A Counsellor-Director offered to assist the CEO in working with other Directors, contacts and experts outside the company to the extent necessary. The Counsellor-Director had been recruited to the board because he had the skills to work as an individual through consensus-building and the forging of alliances.

Neither the Consensus-Builder nor the Counsellor-Director on this board possessed the specific competencies that the Challenger and Change-Agent-Directors had, but they did not need to. The board had these competencies covered off within functional director behaviours—it had undertaken a Competency and Behavioural Matrix Analysis—that ensured these competencies would be exercised effectively and precisely when they were needed, which was now.

An important point in this fictionalized boardroom situation is that, ultimately, the amended strategy was quite successful and shareholders reaped the rewards of C-B-S-R. This is precisely why it has been, and is, so difficult to measure a causal link between corporate governance and corporate financial performance using metrics such as board size, the differentiation between chair and CEO, having a majority of independent directors, board member age, equity, attendence, *etc.* Given the above example, these types of structural criteria do not measure what really matters for board effectiveness, namely the competencies and behaviours of the directors sitting at the table, how these collective skills play out in real time, how the strategy of the company is shaped as a result, and how the directors with necessary competencies and behaviours are recruited onto and off the board—in short, C-B-S-R. Not only are these types of factors difficult to measure, but they are nearly impenetrable to researchers outside of boardrooms. But these variables matter, and perhaps matter greatly. They may hold the key to unlocking the relationship between corporate governance and corporate financial performance.

Figure 10.1

Linking Director Competency and Behaviour

An Effective Board and an Example of Functional and Dysfunctional
Directors

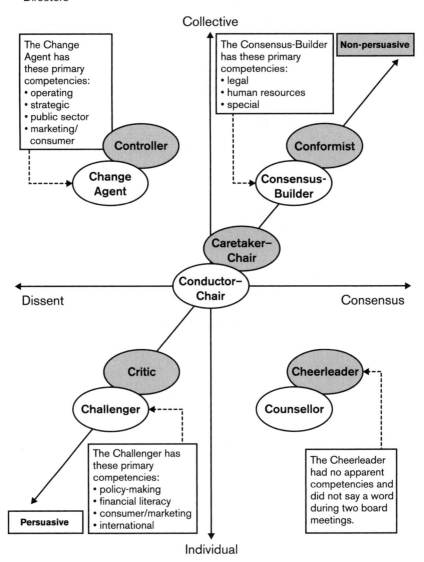

ALIGNING DIRECTOR COMPETENCIES, DIRECTOR BEHAVIOURAL CHARACTERISTICS AND CORPORATE STRATEGY

Corporations are dynamic. They are, or should be, constantly changing as the environment within which they operate changes. Different conditions require different business strategies, and one of the major tasks of the contemporary board of directors is to be involved in setting (or at least in providing strong input into), and approving of, the firm's business plans and strategy. In the final analysis, no firm, whether it articulates it or not, operates without some type of strategy, and the factors underlying its construction usually relate to a company's size and function, its long- and short-term goals, its history and its hoped-for future.

The board of a company with a controlling shareholder whose main objective in life is to maintain the status quo should be, and probably will be, made up of directors with behavioural characteristics different from those of the board of a new start-up company that has as its goal anything but the status quo. Similarly, the behavioural characteristics of additions to a board of a company that has a strategy of rapid acquisitions in many countries should be different from those of an organization that has decided to divest many of its divisions and settle back into a leisurely existence. When creating a board, the realities of the strategic environment in which the corporation is operating must never be neglected.

Consequently, when adding or retiring directors, chairs of nominating committees should know the current and future strategies of the firm and recommend appointment to the board of someone who is capable of evaluating and supporting, or on occasion opposing, the strategies presented to the board. Examples of the relationship between various director behavioural types and different strategies are illustrated in Figure 10.2 that follows. The competencies possessed by the various director types are not shown in this figure, as they will be specific to the company and industry (see Table 10.1 and Figure 10.1).

In many ways, selecting a new director in relation to the strategy of the firm is one of the most difficult tasks of a nominating committee. The reality is that the existing board, upon management's recommendation, has either implicitly or explicitly approved the strategy that the company is following. However, it may well be that certain members of the board feel that a new strategy is needed, but they are neither precisely sure what it should be nor are they willing (as a condition of changing the strategy) to replace the CEO, who may be doing an effective job in most areas of his or her responsibility. Nevertheless, if the competencies and the behavioural characteristics of the board members are appropriate, it is a decided plus when choosing a new director to add someone who supports either maintaining the existing strategy of the organization, or of changing it if that is the goal of the board.

Figure 10.2, based on actual boards, situations and experiences examined for this study, illustrates relationships between the behavioural types of individual directors and corporate strategies for which certain behaviours may be more or less suitable than others. What is being proposed here is that, depending on the degree of strategic change (difficult or less difficult) and the time frame (long-term or short-term), certain director behavioural types and competencies are better-suited for certain strategies. For example, a Consensus-Builder is best suited for long-term, less difficult strategic change (*e.g.*, cooperative strategies); a Counsellor for those strategies involving personal contact and negotiation (*e.g.*, short-term, less difficult strategic change); a Challenger for challenging the status quo (*e.g.*, initiating short-term, difficult strategic change); and a Change Agent for dealing with complex, longer-term strategic change.

If the directors' competencies and behaviours collectively are carefully aligned with the company's strategy, *i.e.*, "C-B-S," the company should perform well. It is through this process of working with management in the formation and adoption of a strategic plan, which in turn reflects the specific competencies and behavioural characteristics of the individual directors, that the board makes its greatest contribution to adding value for the shareholders.

Figure 10.2

Linking Director Competency and Behaviours to the Strategy of a Company

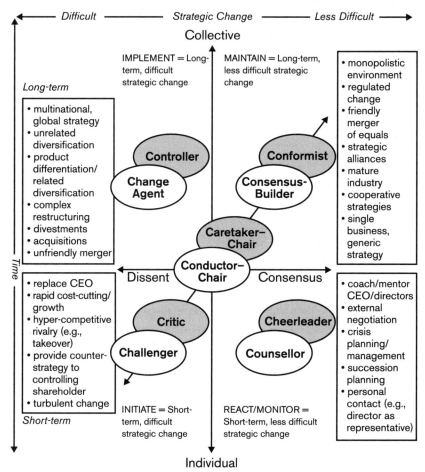

C-B-S-R: LINKING DIRECTOR COMPETENCY, BEHAVIOURAL CHARACTERISTICS AND CORPORATE STRATEGY WITH RECRUITING THE RIGHT DIRECTORS

Choosing directors on the basis of their competencies and behavioural characteristics clearly is more difficult than recruiting them on the basis of how well they are known by members of the board or the public. Interviews with prospective directors must be complete and well-planned. They must be shaped to elicit whether or not the candidate does in fact have the skills, training and experience, as well as the basic behavioural characteristics, required of all functional directors. For example, emphasis in interviewing a candidate for the position of a Consensus-Builder should focus on finding examples of when and how the director was successful in bridging the gap between dissenting groups in relatively difficult situations. On the other hand, when looking for a director with the skills of a Change Agent, one seeks examples of how the director in the past promoted and handled significant issues of complex change. Such questions should be carefully shaped before any interviews are undertaken, and should, of course, always be supplemental to the basic question of whether or not the candidate has the behavioural characteristics that ensure he or she is a functional director. Obviously, questions should be designed to meet the particular needs of the company, but they should not be changed so much that they stray from the underlying task of identifying to the fullest extent possible, what the probable behaviour of the candidate would be as a member of the board of directors. Needless to say, selecting directors in such a fashion takes more time than asking a friend, colleague or acquaintance to join the board.

Candidates for possible selection to a board do not appear to show much resistance to a careful selection process. Getting complete information on potential candidates is not as difficult as it may sound. It does not require the services of a psychologist or psychiatrist—a few in-depth, detailed conversations with a person's current and former colleagues, who are usually more than willing to chat on a confidential basis about their acquaintences or friends, makes classification according to a recognition of individual competencies and behavioural types relatively easy. Interestingly, while many directors interviewed objected considerably to "specific evaluation" of performance of individual directors and boards in general, they were only slightly reluctant to discuss in considerable detail the manner in which they perceived their duties and the way in which they and their fellow directors carried them out.

C-B-S-R IN PRACTICE

The importance of having a board of directors with the appropriate competencies and the behavioural characteristics aligned with the strategy of the corporation cannot be overestimated, as the following examples (based on fictionalized characterizations of actual situations, appropriately disguised and modified to preserve confidentiality) show.

- A high-growth company in the high-technology sector with a Controller-CEO and Caretaker-Chair, and populated by Consensus-Builder, Conformist and Cheerleader directors, embarked at the CEO's urging on a strategy of rapid expansion through acquisitions. The board lacked a Challenger, Critic or Change Agent, and so the strategy was never closely analyzed. Soon, financial difficulties began to appear as the strategy failed. Very few, if any, of the directors had the required competencies necessary to be on the board of this company, and eventually the company went into bankruptcy.
- The Challenger and Critic on a board lacked the specific but necessary competency that the Controller-CEO also did not possess but for reasons of pride thought he did. Thus, unbridled, the Controller-CEO took the wrong strategic approach, to the detriment of the company. Those directors who possessed the competencies to mount a challenge to the CEO were on the consensus side of the behavioural grid, as shown in in Figure 10.2 (Consensus-Builder, Conformist and Cheerleader). The strategy failed and the CEO was eventually replaced. The board had not acted when it should have.
- A company in a natural resources industry, whose board consisted of a Caretaker-Chair and Conformist, Cheerleader and Consensus-Builder directors, needed to rapidly cut costs and divest of some of its divisions. The only dissenting directors were Critics, and there was infighting among them. One Critic resigned and a Challenger and Change Agent with the requisite competencies were then recruited onto the board. The downsizing began and the board began to oversee the CEO in making the necessary

changes. The board is still dysfunctional because it is being led by a Caretaker-Chair and the Critics lack the capacity to become Challengers. The Caretaker-Chair should be replaced by a Conductor-Chair.

- A company in the manufacturing industry, with a Controller-Shareholder serving as chair and CEO, adopted a strategy of expansion. The majority of directors were Cheerleaders, Conformists or Consensus-Builders. There were no Challengers or Change Agents on the board, so the strategy was never effectively questioned. Since the board provided no checks and balances for the proper examination of the strategy, the strategy went ahead and the company failed. If a Challenger with the appropriate competencies had been on the board, the company might well have been saved. The board did not act when it should have.

- A company was moving from a monopolistic strategic environment to one that was becoming more competitive. It had a Caretaker-Chair and a Change Agent CEO, but lacked both another Change Agent to cope with the complexity of the change and a Counsellor to advise the CEO. Other directors were Cheerleaders, Critics and Challengers. The Critics and Challengers did not have the requisite competencies to deal with the strategic situation. Competency and Behaviour Matrix Analyses were conducted; the two Cheerleaders were counselled off the board and one Critic resigned. The Caretaker-Chair was replaced with a Conductor-Chair. A Change Agent with specific operating experience was brought onto the board, as was a Counsellor to mentor the CEO. The company's financial performance is improving.

WHAT DOES IT ALL MEAN?

Since the time public corporations became a dominant force in the economy, problems in corporate performance were deemed to be capable of being solved by specifying the structure of their governing body—the board of directors. And yet board structure in and by itself appears to have little impact on board performance. No one knows *for certain* what leads to outstanding corporate performance, but in this book it is speculated that it is related to the manner in which boards operate—the way they makes decisions. Consequently, if corporate performance is to be improved, corporate chairs, chairs of nominating committees and, if necessary, regulators must accept that sound corporate governance, that is, governance that enhances corporate performance, is related to the competencies and behavioural characteristics of members of the board and how they relate to corporate strategies. While there is no definitive evidence as yet proving there is a link between corporate governance and corporate performance, those who believe that there is (including the overwhelming number of active directors interviewed for this book) should take as their number one task making certain that the board of directors of their company meets C-B-S-R standards.

The traditional approach to corporate governance has proven to be inadequate. The slight evidence that is available indicates that the structure and form of boards of directors simply don't make a meaningful difference in corporate performance, but the way that boards make decisions may do so. Assuring that the proper forces are in play to optimize decision-making in the boardroom should be the goal of everyone interested in improving corporate governance. Somewhere in C-B-S-R—competency, behaviour, strategy and recruitment, and their relationships—may be found the elusive factors linking corporate governance to corporate performance. Focusing on assuring that these factors are considered when boards are created or changed may well lead to the high levels of corporate governance that investors are seeking.

CHAPTER 11

THE COMING REVOLUTION IN CORPORATE GOVERNANCE

It's not only about where you have been but where you're going.

—Director

One of the great paradoxes of the twentieth century is that while enormous progress was made in understanding how economies in general operate[1] and in improving the management of corporations, relatively little was learned about the way in which the people who are by law responsible for the oversight of the corporations, upon which so much of prosperity is based, actually made their decisions. The fifty years between 1940 and 1990 was a period of drought in the study of the governance of corporations. Indeed, the term "corporate governance" itself was not widely used until the mid-1980s.[2] In spite of the importance of good governance for assuring the attraction of capital to the corporate sector through fair and well-functioning markets, there was little in-depth analysis of precisely how boards of directors undertook "the governing of enterprises."

Again, paradoxically, although boards were seldom studied and generally dismissed as relatively ineffective, whenever problems arose within the corporate sector, much of the blame for the difficulties was directed towards the manner in which corporations were

---

1. See, for example, J. M. Keynes, *The General Theory of Employment, Interest and Money* (London: Macmillan, 1936). It is difficult to believe that in the 1930s, there were not even reliable figures on the gross national product of countries, and there was no understanding of the forces leading to full employment and price stability.
2. Robert Tricker, *The Pocket Director.*

245

governed—at boards of directors. Every recession, let alone depression, saw the formation of commissions and study groups charged with the responsibility of making recommendations for improvement in corporate governance.[3] "Where were the directors?" became the rallying call for reform, even though for half a century there was a general view that governance did not matter, that directors were no more than expensive accoutrements required by law who were more like impediments than assistants in assuring the efficient operation of enterprises.

In spite of this irony, when crises did develop and attention was paid to boards, as was the case in the late 1990s, most of the rules and regulations that were enacted with the intention of making boards operate more effectively had to do with board structure. As a result, the number of outside directors on boards was increased; greater transparency about the operations of corporations was achieved;[4] more corporations separated the positions of CEO and chair; and, in general, a great deal more attention was paid by directors, regulators, academics, managers and the media to matters of corporate governance.

Because of the interest generated about boards and the plethora of new regulations put in place since the 1990s, a general view evolved that "boards of directors" were fulfilling their duties more effectively. There was really no evidence to support such a conclusion, but it was widely believed that the pressure from institutional investors, the increase in threats of litigation, the need on the part of management for good advice in more competitive and global markets, the large role played by directors in the unfriendly takeovers movement of the early part of the decade, and particularly new regulations were all bringing about more effective operations of boards of directors.[5]

It was, however, confidence misplaced. As the experience of the early years of the twenty-first century so clearly showed, the

---

3. For an account of the superficiality of one such report, see D. H. Thain, "The TSE Corporate Governance Report: Disappointing."

4. This was done primarily by requiring more extensive reporting to regulatory agencies about the financial activities of corporations and to shareholders about executive compensation.

5. James Gillies, *Boardroom Renaissance*, 19–24.

effectiveness of boards and individual directors has not improved substantially. Despite all the optimistic expectations, there was no general revolution in corporate governance. All the new rules and regulations had, at best, only marginal impact on board perform-ance. The reason that the results (from what appeared to be almost heroic action on the part of regulators, trading exchanges and commissions) were so modest is that board structure in and by itself does not appear to have much impact on the performance of boards. An independent board structure, as it is currently conceptualized, may be a necessary—but certainly not a sufficient—condition for board effectiveness, or for that matter, even individual director effectiveness.

In short, the belief that regulations and recommendations about board structure, transparency, *et al.*, in and by themselves will ensure board effectiveness, and by extension, better financial performance of corporations could well be wrong; indeed, the slight evidence that is available suggests that it is.[6] Directors, while perhaps being something more than "parsley on fish—decorative but useless", are in many instances still far from being selected in such a manner that they col-lectively, as a board, are having a major impact on the way in which corporations are being governed.[7] While the significance of certain specific changes in corporate governance that occurred in the 1990s and the early years of the twenty-first century may be debated, what is not debatable is that no revolution in corporate governance took place during those years. Some minor changes, but no revolution.

WHAT BOARDS REALLY DO
The principal work of a board of directors is to make decisions. Some are trivial—deciding when the next board meeting will be held, the date of the annual meeting, and so on. But, most issues that the board spends (or should spend) a good deal of time on are very important—decisions about strategy, about financing, about removing or hiring a CEO, about acquisitions and divestitures, about writing down the value of a subsidiary. Indeed, they are so

6. See Chapter 5.
7. See Chapter 3.

important that how the board decides many of them is critical to the success or failure of the enterprise.

Given the fact that boards are made up of small groups of individuals, a critical factor in their decision-making is the interrelationship among and between directors, which in turn is largely based on the behavioural characteristics of individual directors. As many directors pointed out in the course of this study, it is individuals, not corporations, who make decisions. Indeed, board dynamics may be the single most important factor in determining the effectiveness of the board in carrying out its duties of overseeing management in the best interests of the corporation. And the success of these dynamics, that is, the effectiveness of the board in making decisions, is clearly influenced by the behavioural characteristics of the directors that make up the board.

From observation of boards in action and interviews with directors, it has been possible to develop a new classification scheme for directors that goes well beyond the traditional method of classification. Ten director types have been identified. Five functional director types—Conductor-Chairs, Change Agents, Consensus-Builders, Counsellors and Challengers—are associated with effective boards, and five—Caretaker-Chairs, Controllers, Conformists, Cheerleaders and Critics—are associated with dysfunctional ones. It is hypothesized that for a board to have efficient board process and effective decision-making, it needs to have a full complement of all five functional director behavioural types.

However, the appropriate mix of functional director types is not in itself a guarantee that a corporation will be governed effectively, when "effective" is defined as making decisions that contribute directly to the success of the enterprise. The board must also include directors with the specific and necessary competencies to deal with the issues that the company faces, in the industry and environment in which the company is lodged, and with the strategies that the firm is pursuing, now and into the future. Consequently, if the goal of the board is to be effective, the selection of directors must be based on how the competencies and individual behavioural patterns of directors are aligned with the company, its environment and its strategy. This is, of course, a far cry from the selection of directors on the basis of who current directors might know or the choice of someone because he or she has a high public profile.

Obviously, if an effective board is to be created, the recruitment process of new directors must be sufficiently rigorous to give directors, nominating committees and director search firms confidence that they have selected the proper candidates, despite the fact that directors might not personally know a particular candidate selected.

Finally, in order to create the best of all possible boards, non-performing directors who refuse to perform, who are incapable of performing, who refuse to augment their competencies or behave in inappropriate ways, given the strategy of the corporation, must, in the interest of good corporate governance and fairness to their colleagues, be asked to step down. The inability or unwillingness of boards, including chairs of the boards and chairs of governance and nominating committees, to rid themselves of dysfunctional members is as serious an issue in corporate governance as is the importance of selecting functional new directors. Counselling non- or under-performing directors off the board is a major task that many directors believe is not being adequately completed.

LEADING THE EFFECTIVE BOARD

An effective board must have, in addition to effective directors, solid leadership. There is no doubt that the leadership skills of the chair of the board are the most important factor in assuring effective board processes and wise decision-making, and in determining the overall effectiveness of the board of directors. Obviously, the selection of the chair is critical. It should not be based on seniority of a director or tenure on the board or ties to management or a high percentage of share ownership, but rather on the independence of mind, competencies, knowledge of the business and leadership effectiveness. The chair should be responsible for fulfilling the duties outlined in the position description and be assessed by fellow directors on the manner in which he or she does so.

Needless to say, the skills necessary for fulfilling the position calls for a Conductor—a person who can lead the setting of the agenda, run the meetings effectively, moderate discussion, manage dissent, work towards consensus, communicate persuasively with colleagues and management, and, most importantly, set the tone and culture for effective corporate governance. Normally these paragons of virtue are individuals who possess the traits of Consensus-Builders, Counsellors, Change Agents and/or Challengers.

Whether the chair is also CEO is less relevant to the effectiveness of the board than is often thought. An executive chair is not necessarily ineffective and a non-executive chair is not necessarily effective. What matters is not the separation of the positions but the demonstrated independence, competencies and the behavioural characteristics of the person or persons who hold them.

C-B-S-R: THE ACRONYM FOR THE EFFECTIVE BOARD

The acronym for building effective boards might well be "C-B-S-R"—the identification of directors with the mix of competencies and behavioural patterns that match the strategy of the firm and then the lively pursuit and recruitment of board members who meet these requirements.

A change from structure-based to competency- and behaviour-based boards of directors will bring about a revolution in corporate governance. The dimensions of the revolution are awesome. It will mean that the era of "directors are like parsley on fish—decorative but useless" will be over. It will lead to no less than a total rethinking of the concept of appropriate corporate governance—from emphasis on form and structure to emphasis on performance and results. It will mean that effective governance will be as much about putting in place strategies and policies that earn satisfactory returns to shareholders as it is about monitoring the activities of the management of the enterprise to conserve or maintain shareholders' wealth. It will mean that the role of the effective board of directors is neither more nor less significant during a crisis than it is at any other time, and it also will mean that the historic role of the board of directors as an active, dynamic representative of the shareholders will be resurrected.

Moreover:

1. It will mark the beginning of the era of penetrating and effective board and director assessments. Effective boards cannot be created without the full knowledge of the behavioural characteristics and competencies of existing board members. Consequently, corporations that wish to have effective boards will develop programs of board and director performance assessments.

2. It will mark the end of the era when casual acquaintance and cronyism is the chief criterion for selection to a board. Directors will be chosen very carefully and specifically for their behavioural characteristics and competencies. No longer will being a member of "the old boy network" be a sufficient criterion for board membership.

3. It will end the practice of retaining ineffective and dysfunctional directors on boards until retirement age simply because it is inconvenient to remove them.

4. It will mean the power that boards have in law will become power in fact. Directors will be chosen for their competencies to contribute to the major functions of the board—monitoring the activities of the corporation in the interests of the stakeholders and contributing to the creation of shareholders' wealth.

5. It will lead to more effective board practices. Directors elected for their specific competency and behavioural characteristics will not tolerate inefficient board operations. Because of their competencies, such directors will demand effective continuing education and orientation programs to the company as they may be cited individually for lack of performance in their areas of competency. They will demand proper board information and effective board mechanics and communications. Directors will make greater use of consultants, educators and advisers. They will know what they need to know in order to fulfill properly their

obligations and will insist that they have access to the best advice available and all the information they deem necessary to make informed decisions. Because of their competencies, they will know what that information is.

6. It will increase the accountability of individual directors to fellow directors and shareholders. Members of various committees of the board will be held more responsible for the activities of the committee, since they are deemed to have the competency to serve on that committee. For example, members of the Audit Committee will have to take more direct responsibility for any mistakes in the financial statements. They cannot hide behind the excuse that their auditors and financial officers were incompetent: *they* were elected to their position presumably because of *their* competence to judge the competence of the auditors and financial officers. Members of the Compensation Committee will have to be competent enough to judge and oversee pay and performance, and ensure that the link between the two is made. Members of the Risk Management Committee will have to have a sound knowledge and understanding of the principal risks to which the company is exposed, and ensure that management has appropriate standards, practices and policies to mitigate against these risks.

7. It will increase the general level of accountability of boards of directors to shareholders. A board specifically elected because of its members' competencies and behavioural characteristics that does not deliver acceptable rates of return to its shareholders will have to explain the reasons for its failure. With greater public disclosure and scrutiny on the process by which boards identify new candidates for board nomination—including the assessment of competencies and behavioural skills of current and prospective directors—shareholders will have greater information upon which to assess the effectiveness of boards and individual directors.

8. It will lead to many more elections of individual directors, rather than slates of directors. Shareholders will know the competency

for which and why a particular director is being nominated. If it is clear that he or she does not have the competency or some other characteristic that is essential for the success of the corporation, shareholders will be inclined to vote against election or re-election.

9. It will lead, because of increasing demands on individual directors, to the growth of a core of professional directors, *i.e.*, people whose major source of employment is serving on boards. Conversely, it will lead to a decline in the number of boards that fully-employed executives will join.

10. It will lead regulators to focus attention on competency and behavioural characteristics of directors when developing policies for corporate governance.[8]

11. It will end the view that certain shareholders, such as institutional investors, should, because of their holdings, automatically have a position on the board.

Most of all it moves the evaluation of effective corporate governance from the static and negative concept of form to the dynamic and positive belief that governance must be evaluated in terms of results.

THE HARBINGERS FOR CHANGE

Will there be a major shift from structure-based boards to performance-based ones? Or is the situation very much as it was in the 1990s, when there was great optimism for reform because of the growth in importance of the institutional investor, the increase in litigation, *etc.*, and yet nothing much really happened? In spite of the spurt of activity with respect to corporate governance as demonstrated by the Sarbanes-Oxley legislation in the United States and the implementation of rules and regulations for listing on exchanges

---

8. This has been done by the Ontario Securities Commission in its proposed policy. See, *e.g.*, Step One and Step Two in section 12 of the "Proposed Multilateral Policy 58-201: Effective Corporate Governance," January 16 and October 29, 2004, on which Dr. Lablanc has advised.

and reporting to governing agencies, will the results be the same as they were in the 1990s? Will anything happen?

There is no question that there are many directors on many boards who believe that they need to change—not because regulators or shareholders or anyone else is telling them that they must, but rather because with the increasing complexity of business they know that under current circumstances they cannot adequately fulfill their duties. The one theme that was constant from interviews and from observing boards in action was that directors are deeply concerned with the ineffectiveness of many of the boards with which they are associated. Even directors on boards of companies with acceptable rates of return for their shareholders and no signs of serious legal or other problems indicate a concern that their boards are not doing as good a job as they intuitively believe they should.

The scandals of the corporate world in the first few years of the twenty-first century have created, within corporations themselves, a climate for change. The problem for many directors and board members is that while they believe there is a need for change if they are to fulfill all their obligations, both legal and practical, they have little general knowledge about what the change should be.

The reason that intuitive feelings on the part of board members have created so much of the climate for change is that, currently, boards are just at the forefront of undertaking a critical self-examination of themselves as boards and as individual directors; so they do not yet know for certain how effective they are. However, the good news for those interested in building better boards is that the number of boards willing to undertake such assessments is growing. So, the first reason to be optimistic that change will come is that thoughtful directors want it.

Second, since the 1990s, there has been a great increase in interest in the concept of corporate governance. Once a forgotten part of the operations of a business, it has now become relatively central. As a result, in response to growing concerns of shareholders and regulators about board activities, there has been considerable change in board practices. More and more boards are writing position descriptions for the board—for directors, the chair and committee chairs. Many also are not only developing board and committee charters, criteria for director effectiveness, and descriptions of the board's role in strategic planning and in setting executive compensation philosophy and levels, but they are publishing them and holding directors accountable for achieving them.

Third, directors are increasingly realizing that, as well as the fiduciary duty to the corporation and its shareholders, they also have a moral as well as a practical obligation to their stakeholders to operate the company in a legal and ethically responsible manner, and they have concluded that the best way of fulfilling that obligation is through full and complete disclosure of their activities.

Fourth, increased disclosure has had the result of increasing shareholder activism, and vice-versa. Both of these activities provide ammunition to those who believe that change is necessary, and is, therefore, a positive step in exerting pressure on boards and regulators to change.[9]

Fifth, and very importantly, the great interest in corporate governance generated by the failures in the early 2000s has generated considerable interest in director education. Many directors, when they join a board, have very little knowledge about the industry and the business in which the corporation is involved and even less about the legal, financial and regulatory environment in which it operates. There is no question that this lack of knowledge about such things as risk management, corporate law, responsibilities of directors, how to undertake CEO assessments, how to ask effective questions, *etc.*, makes it almost impossible for a director initially to make a significant contribution to discussion of many important issues.

However, the situation is changing. Director educational programs are growing in number, and some types of director certification, based on examination and experience, have developed in a number of jurisdictions. And there is no question that the increase in formal education, and the possible requirement of some type of educational qualification for membership on a board, will hasten the movement for change in the manner in which directors are selected.

---

9. See, for example, the activities of the Canadian Coalition for Good Governance in Canada and CalPERS in the United States.

Sixth, directors are being paid more. Consequently, they are expected to spend more time and be more effective. Higher pay brings pressure for better performance.

For all these reasons, there is a climate for change. Consequently, it is possible to be optimistic that there is beginning to be and will continue to be a steady movement from structure-based to competency- and behaviour-based boards.

REGULATIONS WILL NOT BE SUFFICIENT

Searching for and promoting a greater understanding of how boards make decisions and the factors that lead to board and director effectiveness does not imply the imposition of more rules and regulations. Rather, it should lead to fewer. As chairs of nominating committees seek directors not on the basis of their external profiles and relationship to existing board members, but instead on the basis of competence, behavioural characteristics and their fit with the strategic direction of the firm, the need for specific rules should decline. The role of the regulator should move much more towards research on the relationship of corporate governance to corporate performance—on finding the issues that really matter in governance—and to providing information to organizations on how to deal with them. Indeed, moving away from structure-based boards would be a major step in reducing the need for specific, stultifying rule-making. Moving towards competency- and behavioural-based boards would encourage the risk-taking and entrepreneurship that are part of the essence of capitalism. As the change takes place, regulators will be in a position once again to do what they were intended to do in the first place: make certain that there is a level playing field for all.

However, old habits die hard. Despite the evidence to the contrary, as legislation and regulations such as the Sarbanes-Oxley Act and the New York Stock Exchange governance guidelines in the United States so clearly show, regulations still appear to be focused on structure and form, although there is some reason to believe that Canadian regulators are seeing the need to change. Indeed, so many more requirements for reporting various actions of officers and directors have been and are being put in place that a strong reaction will undoubtedly develop against more regulation. It can be argued that many of the new rules not only substantially increase the costs of operations, but more significantly, restrain organizations from taking action to promote growth and development, and therefore have the cumulative effect of retarding economic growth. Inasmuch as there is no evidence that the rules will improve corporate performance, or assure more effective operation of the institutions of capitalism, the concern is well felt.

THE NEXT BIG CHALLENGE: FINDING THE UNICORN

It is the hypothesis of this book that boards would be much more effective if directors were selected on the basis of competency and behavioural characteristics, as well as on the basis of meeting certain structural requirements. Such a change should lead to more effective decision-making, which in turn should lead to more effective corporate performance. But before one can be completely confident in the latter—that is, of the importance of board process to corporate governance and of governance to corporate performance—there must be much more, albeit difficult, research on a broad range of board and individual directors' issues. This study, based on the observation of boards and board committees in real time and almost two hundred interviews with directors, regulators and students of corporate governance over a five-year period, suggests that such work can be undertaken. There are indications that such work may well confirm that there is a causal relationship between governance and performance—that boards constructed on the competencies and behavioural characteristics of individual directors, as suggested in this book, will lead to superior corporate financial performance.

Is it important to find out if the hypothesis is true? The answer is, of course, yes, because everyone—all stakeholders, the community and the economy—benefits from well-run corporations operating profitably within fair, efficient capital markets, and everyone suffers when corporations fail. Most practitioners and scholars agree that there is a relationship between corporate financial returns and a certain pattern of corporate governance, but no one is quite sure what that pattern is. This study is a step towards finding the relationship that, unlike the unicorn, may exist. Continuing research to flesh out the competency, behavioural, strategy and recruitment model developed in this book is the major challenge for the students of corporate governance in the twenty-first century.

Qualitative and Quantitative Research Methodologies: How Do They Differ?

The traditional research methodology used in the natural sciences and strongly favoured in the social sciences is known as "quantitative." It consists of observation, theory building, experimental design, testing, and confirmation or rejection of various hypotheses in efforts to generalize from a random sample to a larger population. A quantitative approach often requires researchers to analyze complex regression equations in an attempt to relate certain variables to one another while holding others constant.

Conversely, a "qualitative" methodology involves getting "inside" the subject being studied, adopting the role of the learner and drawing out themes and interpretations. The approach requires observation, the suspension of belief, in-depth interviews, dialogues with subjects of shared experiences and longitudinal case studies. It is these principal characteristics that distinguish the qualitative research method from the quantitative one. As Professor John Creswell wrote:

Qualitative research occurs in natural settings, where human behaviour and events occur. . . . Qualitative research is based on assumptions that are very different from quantitative designs. Theory or hypotheses are not established a priori. . . . The researcher is the primary instrument in data collection rather than some inanimate mechanism (Eisner, 1991; Fraenkel &

Wallen, 1990; Lincoln & Guba, 1985; Merriam, 1988). . . . The data that emerge from a qualitative study are descriptive. That is, data are reported in words (primarily the participant's words) or pictures, rather than in numbers (Fraenkel & Wallen, 1990; Locke et al., 1987; Marshall & Rossman, 1989; Merriam, 1988).

Objectivity and truthfulness are critical to both research traditions. However the criteria for judging a qualitative study differ from quantitative research. First and foremost, the research seeks believability, based on coherence, insight and instrumental utility (Eisner, 1991) and trustworthiness (Lincoln & Guba, 1985) through a process of verification rather than through traditional validity and reliability measures.[1]

The purpose of qualitative research is not to test hypotheses deductively in the traditional scientific method, nor is it to generalize from a sample to a population. The "intent of qualitative research is not to generalize findings, but to form a unique interpretation of events."[2]

When discussing the purpose of qualitative research, Creswell went on to write that:

The intent of qualitative research is to understand a particular social situation, event, role, group, or interaction (Locke, Spirduso, & Silverman, 1987). It is largely an investigative process where the researcher gradually makes sense of a social phenomenon by contrasting, comparing, replicating, cataloguing and classifying the object of study (Miles & Huberman, 1984). Marshall and Rossman (1989) suggest that this entails immersion in the everyday life of the setting chosen for the study; the researcher enters the informants' world and, through ongoing interaction, seeks the informants' perspectives and meanings.[3]

1. J. W. Creswell, *Research Design: Qualitative & Quantitative Approaches* (Thousand Oaks, CA: Sage Publications, 1994), 162–163.
2. *Ibid.* at 158-159, from Merriam, 1988.
3. *Ibid.* at 161, from Miller, 1992.

Lastly, a final distinction between quantitative and qualitative research is the legitimacy with which data is collected and analyzed and interpretations are viewed. Quantitative researchers speak of "validity" and "reliability," whereas qualitative researchers speak of "establishing trustworthiness" (Lincoln and Guba, 1985).

To summarize, first, both quantitative and qualitative methodologies differ significantly in how the researcher engages his or her subject in their fundamental assumptions, in their knowledge claims, and ultimately in what each method intends to accomplish. Second, given these distinctions and the researcher's intent to observe and investigate inner board membership, processes and decision-making, a qualitative methodology is an appropriate means of doing so. Third, the data generated by a qualitative research design should not be judged using criteria arising from assumptions underlying the quantitative method.

In its most simple terms, because scholars need to interact with corporate directors in a more intense way to determine with greater precision how directors see their roles, tasks and actions within their frame of reference and the world around them, a qualitative methodology facilitates linkages between the two worlds of researchers on the one hand and practitioners on the other, so that each may inform one another in more useful ways.

THE RESEARCH PROCESS: GETTING INTO THE BOARDROOMS, OBTAINING THE INTERVIEWS AND ANALYZING THE DATA

CONFIDENTIALITY AND RESEARCH ETHICS

There are two major confidentiality problems in this type of study. The first is the source of the data and the second is that the data that is offered is of a confidential nature.

Most of the companies that allowed access by the researcher, Dr. Leblanc, to board and committee meetings did so on the condition of strict confidentiality. Often this assurance of confidentiality was formalized by the researcher signing an explicit agreement drafted by the company's legal department. The corporations' concerns tended to centre on prohibiting by contract, with the possibility of liability by the researcher for breach, the release of any confidential information discussed during board deliberations to third parties or the use of that information by the researcher for self-gain. The confidentiality concern, it must be said, did not relate to the academic nature of the study, *i.e.*, the interpretation and findings of the study, but rather that nothing be written that could identify or harm the company.

The researcher indicated to the respondents orally, during the preliminary interviews, that comments made would not be attributed to them without their permission. If an individual asked that a comment made by him or her remain confidential, it would be. In other words, the respondent would not be identified, but the substance of the comment could be used in the research study, hence the word "(director)" after most of the commentary in this book. At the outset, it was thought that all the respondents could be listed, but comments would not be attributed to anyone individually. A decision had to be made during the data collection phase that, because of the sensitivity of much of the data being collected, neither companies nor individual directors should be identified in this study. In addition, for sensitive quotations, *e.g.*, containing names of individuals, the letters "X" or "Y" were used to replace the name of the individual(s) or instances in which the identity of the individual(s) could be inferred from the quotation. The fact that individuals could not be identified, while making this study less interesting, does not in any way make it less valid.

GAINING ACCESS TO THE BOARDROOM

It is one thing to recognize that a qualitative research methodology is the appropriate one for studying boards of directors. It is another thing to use it. The impediments to doing so are great. The most significant is, as to be expected, gaining access to board and committee meetings—negotiating access to some took between twelve and eighteen months. Gaining interviews with individual directors was almost as difficult.

It became apparent early in the study that the two major impediments to gaining access to board and committee meetings were 1) concerns about confidentiality and 2) that the presence of the researcher in the boardroom would affect the meeting itself. The first of these impediments was most frequently cited as the reason to deny access.

Board deliberations involve discussion of sensitive and "inside" information that, if released, could in certain circumstances irreparably harm the company and the reputation of board members and management. It is rare for an outsider, *i.e.*, not a director, officer, manager or employee of the company or independent adviser, to be permitted to attend a board or committee meeting. Indeed, when the idea was first broached to chairs or chief executive officers, it was clear that, to most, it was something that they had never thought of and certainly something that had never occurred. Most officers were somewhat nonplussed that the request was even made. To allow an outsider to attend a meeting was a risk that was simply too great for most of the companies approached to take. In addition, a number of companies who denied access were concerned that the mere presence of an outsider during a board or committee meeting would affect the meeting by inhibiting candid dialogue.

To address the first concern—confidentiality—it was made clear that there was no interest in learning about the substance of board and committee deliberations in a detailed and technical sense. Rather, from a data collection perspective, the researcher wished to observe overall board process, the "give-and-take" of the discussion and the interplay between the board and management and among individual directors. The researcher offered, and in some cases was asked, to leave the room during very sensitive discussions. In other words, the researcher made it clear to boards that access to meetings did not require that the researcher be present at an entire meeting, but that he could leave for certain agenda items. Finally, the researcher offered, or was required, to sign a confidentiality agreement as a condition of entry to the board or committee meeting. Boards wanted to receive explicit assurance that the researcher fully understood the confidential nature of the undertaking and that the researcher would maintain such confidences.

The second concern about granting access was that the presence of the researcher would affect the meeting. It was suggested that directors who were normally fairly silent might become more talkative when the researcher was present. As well, some directors who did speak might look to the researcher to see if notes were being taken on their comments.

Addressing the above two concerns did not guarantee access; at a minimum, doing so simply enabled the conditions for access to occur. More was often needed.

Four additional interdependent means were developed. In almost all cases, a combination of a number of these was necessary to gain the needed access.

THE FORMAL ROUTE

A letter explaining the purpose of the study was sent to the chairs of 428 Canadian and American corporations. Of the 428 letters, 279 were sent to the largest publicly-traded corporations in the "FP [*Financial Post*] 500" list; forty-nine letters were sent to the largest U.S. corporations as ranked on the "S&P 500" list; twenty-five letters were sent out to U.S. companies on the "worst boards of directors" list, according to a *Business Week* survey; and seventy-five letters were sent to the following: former government officials, managing partners of professional service firms (law, consulting, accounting, investment banking), academics known (by the researcher) to serve on boards, university presidents, deans of business schools, media publishers, institutional shareholders, and other corporate directors whom the researcher knew.

Of the individuals responding to these 428 letters sent out for the purpose of initiating access to a board of directors meeting(s), 103 sent rejection letters and thirty-six expressed initial interest in the project or a desire to participate. Of these latter companies, about half resulted in access being successfully negotiated and their boards of directors eventually being studied. For the remaining companies, who were not part of this original mailing, access was initiated and negotiated by means other than an initial letter.

No company granted access to a board or committee meeting on the basis of the letter alone. Nor did a company permit access to a board or committee meeting without first conducting an in-person interview between the researcher and the point of contact at the company, usually the chair of the board, an outside director, the CEO or the corporate secretary. In many cases, therefore, this "formal" route served only to open a door for further contact.

UNIVERSITY GUEST LECTURING

Directors generally enjoy coming back to universities and sharing their expertise with graduate students and executives, and many of them will volunteer to do so. Having experienced directors who guest-lectured on the topic of boards of directors provided the researcher the opportunity to meet directors, establish contacts and have the directors see the researcher in a teaching setting. As a result, the researcher was able then to pursue these guest speakers with a view to accessing the boards of which some of these directors were members.

THE INFORMAL ROUTE

Accessing board or committee meetings by means of an informal route proved to be the most effective means. There reached a point where the researcher knew numerous directors—some moderately well, including those whom he had interviewed and those who had guest-lectured for him. It became productive for the researcher to focus on a particular director or group of directors who could—on the researcher's behalf—negotiate access to a board for him. This "second-level" route meant that the researcher would target the individual who could sponsor the researcher's request to the board member's colleagues. The strength of access was determined by the credibility that the researcher had with the sponsoring director, and, in turn, the credibility that that director had with the rest of the board.

This informal route proved to be more effective than negotiating access directly because it is relatively risk-free for a chair of a board to deny access directly to a PhD researcher (in aid of obtaining his doctorate). Refusal becomes more difficult, however, if a peer of that director asks that the researcher be given access.

Focusing on a director or the chair of a board did not have to happen through a director on that particular board, although it most often did. In one instance, a letter of rejection was sent by the chair of a board to the researcher. The researcher knew a former colleague and close personal friend of the chair, who also happened to be a close colleague of the researcher. The researcher then asked this person—the "sponsor"—to arrange a meeting between the chair of the board, the researcher and the sponsor so that the researcher could explain in person to the chair the nature and value of the researcher's study. At the meeting, after the chair met the researcher in person, he asked the researcher for a second letter requesting access. As it turned out, access to three meetings (two board and one committee) on which that director sat, either as a chair or as a director, was subsequently granted to the researcher.

THE PEER PROCESS

Directors frequently serve on multiple boards and are often inter-connected through various charitable, social and business activities. As a group, directors are fairly homogeneous in terms of race, gender and socio-economic class. Interrelated directors often know one another on a first-name basis and are members of the same social circles. As such, there exists a "peer" or "club" mentality among them. Frequently, when negotiating access to a board or committee meeting, the researcher would be asked, "Have other boards let you in?" Although confidentiality was maintained, often during director interviews the question would be asked, "What other directors have you interviewed?" In the opinion of the researcher, these queries went beyond mere interest. They indicated that they might or might not participate in the venture if the venture had received the endorsement of members of their peer group. The researcher used this peer interest to his advantage in negotiating access, while maintaining confidences, both for boards and for directors.

For example, in accessing board or committee meetings in the financial services industry, negotiating access to a board meeting of the first company was most difficult. The particular company that was targeted was the one at which the researcher had the best board contacts and access to it was the most likely of all firms in the industry. Once access to a board meeting of this first company occurred, access to a second financial services board meeting was negotiated successfully, and then a third (board meeting), and finally a fourth (committee meeting).

OBTAINING THE INTERVIEWS

For access to individual directors, the researcher employed a similar strategy of escalating access to the more difficult directors and emphasizing peer groups as the researcher interviewed more directors. For example, there was one chair and CEO in particular whom the researcher was targeting for an interview. This individual had an avid interest in corporate governance, had revamped the company's board of directors, was high profile, and had spoken and written publicly about the topic on several occasions. However, access was expected to be difficult. The researcher then interviewed the vice-chair, lead director and one other outside director. In addition, the president of that company had guest-lectured for the researcher at the university. When requested by the researcher, the chair and CEO subsequently granted a forty-five minute interview.

As a last example of accessing an outside director, the researcher targeted one government official who sat on a number of boards but, as his executive assistant had indicated, generally had declined interviews since leaving office. Before interviewing the respondent, the researcher interviewed six former government officials. A telephone interview was then granted.

ORGANIZING THE RESEARCH

The Pilot Project
The purpose of the pilot project was to address methodological and data collection issues prior to executing the study. As Dr. Robert Yin pointed out, the pilot study:

> *helps investigators to refine their data collection plans with respect to both the content of the data and the procedures to be followed. In this regard, it is important to note that a pilot test is not a pretest. The pilot case is used more formatively, assisting an investigator to develop relevant lines of questions—possibly even providing some conceptual clarification for the research design as well. In contrast, the pretest is the occasion for a formal "dress rehearsal," in which the intended data collection plan is used as faithfully as possible as a final test run.* (R. K. Yin, Case Study Research: Design and Methods, 2nd. ed. (Thousand Oaks, CA: Sage Publications, 1994), 74).

Four initial research questions were developed, followed by a questionnaire consisting of ten questions, and a series of mock interviews were conducted. Next, access was negotiated with three boards of directors, including attending board and committee meetings of two boards and interviewing directors of a third.

The Initial Research Questions

Four preliminary questions, together with sub-questions that flowed from these questions, were designed as part of the pilot project. These initial questions were general and rather speculative in nature and were used to determine how the system worked with people who were not used to talking about this topic. The questions were eventually reconstituted into more precise questions and approaches as the pilot study was completed, the data were collected and observations were made at board meetings. The pilot project served its purpose of determining the nature and form of the interview process and questionnaire.

FIELD WORK DIFFICULTIES

The following difficulties in the fieldwork became apparent after attending four board and committee meetings and interviewing eight directors.

First, there was strong resistance by many directors to the use of a tape recorder.[1] A greater level of candour was obtained when the researcher took notes during interviews rather than taping individual directors. Directors also tended to speak longer when the researcher took notes. It became obvious that taping would result in less candid data. There also existed a risk that taping had the potential to conflict with confidentiality agreements that the researcher was beginning to negotiate with various companies.

Second, the researcher's continuous note-taking during board meetings at certain times appeared to be affecting the meeting. On a few occasions, directors glanced at the researcher as he was writing. In one instance, a director made a comment and then looked to

---

1. Parenthetically, data collection strategies extended beyond eliminating the use of the tape recorder. Another important finding with methodological implications included a reluctance expressed by directors to reduce certain things to writing and to fill out surveys because of possible reputational harm and legal liability. (For this reason, survey completion was not asked of respondents in this study.) Methodologically, therefore, when investigating board process, quantitative-type surveys used to assess corporate governance variables may lack some validity for two reasons: 1) by using a written survey, the researcher may miss much of the richer data that could be obtained by observing boards in action and by interviewing directors orally and taking notes; and 2) directors are reluctant to express candid opinions in writing. As Zahra and Pearce (1989:330) note:

> "Thus far, secondary references and surveys completed by management dominate the literature. We recognize the importance and richness of these data sources, but we urge researchers to consider incorporating directors' views in the study of board behaviours. . . ."

the researcher to determine whether the researcher was writing it down. The researcher realized that note-taking during a board meeting would need to be judicious in nature. In order to reduce the apparent extent of the note-taking, key words and phrases were developed and used by the researcher. The shortened notes were transcribed into full text immediately following each meeting.

Third, the ten questions from the questionnaire also proved to be inadequate in certain respects. For instance, during the interviews, many directors began to talk about corporate governance issues in a more open-ended fashion rather than addressing the researcher's specific questions. In addition, as the researcher began to recognize recurring themes and patterns, follow-up questions that deviated from the formal script were developed. It was also impolitic to adhere to a formal script. The initial script, however, did form the basis for the beginning of the interviews, and was necessary for those directors who preferred to respond to questions rather than initiate dialogue.

THE RESEARCH PROCESS

Once the pilot project was completed, it was possible to begin the study. Unlike in a quantitative study, there was no attempt to draw a sample from the total population of directors. Rather, the selection of boards to be studied and individuals to be interviewed was purposeful and strategic (Gilchrist: 1992, 87). There were no set rules for determining subject size and the number of interviews.

The principal decision that had to be made in this study was whether or not a large or a small number of boards and individuals should be studied—that is, a decision of scope versus depth. For instance, it would have been possible to study in significant depth only two boards of directors across time for a two-year period and interview all the directors on each board on a number of occasions. The benefit of studying a subject in depth is that key learning insights tend to surface under more in-depth forms of scrutiny. The benefit of studying a scope of subjects is that the data obtained would provide a good basis from which patterns of behaviour and relationships could be distilled.

Given the access success that the researcher was fortunate enough to negotiate (thirty-nine boards and 194 respondents) and the realities of the research setting (*e.g.*, low response rate and varying degrees of access), a research design was constructed to capture both the benefits of studying a range of boards of directors and at the same time the advantages that come from more in-depth study.

It is very important to remember that access to, and ultimate selection of, respondents to be interviewed were not random but strategic in nature. The choice of respondents was based on a number of criteria: first, from the thirty-nine boards of directors, depending on availability and access, the intention was to interview the chair, the CEO, the significant shareholder (if applicable), a number of outside directors and the corporate secretary. Second, the intention was to interview those respondents who, in the opinion of the researcher, would provide the most useful data, based on expressions of interest by the respondents and their willingness to share their views with the researcher. Third, the intention was to obtain a mixture of respondent backgrounds, including regulators, shareholders and corporate governance researchers, as well as directors. The vast majority of respondents interviewed for this study, however, were directors.

As a result of the pilot project, the questionnaire was broadened and became more open-ended. When appropriate, the researcher also posed "probing questions" to respondents to assist in surfacing key insights. Discussions tended to converge around issues of corporate governance.

The majority of interviews were conducted face-to-face between the respondent and the researcher. The researcher needed, however, to accommodate the schedule restrictions and geographical limitations of some respondents and, in doing so, telephone interviews occurred. One interview occurred via non-interactive voicemail that was subsequently transcribed. Email was used, although infrequently. Generally, the data obtained via a face-to-face interview were of a higher quality and quantity than those obtained over the telephone and electronically, although not always. Eighteen of the 194 interviews occurred by telephone and the remaining 176 were done in person.

The shortest interview was less than eight minutes and occurred by telephone. The longest interviews were over one-and-a-half hours in length and occurred in person at the respondents' offices. The majority of the interviews tended to range between half-an-hour or so and one hour in length. As was the case with face-to-face interviews, longer interviews generally resulted in higher quality data, although not always. A shorter interview, in a moment of candour after a board meeting for example, resulted in equally rich data.

The interviews were conducted within Canada, the United States and the United Kingdom. Cities were not named as they could signal head office locations and hence the identity of companies and boards.

The majority of interviews were undertaken by the researcher visiting the respondent's office. In some cases, interviews occurred at the respondent's home. Others occurred over dinner/lunch/coffee at restaurants and at private clubs. Interviews in private corporate dining rooms over lunch and dinner also occurred, both before and after board meetings. In private corporate dining rooms, as in private clubs, note-taking was inappropriate and the researcher transcribed notes after the interview. In almost all cases at public restaurants, the researcher took notes in real time.

The researcher, as a matter of practice, suggested that the interview occur at the respondent's office but was amenable to wherever the respondent felt most comfortable, such as clubs and restaurants, in order to obtain richer data in a more relaxing environment. Often, opinions were more candid in these types of settings. There was great advantage gained by interviewing directors in their offices shortly after a board or committee meeting(s), when events were fresh in their mind and access was easier. Interviews occurred at an airport, in the waiting area outside a boardroom, in an elevator in a discussion that continued after a board meeting, and in one case in the researcher's car as he drove a chair of the board from his home to a downtown dinner meeting. The intent was for the researcher to immerse himself in the respondents' environment to maximize convenience and comfort for the respondents and to enrich the quality of data collection.

THE NATURE OF THE DATA

It soon became apparent that the amount of data being collected was enormous and varied significantly among respondents and boards. Consequently, it was necessary to develop a method for classifying it according to its quality and source.

The four sources were:

1. a brief encounter;
2. a single board or committee meeting or interview;
3. multiple board or committee meetings and interviews; and
4. surrogate data.

Moreover, the data obtained from each source was not all of the same quality. Consequently, it was necessary to classify the data not only by source but by quality. Three classes were:

1. objective, "factual" data;
2. "socially-constructed" data offered by respondents; and
3. the researcher's interpretations based on the first two classes.

There is no relationship between the four sources of data and the three classes of data. Classes of data could originate from any source.

THE SOURCES OF THE ORIGINAL DATA

SOURCE ONE: BRIEF ENCOUNTER

Source one consisted of an initial contact between the researcher and the company's board of directors, usually in the form of an in-person interview with the chair of the board, lead director, the CEO, general counsel or corporate secretary. This source included between one and four respondent interviews per board site but did not involve attending an actual board or committee meeting. Eighteen of the thirty-nine boards studied provided data via this source.

SOURCE TWO: SINGLE BOARD OR COMMITTEE MEETINGS AND INTERVIEWS

Source two consisted of attending at least one board or committee meeting and interviewing a number of directors, ranging from between one and six. Twenty-one of the thirty-nine boards provided data via this source.

SOURCE THREE: MULTIPLE BOARD OR COMMITTEE MEETINGS AND INTERVIEWS

Source three consisted of attending between two and three board or committee meetings of a single company over time, as well as interviewing individual directors. Eight of the twenty-one boards of directors from source two provided data via this source.

SOURCE FOUR: "SURROGATE" DATA

Source four consisted of going back to the field and interviewing selected key informants to assess the interpretations made by the researcher. Themes, ideas and emerging patterns developed by the researcher were further refined. The key informants confirmed, contradicted and re-framed the researcher's interpretations.

In addition, other sources of external data and verification of the researcher's findings and conclusions occurred during this study, including public assessments of boards of directors by commentators and groups, media reports, actions by regulatory and other bodies, and the views of other corporate governance stakeholders.

The purpose of the above three sources, unlike the fourth, was to identify key themes or patterns that emerged from the data. A progression from source one to source three involved getting inside and adopting the role of the subjects, listening, watching, mapping the terrain and fleshing out key governance issues.

There generally existed richer data as the researcher progressed from source one through to source three, but not always. An example illustrates this point: a company that experienced an unfriendly takeover during the course of this study remained in source one because access to a board meeting by the researcher was negotiated with the chair but could not be negotiated between the chair and the rest of the board, given the takeover. The chair of the board nonetheless kept the researcher regularly informed in confidence (via voicemail, email and in person) of the issues and the chair's opinion on them as the takeover progressed. The researcher had a final debriefing interview with the chair once the acquirer had succeeded in taking the company over. The interview was productive, as the chair summarized what lessons he had learned as a result of the takeover.

THE ANALYSIS OF THE ORIGINAL DATA
The data varied immensely among and within sources, so a further classification had to take place. The data were either:

1. factual;
2. informed opinion, *i.e.*, socially constructed; or
3. the result of analysis on the part of the researcher.

CLASS ONE: FACTUAL DATA
Class-one data were factual in nature, objective and indisputable. For example, at a board meeting, if the researcher observed a director with his eyes shut and breathing heavily and slowly (arms folded, chest heaving up and down), with fellow directors looking at the researcher and then at other directors and the chair chuckling quietly, these were facts. When a board member (of another board) sat with his arms folded for an entire two-hour meeting and his binder of materials in front of him was shut and (what appeared to be) facing in the wrong direction, and he did not say anything during the meeting, then these were also considered to be facts. And the number of women around a board table was a fact.

CLASS TWO: ORAL COMMENTARY DATA
PROVIDED BY THE RESPONDENTS
This data source included notes taken by the researcher on what was said during respondent interviews, during board and committee meetings, and during guest lectures. When confidential quotes

are used in this book (without the respondent being identified), the origin of the quotation is the researcher's working notes, as the researcher used shorthand in real time in the above settings when interviewing respondents. While it certainly is possible that the researcher inadvertently misquoted a respondent—given that tape recorders were not used and that the researcher was reproducing the quote in real time, with subsequent editing if required,—this likelihood is believed to be minimal, as the researcher was especially careful during the note-taking component of the data collection. If there was any uncertainty concerning the content of the quotation, then the researcher verified the contents of the quote with the respondent who said it.

These data consisted of respondents' views on the factual data above, as well as their views on corporate governance issues, broadly speaking. This data class was the "reality" of the respondents. As the outset to this methodology has indicated, the respondents' reality is "socially constructed" because different people perceive the "objective" world differently based on their frames of reference and experience. Continuing the two examples above will serve to illustrate.

First, when the researcher asked the chair if a particular director was asleep during a board meeting (referred to above), the chair indicated how embarrassed he was and went on to say that the director came onto the board because "he was a golfing buddy of [X]." This datum represented the chair's interpretation of that director's non-performance and the reason that the director was on this particular board.

In the context of another example—women on boards of directors—if a chair of a board of a company said at a guest lecture at a university that "There are only twenty women in Canada who are board-ready," this then was a class-two datum, because it was this chair's socially constructed reality. It was his interpretation of women's ability to serve on boards. If the CEO of that same company said during an interview with the researcher that women are on the board because they are "dresses," and "as CEO of a public company, this is a requirement that has to be met [women on boards] so I meet it," then this quote also serves as a class-two datum.

To extend this example for illustrative purposes, the chair of another company remarked during a board meeting that a female candidate director was "very attractive," followed by a fellow director saying that "we all loved the 50s," followed still by another director saying, "she likes skiing and sailing so she'll be a good board member." All of these comments were classified as class-two data. They were class-two data because they were the respondents' reality, more specifically their views of women, their ability to serve on boards and what the criteria may be at that board for being an effective director.

CLASS THREE: INTERPRETATION OF THE DATA

Class-three data consisted of the researcher's interpretation of class-one and class-two data. Class-three interpretations, or themes, were supported by class-one and class-two data, including respondents' commentary shared with the researcher during interviews and observations that the researcher made during board and committee meetings.

For example, to continue with women on boards, a number of the comments made by respondents who shared similar views to the preceding class-two examples above were compared with what other respondents said regarding the role of women on boards; these included the views and experiences of female directors. Because interpretations of the data were derived inductively from the data in this fashion, in this type of qualitative research, the study's findings, including the generation of categories, themes, patterns and explanation-building (Yin, 1994:33) became "grounded" and validated by the data themselves.

This class of data also included observations and descriptions made by the researcher, documented in a very detailed way, during or after the following: board or committee meetings; director meetings when management was not present; informal meetings and social gatherings of the company; and respondent interviews. Recollections made by the researcher that were not documented in real time, nor shortly thereafter, for one reason or another, including circumstances where note-taking was not politic, were also included.

"Key informants"[2] and "member checks"[3] were also used, as the boards that were studied had cultures consisting of formal and informal processes, political alliances, power centres and historical working relations not readily observable to an untrained outsider. Without the assistance of directors to attach deeper meaning to the various cultural "signals," both inside and outside of the board-room, they could not have been uncovered.

LIMITATIONS ON THE ORIGINAL DATA COLLECTION AND ANALYSIS

Collecting and analyzing the raw data from the board and commit-tee meetings and interviews required the use of a proper filing system. This included data organization—categorically and chrono-logically, by respondent and site—and the repeated review and coding of the data. Adhering to the research design of three classes and four sources of data, above (particularly the third class and fourth source) assisted in ensuring that the interpretations made by the researcher possessed integrity and were trustworthy.

CONFIDENTIALITY AND THE RELIABILITY OF THE DATA

As mentioned earlier, in order to gain access to companies' boards and committee meetings, in most cases the researcher had to abide by explicit confidentiality agreements. The effect of confidentiality granted to companies and individuals, and the necessary decision by the researcher to shield the names of all boards examined and direc-tors interviewed, has meant that "who said what" has been refined largely to "what." As a result, part of the data could not be repro-duced because of this sensitivity. It is no doubt more interesting to have both components—the "who" and "what"—as the respon-dents interviewed for this book included dozens of Canada's senior directors of significant entities. However, the focus of this study had to be on what was being said rather than on who said it.

---

2. Key informants (Creswell, 1998:60) are "individuals who provide useful insights into the group [board] and can steer the researcher to information and contacts."
3. In "member checking" (Stake, 1995:115), "the actor is requested to examine rough drafts or writing. . . . The actor is asked to review the material for accuracy and palatability."

Ideally, the strength of an idea rests primarily on the idea per se, rather than who is putting the idea forward. The reality in the business world, however, is that "who" says what matters, and is weighted by the credibility that person possesses as a result of past accomplishments, experience and the views of that person's peers. Assessment of the substance of what is being put forward is based in part on the credibility of the person who said it.

INTERPRETATION AND ROLE OF THE RESEARCHER

The possibility always exists that the researcher may have subconsciously biased or prompted respondents during interviews by reacting favourably or unfavourably through body language to responses that they gave. Another response bias could have been that the researcher deliberately chose those companies or respondents who favoured a particular point of view. In a study of this sort, with access driving much of the data collection, both for boards and individuals, this risk was minimal.

LIMITED NUMBER OF RESPONSES

The number of boards of directors examined (thirty-nine) and the number of respondents interviewed (194) comprised a very large qualitative study. The three previous, well-known, similar studies (Mace, 1971; Lorsch, 1989; and Demb and Neubauer, 1992) had seventy-five, approximately 100, and seventy-one respondent interviews, respectively, and no observations of boards in action.

As mentioned, this study lacked randomness of selection, both for the boards examined and for individual respondents. Randomness is, to reiterate, a requirement in a quantitative study when attempting to draw inferences from a sample to a population. This is not the case here.

However, because this is not a random selection, there exists the possibility that those companies who elected to participate in the study did so in part because of their interest in corporate governance. Therefore, the companies may, in fact, not be representative of the population as a whole, but may be those companies that believe in effective corporate governance, and therefore their practices may not

280

be representative of the general population. The same social desirability bias existed for individual respondents. The researcher thus attempted to balance this study by examining a range of boards and respondents, including dysfunctional boards and non-performing directors.

VALIDITY AND RELIABILITY CONCERNS

Quantitative researchers refer to "validity" and "reliability" to provide confidence that the researcher is measuring what he or she is purporting to measure, and that the same findings would occur if someone else replicated the researcher's study. Naturalist researchers would do so by "establishing trustworthiness" (Lincoln and Guba, 1985). As Creswell states:

> *Early qualitative researchers felt compelled to relate traditional notions of validity and reliability to the procedures in qualitative research (e.g., see Goetz & LeCompte, 1984). Later qualitative writers developed their own language to distance themselves from the positivist paradigms. Lincoln and Guba (1985) and, more recently, Erlandson, Harris, Skipper, and Allen (1993) discuss establishing quality criteria such as "trustworthiness" and "authenticity." These are all viable stances on the question of validity and reliability.* (1994:157-158).

Nevertheless, the researcher addressed validity and reliability issues. The following steps were taken to address the validity of this study:

- triangulating or converging data sources, including observations, interviews and text. Triangulation is defined by Denzen as "the combination of methodologies in the study of the same phenomenon" (in Jick, 1979:602);
- establishing an audit trail of key decisions and a chain of evidence made during the research process, including why decisions were made;
- developing data analysis strategies, including organizing and repeatedly reviewing the study's data, categorically and chronologically;

- having prolonged engagements and repeated observations of phenomena made at several board sites as part of the qualitative research design;
- clarifying the role and possible biases of the researcher and having strategies to minimize them (*e.g.*, the effect that the researcher may have on board or committee meetings);
- generating themes, patterns, relationships, models, categories and explanation-building (Yin, 1994:33) and testing these in the field in order that they be confirmed, refuted or reformulated;
- searching for contrary evidence and opinions;
- having ongoing checks occur by key informants of the researcher's interpretation of the informants' reality in order to contribute to the truth value of the data;
- other participatory modes of qualitative research (Creswell, 1994: 168), such as key informants and respondents providing input during the interpretation and conclusion phases and reviewing the proposed model of board effectiveness.

The following steps were taken to address the reliability of this study:

- providing a detailed description of the focus of the study, the researcher's role, the basis for subject selection, and the context in which the data were gathered;
- selecting subjects purposefully and strategically, which contributed to "thick description." Thick description is defined by Guba and Lincoln as "a thorough description of the context or setting within which the inquiry took place and with which the inquiry was concerned . . . [and] a thorough description of the transactions or processes observed in that context that are relevant to the problem, evaluand, or policy option" (in Kuzel and Like, 1991:153);
- using such rich, detailed "thick description" that anyone interested in transferability will have a solid framework for comparison (Merriam, 1988, in Creswell, 1994:168);
- triangulating and utilizing multiple methods of data collection and analysis, with full detailed reporting of the methods used in this study (Merriam and Creswell, *ibid.*);

- providing a comprehensive description of the data collection and analysis techniques in order to provide a clear and accurate picture of the methods used so the results may be replicated in another setting;
- using and maintaining handwritten notes, computer files, photocopies, methodological notes, interview transcripts, observation notes and notes on themes, preliminary models, *etc.* as they emerged, so the researcher's journey may be replicated (Christenson, 1996:83);
- having peers provide input and an experienced qualitative researcher review the data analysis and interpretation design.

The purpose of this study is not to test hypotheses a priori in the traditional scientific method, nor is it to generalize from a sample to a population. Its purpose is to build inductively from the data and the study of the boards examined within this closed system. In other words, after an in-depth, well-documented and thorough qualitative investigation—across multiple boards in different situations in which different processes were experienced—based on the data, the research questions have been addressed. The data are used to propose a model for board effectiveness and a new classification scheme for types of directors.

OTHER SOURCES OF DATA

Print sources for this study included the following:

- management books and periodicals;
- legal texts, journals, statutes and case law;
- academic working papers;
- print material from academic and professional conferences and workshops;
- publications of professional firms and institutes;
- government publications;
- newspapers;
- texts of written speeches on corporate governance.

The researcher read a wide range of materials, including case histories of companies whose board actions have been reported in the public media in both Canada and the U.S.

Publicly available corporate documentation also was used, such as annual and quarterly reports, annual information forms, management proxy circulars, shareholder communications and corporate governance commentary and guidelines publicly distributed by companies. Private documents made available confidentially to the researcher were also used, including board and committee meeting agendas and material, internal communications such as board and individual director evaluations, copies of management presentations handed out during board meetings, and correspondence between the researcher and companies.

BIBLIOGRAPHY

The following includes a select list of books and articles on corporate governance. No books or articles published before 1995 are included. Anyone wishing a more detailed bibliography should please contact rleblanc@yorku.ca.

Anderson, B., and B. H. Kleiner. "How to Evaluate the Performance of Chief Executive Officers Effectively." *Management Research News* 26:2-4 (2003): 3-11.

Australian Stock Exchange Corporate Governance Council. *Principles of Good Corporate Governance and Best Practice Recommendations.* Sydney: March, 2003.

Bakan, J. *The Corporation: The Pathological Pursuit of Profit and Power.* Toronto: Viking Canada, 2004.

Baliga, B. R., R. C. Moyer, and R. S. Rao. "CEO Duality and Firm Performance: What's the Fuss?" *Strategic Management Journal* 17:1 (1996): 41–53.

Barrett, M. W. "Shaping a Board of Directors for the Future: Restructuring the Board of Directors at Bank of Montreal." In James Gillies, ed., *Success: Canadian Leaders Prepare for the Next Century.* Toronto: Key Porter, 1996, 118–130.

Bebchuk, L., and J. Fried. Pay Without Performance: *The Unfulfilled Promise of Executive Compensation.* Cambridge, MA: Harvard University Press, 2004.

Bhagat, S., and B. Black. "The Non-Correlation Between Board Independence and Long-Term Firm Performance." *Journal of Corporation Law* 27:2 (Winter 2002): 231-273.

Blair, M. M., *Ownership and Control: Rethinking Corporate Governance for the Twenty-First Century*. Washington: Brookings, 1995.

Brountas, P. P. *Boardroom Excellence: A Commonsense Perspective on Corporate Governance*. San Francisco: Jossey-Bass, 2004.

Cadbury, A. *Corporate Governance and Chairmanship: A Personal View*. Oxford: Oxford University Press, 2002.

Carey, D. C., and D. Ogden. *CEO Succession: A Window on How Boards Can Get It Right When Choosing a New Chief Executive*. New York: Oxford University Press, 2000.

Carter, C. B., and J. W. Lorsch. *Back to the Drawing Board: Designing Corporate Boards for a Complex World*. Boston: Harvard Business School Press, 2004.

Carver, J. *On Board Leadership*. San Francisco: Jossey-Bass, 2002.

Carver, J. *Boards That Make a Difference: A New Design for Leadership in No-profit and Public Organizations*, 2nd ed. San Francisco: Jossey-Bass Publishers, 1997.

Carver, J. and C. Oliver. *Corporate Boards That Create Value: Governing Company Performance from the Boardroom*. San Francisco: Jossey-Bass, 2002.

Carver, J. and M. M. Carver. *Reinventing Your Board: A Step-by-Step Guide to Implementing Policy Governance*. San Francisco: Jossey-Bass, 1997.

Charan, R. *Boards at Work: How Corporate Boards Create Competitive Advantage*. San Francisco: Jossey-Bass Publishers, 1998.

Chingos, P. T. *Responsible Executive Compensation for a New Era of Accountability*. Hoboken, NJ: Wiley, 2004.

Clarke, T., ed. *Theories of Corporate Governance: The Philosophical Foundation of Corporate Governance*. London: Routledge, 2004.

Clarkson, M. B. E., ed. *The Corporation and Its Stakeholders: Classic and Contemporary Readings*. Toronto: University of Toronto Press, 1998.

Coles, J. W. "Independence of the Chairman and Board Composition: Firm Choices and Shareholder Value." *Journal of Management* 26:2 (2000): 195.

Colley, Jr., J. L., J. L. Doyle, G. W. Logan, and W. Stettinius. *What Is Corporate Governance?* New York: McGraw-Hill, 2005.

Colley, Jr., J. L., J. L. Doyle, G. W. Logan, and W. Stettinius. *Corporate Governance*. New York: McGraw-Hill, 2003.

Committee on Corporate Laws, ABA Section of Business Law. "Corporate Director's Guidebook, Fourth Edition." *The Business Lawyer* 59:3 (May 2004): 1057-1120.

Conger, J. A., E. E. Lawler III and D. L. Finegold. *Corporate Boards*. New York: Jossey-Bass, 2001.

Conger, J. A. "Appraising Boardroom Performance." *Harvard Business Review* 76:1 (January/February 1998): 136–148.

Council on Corporate Disclosure and Governance. "Consultation Paper on Proposed Revisions to the Code of Corporate Governance." Singapore: December, 2004.

Daily, C. M., and D. R. Dalton. "CEO and Board Chair Roles Held Jointly or Separately: Much Ado About Nothing?" *Academy of Management Executive* 11:3 (1997): 11–20.

Daily, C. M., D. R. Dalton, and A. A. Cannella Jr. "Introduction to Special Topic Forum—Corporate Governance: Decades of Dialogue and Data." *Academy of Management Review* 28:3 (2003): 371–382.

Dallas, G. S., ed. *Governance and Risk: An Analytical Handbook for Investors, Managers, Directors & Stakeholders*. New York: McGraw-Hill, 2004.

287

Dalton, D. R. *et al.* "Number of Directors and Financial Performance: A Meta-Analysis." *Academy of Management Journal* 42:6 (December 1999): 674–686.

Dalton, D. R. *et al.* "Meta-Analytic Reviews of Board Composition, Leadership Structure, and Financial Performance." *Strategic Management Journal* 19:3 (March 1998): 269.

Daniels, R. J., and R. Morck, eds., *Corporate Decision-Making in Canada.* Calgary: U. Calgary Press, 1995.

Davis, M., and A. Stark, eds., *Conflict of Interest in the Professions.* New York: Oxford University Press, 2001.

Denis, D. K. "Twenty-Five Years of Corporate Governance Research... and Counting." *Review of Financial Economics* 10 (2001): 191-212.

Dimma, W. A. *Excellence in the Boardroom: Best Practices in Corporate Directorship.* Toronto: Wiley, 2002.

Donaldson, G. "A New Tool for Boards: The Strategic Audit." *Harvard Business Review* 73:4 (July/August 1995): 99–107.

Duca, D. J. *NonProfit Boards: Roles, Responsibilities and Performance.* New York: John Wiley & Sons, 1996.

Dulewicz, V. "Appraising and Developing the Effectiveness of Boards and Their Directors." *Journal of General Management* 20:3 (Spring 1995): 1–19.

Eisenberg, T. "Larger Board Size and Decreasing Firm Value in Small Firms." *Journal of Financial Economics* 48:1 (April 1998): 35–54.

Elliott, C. W. "21st Century Corporate Board." *Academy of Management Executive* 11:1 (February 1997): 131–132.

Elson, C. M. "What's Wrong with Executive Compensation?: A Roundtable Moderated by Charles Elson." *Harvard Business Review* (January 2003): 68-77.

Elson, C. M., and C. J. Gyves. "The Enron Failure and Corporate Governance Reform." *Wake Forest Law Review* 38 (2003): 855-884.

Epstein, M. J., and M. J. Roy. "Improving the Performance of Corporate Boards: Identifying and Measuring the Key Drivers of Success." *Journal of General Management* 29:3 (Spring 2004) 1-23.

Ericson, R. N. *Pay to Prosper: Using Value Rules to Reinvent Executive Incentives*. Scottsdale, AZ: WorldatWork, 2004.

Fay, C. H., M. A. Thompson, and D. Knight, eds. *The Executive Handbook on Compensation: Linking Strategic Rewards to Business Performance*. New York: The Free Press, 2001.

Financial Reporting Council. *Audit Committees: Combined Code Guidance*. A Report and Proposed Guidance by an FRC-Appointed Group, Chaired by Sir R. Smith. London: January, 2003.

Financial Reporting Council. *The Combined Code on Corporate Governance*. London: July, 2003.

Forbes, D. P. "Cognition and Corporate Governance: Understanding Boards of Directors as Strategic Decision-Making Groups." *Academy of Management Review* 24:3 (July 1999): 489–505.

Gandossy, R., and J. A. Sonnenfeld, eds. *Leadership and Governance from the Inside Out*. Hoboken, NJ: Wiley, 2004.

Garratt, B. "Developing Effective Directors and Building Dynamic Boards." *Long Range Planning* 32:1 (February 1999): 28–35.

Garratt, B. *The Fish Rots From the Head: The Crisis in Our Boardrooms: Developing the Crucial Skills of the Competent Director*. London: Harper Collins Business, 1996.

Gillies, James and D. Morra. "Does Corporate Governance Matter?: A Review of Recent Research in Corporate Decision-Making in Canada Suggests We Don't Yet Have All the Answers." *Business Quarterly* 61:3 (Spring 1997): 71.

Glasbeek, H. J. "More Direct Director Responsibility: Much Ado About ...What?" *Canadian Business Law Journal* 25:3 (1995): 416–459.

Hansell, Carol. *What Directors Need to Know: Corporate Governance*. Toronto: Carswell, 2003.

Hansell, C. *Directors and Officers in Canada: Law and Practice*, vols. 1 and 2. Toronto: Carswell, 1999.

Hazard, Jr., G. C., and E. B. Rock. "A New Player in the Boardroom: The Emergence of the Independent Directors' Counsel." *The Business Lawyer* 59:4 (August 2004): 1389-1412.

Higgs, D. *Review of the Role and Effectiveness of Non-Executive Directors. Department of Trade and Industry.* London: January, 2003.

Howe, F. *Welcome to the Board: Your Guide to Effective Participation.* San Francisco: Jossey-Bass Publishers, 1995.

Institute of Chartered Accountants in England & Wales, Internal Control Working Party, Chaired by Nigel Turnbull. *Internal Control: Guidance for Directors on the Combined Code.* London: September, 1999.

Jennings, M. *The Board of Directors.* New York: Lebhar-Friedman, 2000.

Johnson, J. E., C. M. Daily, and A. E. Ellstrand. "Boards of Directors: A Review and Research Agenda." *Journal of Management* 22:3 (1996): 409–438.

Joint Committee on Corporate Governance. *Final Report: Beyond Compliance: Building a Governance Culture.* Toronto: November 2001.

Joint Committee on Corporate Governance. *Interim Report: Beyond Compliance: Building a Governance Culture.* Toronto: March 2001.

Kaplan, R. S., and D. P. Norton. *The Balanced Scorecard: Translating Strategy Into Action.* Boston: Harvard Business School Press, 1996.

Kazanjian, J. "Assessing Boards and Individual Directors." *Ivey Business Journal* 64:5 (May/June 2000): 45–50.

Keasey, K., and M. Wright, eds. *Corporate Governance: Responsibilities, Risks and Remuneration.* Chichester: Wiley, 1997.

Kiel, G. C., G. J. Nicholson and M. A. Barclay. *Board, Director and CEO Evaluation*. Sydney: McGraw-Hill, 2005.

Kiel, G. C., and G. J. Nicholson. *Boards That Work: A New Guide for Directors*. Sydney: McGraw-Hill, 2003.

Koehnen, M. *Oppression and Related Remedies*. Toronto: Carswell, 2004.

Korac-Kakabadse, N., A. K. Kakabadse, and A. Kouzmin. "Board Governance and Company Performance: Any Correlations?" *Corporate Governance* 1:1 (2001): 24.

Lear, R. W. "Boards: Going From Good to Great." *Chief Executive* Iss. 148 (New York: October 1999): 14.

Lechem, B. *Chairman of the Board: A Practical Guide*. Toronto: Wiley, 2002.

Leighton, D. S. R., and D. H. Thain. *Making Boards Work: What Directors Must Do to Make Canadian Boards Effective*. Toronto: McGraw-Hill Ryerson, 1997.

London Stock Exchange Committee on the Financial Aspects of Corporate Governance. *Report of the Committee on the Financial Aspects of Corporate Governance*. London: Gee, 1992.

Lorsch, J. W., A. S. Zelke, and K. Pick, "Unbalanced Boards." *Harvard Business Review* (February, 2001).

Lorsch, J. W. "Empowering the Board." *Harvard Business Review* 73:1 (January 1995): 107–117.

Maas, J. "Boards at Work: How Corporate Boards Create Competitive Advantage." *Sloan Management Review* 39:4 (Summer 1998): 109–111.

Mackenzie, M. A. "The Evolving Board: The Mechanisms of Board Oversight." *Canadian Business Law Journal* 26 (1996): 140–145.

Madura, J. *What Every Investor Needs to Know About Accounting Fraud*. New York: McGraw-Hill, 2004.

McCarthy, M. P., and T. P. Flynn. *Risk: From the CEO and Board Perspective*. New York: McGraw-Hill, 2004.

McLean, B., and P. Elkind. *The Smartest Guys in the Room: The Amazing Rise and Scandalous Fall of Enron*. New York: Portfolio, 2004.

Meyer, H. "Boards Take on the Heavy Lifting." *Journal of Business Strategy* 21:4 (July/August 2000): 18–21.

Moeller, R. R. *Sarbanes-Oxley and the New Internal Auditing Rules*. Hoboken, NJ: Wiley, 2004.

Monks, R. A. G., and N. Minow. *Corporate Governance* (3rd ed.). Malden, MA: Blackwell Publishing, 2003.

Monks, R. A. G., and N. Minow. *Watching the Watchers: Corporate Governance for the 21st Century*. Cambridge: Blackwell, 1996.

Monks, R. A. G., and N. Minow. *Corporate Governance*. Cambridge: Blackwell, 1995.

Morgan, G. *Images of Organization*. Thousand Oaks, CA: Sage Publications, 1997.

Mueller, R. K. "A Cure for 'Unprofessional Board Syndrome.'" *Directors and Boards* 23:4 (Philadelphia: Summer 1999): 96.

Nadler, D. A. "Building Better Boards." *Harvard Business Review* 82:5 (2004): 102.

Nadler, D. A. "What's the Board's Role in Strategy Development? 'Engaging the Board in Corporate Strategy.'" *Strategy and Leadership* 32:5 (2004): 25-33.

National Association of Corporate Directors. *Various Reports of NACD Blue Ribbon Commissions*. Washington: National Association of Corporate Directors, 2001–2005.

New York Stock Exchange Corporate Accountability and Listing Standards Committee. "Report of the NYSE Corporate

Accountability and Listing Standards Committee." New York: New York Stock Exchange, June 6, 2002.

New Zealand Securities Commission. *Corporate Governance in New Zealand: Principles and Guidelines*. Wellington: February 16, 2004.

Newquist, S. C., with M. B. Russell. *Putting Investors First: Real Solutions for Better Corporate Governance*. Princeton, NJ: Bloomberg Press, 2003.

Nikos, V. "Board Meeting Frequency and Firm Performance." *Journal of Financial Economics* 53:1 (July 1999): 113–142.

Nofsinger, J., and K. Kim. *Infectious Greed: Restoring Confidence in America's Companies*. Upper Saddle River, NJ: Financial Times Prentice Hall, 2003.

O'Callaghan, Patrick *et al. Corporate Board Governance and Director Compensation in Canada*. Vancouver: Patrick O'Callaghan & Associates, 1995–2004.

Ontario Securities Commission. Proposed National Policy 58-201 Corporate Governance Guidelines, and Proposed National Instrument 58-101 Disclosure of Corporate Governance Practices, Forms 58-101F1 and 58-101F2, Notice, Request for Comments. (2004) 27 OSCB 8825-8858.

Organisation for Economic Co-operation and Development, OECD Steering Group on Corporate Governance. *OECD Principles of Corporate Governance*. 2004.

Park, J. C. "Reengineering Boards of Directors." *Business Horizons* 38:2 (March 1995): 63–69.

Partridge, W. G. R. "Getting the Board to Measure Up." *Association Management* 52:1 (Washington: January 2000): 59–63.

Phan, P. H. *Taking Back the Boardroom*. Singapore: McGraw-Hill, 2000.

Pierce, C., ed. *The Effective Director: The Essential Guide to Director & Board Development*. London: Kogan Page Limited, 2001.

Porter, M. V. "6 Strategies for Better Boards." *Association Management* 52:5 (Washington: May 2000): 52–54.

Rechner, P. L. "Boards at Work: How Corporate Boards Create Competitive Advantage." *Academy of Management Review* 24:1 (January 1999): 151–153.

Rhoades, D. L., P. L. Rechner, and C. Sundaramurthy. "Board Composition And Financial Performance: A Meta-Analysis Of The Influence Of Outside Directors." *Journal of Management Issues* 12:1 (Spring 2000): 76-91.

Robinson, M. K. *Nonprofit Boards that Work: The End of One-Size-Fits-All Governance*. New York: Wiley, 2001.

Rosenstein, S. "Inside Directors, Board Effectiveness, and Shareholder Wealth." *Journal of Financial Economics* 44:2 (May 1997): 229–250.

Sabia, M. J., and J. L. Goodfellow. *Integrity in the Spotlight: Opportunities for Audit Committees*. Toronto: Deloitte & Touche, 2002.

Saloman, W. J., J. W. Lorsch *et al. Harvard Business Review on Corporate Governance*. Boston, MA: Harvard Business School Press, 2000.

Shaw, J. C. *Corporate Governance & Risk: A Systems Approach*. Hoboken, NJ: Wiley, 2003.

Shivdasani, A. "CEO Involvement in the Selection of New Board Members: An Empirical Analysis." *Journal of Finance* 54:5 (October 1999): 1829–1853.

Shultz, S. F. *The Board Book*. New York: Amacom, 2001.

Sonnenfeld, J. A. "Good Governance and the Misleading Myths of Bad Metrics" *Academy of Management Executive* 18:1 (2004): 108-113.

Sonnenfeld, J. A. "Comment" *IR Magazine* (July 2003): 27.

Sonnenfeld, J. A. "What Makes Great Boards Great" *Harvard Business Review* 80:9 (September 2002): 106-113.

Stiles, P., and B. Taylor. *Boards at Work: How Directors View their Roles and Responsibilities*. London: Oxford, 2001.

Tapp, L. G. "It's Time for a New Breed of Director." *Business Quarterly* 60:3 (Spring 1996): 7.

Tapsell, S. "Uninformed Boards—Mushrooms in the Dark?" *New Zealand Management* 47:4 (Auckland: May 2000): 50–51.

Thain, D. H., and D. S. R. Leighton. "Why Boards Fail." *Business Quarterly* 59:3 (Spring 1995): 71–77.

Toronto Stock Exchange and Institute of Corporate Directors. "Report on Corporate Governance, 1999: Five Years to the Dey.'" Toronto: Toronto Stock Exchange, December 1999.

Toronto Stock Exchange Committee on Corporate Governance in Canada. "Report: 'Where Were the Directors?' Guidelines for Improved Corporate Governance in Canada." Toronto: Toronto Stock Exchange, December 1994.

Thompson, R. W. "Catalyst Expands Survey Involving Women Directors." *HRMagazine* 45:2 (February 2000): 12.

Tricker, R. I. *The Essential Director: An Economist Guide*. London: Economist Books, 2003.

Tricker, R. I. *Pocket Director*. London: The Economist and Profile Books Ltd., 1999.

Useem, M. "Corporate Governance is Directors Making Decisions: Reforming the Outward Foundations for Inside Decision Making." *Journal of Management & Governance* 7 (2003): 241-253.

Vafeas, N. "Board Meeting Frequency and Firm Performance." *Journal of Financial Economics* 53:1 (July 1999): 113–142.

Van den Berghe, L. A. A., and A. Levrau. "Measuring the Quality of Corporate Governance: In Search of a Tailormade Approach?" *Journal of General Management* 28:3 (Spring 2003): 71-83.

Veasey, E. N. "Separate and Continuing Counsel for Independent Directors: An Idea Whose Time Has Not Come as a General Practice." *The Business Lawyer* 59:4 (August 2004): 1413-1418.

Ward, R. D. *Saving the Corporate Board: Why Boards Fail and How to Fix Them.* Hoboken, NJ: Wiley, 2003.

Ward, R. D. *Improving Corporate Boards.* New York: Wiley, 2000.

Ward, R. D. *21st Century Corporate Board.* New York: Wiley, 1997.

Waring, K., and C. Pierce, ed. *The Handbook of International Corporate Governance: A Definitive Guide.* London: Kogan Page, 2005.

Webb, P. "Should Executive Directors Hold Other Board Positions?" *New Zealand Management* 47:5 (Auckland: June 2000): 70–72.

Weir, C., and D. Laing. "Governance Structures, Director Independence and Corporate Performance in the U.K." *European Business Review* 13:2 (2001): 86.

Weisman, C. "Where Can You Find Good Board Members?" *Nonprofit World* 17:5 (September/October 1999): 6–7.

Westphal, J. D. "Second Thoughts on Board Independence: Why Do So Many Demand Board Independence When It Does So Little Good?" *The Corporate Board* 23:136 (September/October 2002): 6–10.

Westphal, J. D. "Collaboration in the Boardroom: Behavioral and Performance Consequences of CEO-Board Social Ties." *Academy of Management Journal* 42:1 (February 1999): 7–24.

Westphal, J. D. "Board Games: How CEOs Adapt to Increases in Structural Board Independence From Management." *Administrative Science Quarterly* 43:3 (September 1998): 511–537.

Westphal, J. D., and E. J. Zajac, "Defections From the Inner Circle: Social Exchange, Reciprocity and the Diffusion of Board Independence in U.S. Corporations." *Academy of Management Journal* (1995): 281–285.

Wood, M., and T. Patrick. "Jumping on the Bandwagon: Outside Representation in Corporate Governance." *Journal of Business & Economic Studies* 9:2 (2003): 48-53.

Yermack, D. "Remuneration, Retention, and Reputation Incentives for Outside Directors" *The Journal of Finance* 59:5 (October 2004): 2281-2308.

Zajac, E. J., and J. D. Westphal, "Director Reputation, CEO-Board Power, and the Dynamics of Board Interlocks." *Administrative Science Quarterly* 41:3 (September 1996): 507–529.

INDEX

defined, 107-108, 156

directors and strategy, 62-63

directors' views on, 116, 142-143

important factors, 157, 158, 247, 248-249

mix of directors, 147, 148-149, 156

model for, 137-153, 283

requirements for, 157, 158, 170, 248, 257

threats to, 186

effectiveness

assessment of, 97-105, 123

of board practices, 251-252

of boards, 142-143

of chair, 209, 210-211, 216-217

director experience and, 112, 126, 147-148

directors' behavioural characteristics and, 86, 144, 148-149, 152, 153, 157-170

of governance, determining, 25

increasing directors,' 75-79

independence and, 126

lack of improvement in, 246-247

model for boards, 137-153

related to board process(es), 152, 157, 158, 202

strategy, assessing board's, 64-66, 101

threats to, 186

environmental damages, 18

equity, 37-38, 40, 123

executives

compensation of, 59-62, 255

power of, 46

sessions/meetings, 88, 92, 176, 189, 233

see also chief executive officer

exogenous events, 4, 7, 60, 137

F

failure, 7, 21, 24, 45, 112

family/individually controlled companies, 37-41

family/individually owned companies, 36-37

fiduciary duties

acting in company's best interests, 34, 110, 221

duty of care, 17, 34-35, 38, 46, 80, 85, 86, 213

loyalty, 17, 38, 46, 85, 86

maximizing share value, 16, 19, 20, 80, 104, 136, 142

not fulfilling, 16, 17

oversight, 42, 89, 92, 109, 136, 137

to shareholders, 12, 16, 19, 20, 40, 41, 80, 104, 110

financial audit committee, 22, 55-56

literacy, views on, 57-58

performance, 55

practices, inappropriate, 56, 57

schemes, 15

sophistication, lack of, 57

statements, 55-56

fraud, 8-11, 21, 57, 137, 222

G

governance

adopting rules and regulations, 108

best practices, 83-84, 85

better, 137

chair's role, 88

changes in, 247

characteristics of, 107

codes, 1

committee, 62, 102, 103, 104

and controlling shareholders, 39